Get Your Life Back

Fiona Kennedy
and
David Pearson

ROBINSON

ROBINSON

First published in Great Britain in 2017 by Robinson

3 5 7 9 10 8 6 4 2

A CIP catalogue record for this book
is available from the British Library.

Important note
This book is not intended as a substitute for medical advice or
treatment. Any person with a condition requiring medical attention
should consult a qualified medical practitioner or suitable therapist.

ISBN 978-1-47213-734-0

Typeset in Gentium by Initial Typesetting Services, Edinburgh EH13 9PH
Printed and bound in Great Britain by CPI Group (UK) Ltd, Croydon CR0 4YY

Papers used by Robinson are from well-managed forests and
other responsible sources

MIX
Paper from
responsible sources
FSC
www.fsc.org   FSC® C104740

Robinson
An imprint of
Little, Brown Book Group
Carmelite House
50 Victoria Embankment
London EC4Y 0DZ

An Hachette UK Company
www.hachette.co.uk

www.littlebrown.co.uk

*We would like to dedicate this book to our mothers,
Marguerite and Vera, our children, Adam, Lorna, Jude, Marie, Bibi,
Joanna and Simon, and our grandchildren.*

*We are grateful for all your love and for everything
you have taught us.*

Contents

Chapter 1

How and Why to Use this Book

Let us take a look at some problems and find out how this book can help

All of us have problems, things we do too much or too little of, or avoid doing altogether. They are *problems* because they cost us dearly; they stop us from being the person we want to be and living the life we want to live. This is a self-help book for people who struggle to control their behaviour and manage their emotions (in other words, all of us). If you find your life derailed by unsuccessful attempts to feel better, you will get a lot from reading on. This book can be used by people in therapy, as well as by all of us who want to get our lives back. We do not wish to be slaves to repetitive, addictive, unhelpful behaviour, nor to hide away from life as it passes us by.

Problems are caused by our lives being driven by our *thoughts and feelings*, rather than by the *actions we value* and the things we want to achieve. Fear, anger, resentment, guilt, grief, sadness and hatred can all end up in charge of our lives. Unwanted thoughts or feelings can dictate how we behave, so that we are unable to act as we want to, or to be who we want to be. We may use drugs, alcohol, over-exercising, eating, self-punishment, sex, shoplifting, aggression, self-harm or bullying others to manage our inner state. Although all of these can 'help' in the short-term, they are a great way to lose your self-respect and descend into a cycle of hopelessness and self-loathing.

1

Those of us who struggle with self-control are often ashamed of the fact and do not tell others about our struggles. These might range from eating disorders to over-use of alcohol. Anxiety (worrying about the future) and depression (hopelessness about the past and the future) often accompany such behaviours. Some of us have too much control; we have narrowed our lives into tiny spaces where we try to hide away from pain. Some of us have too little control.

All of us have some behaviours which are not fully under our control all of the time, even if it is just being unable to stop eating chocolate until the whole bar is gone! When these out-of-control behaviours start interfering with our lives, with who we want to be, we need this book. When we turn away from opportunity and excitement in case it makes us anxious, we lose the joy in our lives and can experience misery and depression as well as, oddly, even more anxiety.

The book covers how to take control of your life using mindfulness, acceptance and behaviour change. The professional understanding and techniques we share are tried and tested. They are supported by research evidence and drawn from the most effective treatments to date.[1] Step by step, the book takes us through how to *accept* our own unhelpful patterns, *understand* how they work and so learn how to *change* them.

This chapter gets things started by helping us identify the problems we need to tackle to get our lives back. We aim to assist you to become more loving and more kind towards yourself as you go through the exercises suggested all through the book. In the following pages we ask you to begin to think about why you really need to change. Then we ask you to describe your thoughts and feelings about trying to change, since these can often get in the way. We also provide an outline of all the things we will be working on together in the book.

Have a look at this list of problems (most of us struggle with some of them):

---

1   *CBT – Cognitive Behavioural Therapy, DBT – Dialectical Behaviour Therapy, CFT – Compassion Focused Therapy, ACT – Acceptance and Commitment Therapy)*

Doing too much

Eating: bingeing, using laxatives, eating rubbish food, dieting

Gambling / Driving recklessly / Lying / Spending

Hoarding / Smoking / Drinking / Drugs / Self-harm

Risky relationships (staying in abusive relationships, selecting no-good partners, etc.)

Pleasing others at great cost to myself

Sexual behaviours (sleeping around, sex with strangers, etc.)

Anger (losing my temper, feeling angry all the time, planning revenge)

Putting others down / Putting myself down / Gossiping (the nasty stuff)

Hearing voices which upset me / Being addicted to porn

Doing too little

Eating: restricting (not eating enough)

Avoiding risks (e.g. relationships, job interviews, adventures)

Not leaving the house or really not wanting to

Turning down opportunities (jobs, relationships, etc.)

Not trusting anyone / Not socialising / Not asking for my needs to be met

Not looking after myself (washing my hair, cleaning my teeth, etc.)

Not exercising / Not seeking opportunities (applying for jobs, etc.)

Not allowing myself any leisure time / Not appreciating other people

Not noticing beautiful things around me

Not calming myself down when I need to

Anxiety

Obsessive Compulsive Disorder (OCD): checking (plugs, locks, etc.)
Compulsive behaviours (hand washing, hair-pulling, etc.)
Rituals (counting, doing things in a rigid order, etc.)
Compulsive thoughts, 'What if?' thoughts, angry thoughts, etc.
Illness behaviours (thinking I'm sick, keep on seeing the doctor, etc.)
Worrying (about disasters, about being ill, about being mad, about money, etc.)
Panicking, having panic attacks
Being paranoid (thinking others are out to get me)
Clinging to people
Fearing abandonment, that a loved one might leave me
Predicting disaster
Being afraid of everyday things (going out, being close to others, etc.)
Making plans to deal with every 'What if?' thought
High levels of anxiety after trauma

Hopelessness

Hopeless thoughts such as 'It will never work',
'I can't do it', 'What's the point?'
Self-loathing (I am worthless, no good, a failure, stupid, etc.)
Rumination (dwelling on the past – if only, I should have . . .)
Believing I do not deserve things
Can't see a way forward
Envy (I wish I were my rich neighbour, etc.)
Bitterness (life has treated me badly)
Feeling depressed
Jealousy (I don't trust my partner)
Staying in bed all day
Zoning out

Law breaking

Shoplifting

Stalking

Porn (illegal stuff)

Criminal damage

Stealing

Being in a gang and doing law-breaking stuff

Fighting

Physically abusing my partner

Thinking about or planning to harm other people

Harming other people

Cyber-bullying

Trolling

Trauma (after bad things happen)

Flashbacks (reliving parts or all of horrible events)

Images and sensations from the trauma/Nightmares

Numbing out (not feeling anything)

Feeling unreal (body unreal or world feels unreal)

Being as if in a fog ('depersonalisation')

Thinking I'll never feel safe again

Staying over-alert for danger

Bad thoughts of blaming myself or others

Irritability / Mood swings

Being jumpy and startling easily

Problems remembering parts or all of the trauma

Concentration problems

Avoiding trauma-related things (the place, people, thoughts, talking about trauma)

Pick up a pen and draw a circle round those problems that apply to you. If you are concerned about privacy, take a piece of paper and write them down there or write them down on your computer. If your problem is not on the list, write it down anyway. Try to notice any thoughts, feelings, urges or body sensations as you are doing this. Depressing, huh? You have just taken a courageous step: you have been willing to stand back and take a real look at how things are. All of us have some of these problems. Many, many people have struggled with these problems before – a quick look on YouTube will tell you that. There is most definitely hope.

Why use this book?

So why bother to use this book and get involved in all the work it is going to take to change your life? Why not just carry on as you are? Write your own answer here:

_____

_____

_____

Remember this answer. We will need it when you reach a low point further on and wonder why you ever started! It will help to keep you going. So what floats your boat? Why do you bother to get up in the morning? What gives you delight, joy and satisfaction? If your mind is telling you 'Nothing', think back to when you did get joy, delight and satisfaction from life. What did it for you then?

Write your own answer here:

_____

_____

_____

This answer is also important. It is the description of the kind of life you want, giving some direction to getting your life back. We will come back to this later.

'OK, I am interested,' we hear you say. So what is in the rest of the book? Here is a brief description to give you an idea of what to expect.

The book is divided into four sections. Part One, 'Stories', tells the stories of some people who have problems they are working on. It also gives an update on their struggles and successes so far. Part Two, 'Reasons to change and acceptance', helps us get clear about the things we value most in life, and about what we want to achieve. Then it shows how to practise acceptance, using mindfulness and validation (do not worry, these are explained a lot more in the chapters). Part Two asks us to lay out our own personal resources, the things we already have and can do, which will help us on our way. Part Three, 'What and how to change', begins with how to understand problem behaviours. Then it takes us step by step through how to change them. Deciding which problem to work on first is important. The pattern of the behaviour and how feelings and thoughts play their part is described here. Part Three gives us skills for developing self-control. Part Four, 'Getting your life back', helps us really commit to taking action. Good action planning is the key. Part Four also shows how to build and keep motivation. It explains how to cope when we feel like giving up and how to deal with setbacks. You will be invited to have another look at your own personal story, using new ways to understand yourself. There are FAQs, resources to read and sources of support in this section. Lastly, a glossary lists many of the words and terms used in the book so that you can quickly check when you need to.

Part One: Stories

To show how we are all in the same boat, **Part One** tells stories. **Chapter 2** tells the stories of some people who struggle. We, the authors, are both clinical psychologists and the characters are based on our real life experience with our clients and with ordinary people in our lives. Each character is a mix of different people we have met and not directly based on any one person. We will take a look at your own personal story too. This might show us what you have learned about yourself, growing up. Most of us learn things in our earlier years which can be less than helpful in our adult lives. We can learn how to put ourselves down or compare ourselves negatively with other people. You will be invited to write a statement of kindness to yourself at the end of this chapter. **Chapter 3** tells some success stories to show how life can be a daring adventure rather than a fearful ordeal. How can you drive your car with the top down, so to speak, instead of worrying about the rain? How can you live a life with meaning and purpose in it? Though called 'Success Stories', this chapter is actually about ongoing work. We need to keep on and on, stepping towards getting our lives back.

Part Two: Reasons to change and acceptance

Motivation building happens in **Chapter 4**, 'Why Change? Values and Goals'. Here, we get maximum clarity on why we want to get our lives back and what that life will look like. What gets you up in the morning? What has meaning for you? Getting this clear means we know which direction to travel towards the life we want. Even when life is being cruel we will know how we want to behave and who we want to be. We will encounter obstacles to our progress. These will include thoughts, feelings and behaviours which hold us back, so we need to disentangle ourselves from them. *We need to be in charge of our lives, not our problem behaviours.* **Chapters 5 and 6** cover acceptance. Which might seem odd, given we are all about change. But as you might have noticed from circling your problems, being willing and able to describe exactly how things are right now is essential. Otherwise, how can we think about it? If we only think about it whilst beating ourselves up or blaming the world or other people, we just get nowhere.

Write down what you think about your problem here. For example, 'I drink too much every evening. My problem will never go away, I have tried so hard, and it is hopeless'. Write down your description of your problem here:

_____

_____

_____

Now try describing exactly what your problem behaviour is, *just as it is*, without any judgement words here (e.g., *should* be able to, *ought* to, *never can*, *always* have to). For example, 'I drink four gin and tonics every day. I think my problem is very difficult to change. So far I have not managed to change it'. The difference here is that we have just described the current situation and taken out the *judgements* about how it will never change and it being hopeless. Write down your description of your problem here, leaving out your judgement thoughts:

_____

_____

There is much more about this coming up and we will get better at it as we go along.

Chapter 5 teaches 'mindfulness' skills and **Chapter 6** 'validation' skills. These are both ways to increase *willingness and acceptance*. Willing acceptance of experience, good and bad, pleasurable and painful, is what we are aiming for. This is the key to freedom from struggling against the way things are. Not that we have to like how things are, or not want to change them, just that we need to get in touch with them. If you are in quicksand and you struggle, you will sink faster: you need to stretch out your arms and make maximum contact with the quicksand. Similarly, we need to get in touch with our experience, but not get overwhelmed by it. Your mind may now be telling you that this is impossible. Thank your mind for that thought and read on. **Chapter 7** lays out your personal resources and strengths, the treasure trove of things you know and can do, people who love you, groups who support you, past achievements, etc. These are your provisions for the journey ahead.

Part Three: What and how to change

Part Three looks at exactly *what* to change: which behaviours are causing misery in your life? You will learn to identify them precisely. Then we can analyse how they work: in other words, why you keep doing them! All of our behaviours work for us in some way, even though we might not see how right now. **Chapter 8** looks in detail at *specific problems*, such as those you have circled. You will prioritise which problem to work on first. **Chapter 9** explains how *feelings* are tied up in it all. Many behaviours work by helping us to avoid painful feelings. **Chapter 10** shows you how to understand the problem behaviours which are ruining your life. We do this by working out the pattern of each behaviour. Behaviours tend, boringly, to keep repeating themselves. Once we have worked out the pattern, we can see exit points where we can break free.

Mindfulness comes back again as **Chapter 11** shows you how to make these changes with *acceptance, understanding and kindness* to yourself (*compassion*). We need to be patient and kind to ourselves as we learn new things. Imagine having a new puppy and beginning to train him. Would you do this with loving kindness and patience? So, you have just the same right to be treated kindly as your imaginary puppy does. **Chapter 12** is about practical ways to handle difficult thoughts. **Chapter 13** illustrates tried and tested skills for developing *self-control*. These skills really are skills – they can be learnt, just as we can learn to use a new computer or to cook. Self-control skills are things like how to calm ourselves down, resist urges, deal with conflict and look after ourselves physically. **Chapter 14** demonstrates how to make a behaviour chain about your problem behaviour, showing the links made up of thoughts, feelings, body sensations, urges and behaviour that lead up to the problem behaviour itself. **Chapter 15** shows you how to use this chain to decide to break some of the links that lead up to it. Next time the behaviour starts up, we can *do something new*. Often this takes a few goes, but guess what? We always get another go as long as the behaviour is still hanging around. So we can always try again. Eventually, our brains learn new habits. The new behaviours we are practising come to replace the old ones.

Part Four: Getting your life back

Part Four of the book reflects on the life you want and invites you to *commit* to getting it. **Chapter 16** is called 'Taking Action to Get Your Life Back'. We do some more work on getting clear what we want and how we want to be. Then we make decisions to move each day towards that life. We lay out practical, achievable steps that we can take in the direction we have chosen. We invite you to commit to following your chosen path with *willingness* to experience fully all that it will bring you, good and bad, including wanted and unwanted feelings.

Write here any thoughts you have right now about being able to get your life back, along with any feelings (anger, frustration, sadness, despair, excitement, etc.):

Thoughts _____

_____

_____

Feelings _____

_____

_____

Take a moment to notice these thoughts and feelings, and also anything going on in your body right now (tension, headaches, knots in the tummy, etc.). Notice how your mind judges things very quickly and easily. Try to stand back and look at the thoughts and feelings as if they are emails arriving in your inbox: they could be junk or they could be useful. If the thoughts are not useful right now, they are probably junk. Just because you think them does not make them true! Thank your mind for sending them to you. It is doing its best. Let us notice they are there (for all of us), and move on.

In **Chapter 17** we notice that progress is not always smooth. It is not 'every day in every way I get better and better'. Life is just not like that. We hear about good days and bad days. We discover that 'bad' days can be great opportunities to put our new skills into practice. Also, that we are in for a marathon, not a sprint. Taking a longer view and being able to see our progress over time is important.

Now we have come this far, it is time for **Chapter 18**, 'Revisiting Your Story'. Here, we take another look at your own personal story. This time it is about how our stories might hold us back. For example, my mind might say to me, 'You can never be a [writer/good mother/businessman/lover], because you had such a bad childhood you will never recover'. That kind of stuff is going to hold me back, prevent me from going for the things I want in my life. I need to stand back and see what is going on here. Then I need to write my story differently, so that it will not hold me back. I might say, 'I've been through the mill and I have so much to say as a writer' or 'I want to use the determination I learned as a child to help me drive my business towards success'.

Any new skill needs to be practised so **Chapter 19** gives us the chance to practise our new behaviours in lots of different ways. We look around at our world and think, 'Where could I use my new asking for things skill?' or 'How might my new mindfulness skills help in tonight's date?' Practice does not always make perfect, but it certainly makes us better at what we are doing.

As we journey along our new, chosen roads, we will come across obstacles. **Chapter 20** is especially for those who experience flashbacks. These can be big obstacles to getting our lives back. Here, there are techniques for handling flashbacks and advice about when to seek further help. **Chapter 21**, 'When Things Go Wrong', will help us in our journey. On a real road, there will be potholes, mud and road closures. We might be tempted off the road to take alternative directions that seem to offer an easier way forward. Other things may make us feel that the journey is impossible, such as getting ill, feeling worn out or making slow progress. We might be tempted to take a turn back towards our old habits (old habits can seem very appealing from a distance). This will probably happen along the way. Giving a big sigh and travelling back onto our chosen road is the thing to do. This chapter offers hints and tips about what to do when things go wrong.

Chapter 22 gives answers to some frequently asked questions about getting your life back. **Chapter 23** gives you more resources, including books to read, support organisations and the chance to go public and support each other. We know that if we make a public statement about our goals, they are more likely to be reached. This is a great way to keep commitment going. You can build your personal community of support using the website www.getyourlifeback.global. For example, you can blog about your own journey, share stories with others and receive support. You can also download free mindfulness, validation and other exercises. All the tables and worksheets from this book are there too. **Chapter 24** is a glossary of terms used throughout this book. We have done our very best to be jargon-free, but you may want to glance here if you need to know what a word means.

As you go through the book you will find places to write things down. There are exercises to do as you read. You will make plans to take action out there in the real world between your readings. It is best to work through this book from one end to the other: we are building a 'tower of change' and we need to lay down the foundations first. You could also think of it as getting a 'toolkit for life'. First, put on the tool belt, then add into it one tool at a time. Eventually, you will have all the tools you need and know which tool to use for what job.

Getting your life back is not a one-off effort. We can all choose to step towards our valued life every day until we have no time left on this earth. So let us get started!

Chapter 2

My Story

Introduction

We all have a story. Our story helps us explain who we are, how we think and why we do things. Some stories are good and others not so good. Most stories have some negative stuff. The negative stuff can relate to our problems here and now. Our stories can be as old as we are, or they may be quite short, as they can start at any point in our lives.

In this chapter there are short stories about people who have problems. Each character is a mix of different people we have met and not directly based on any one person. None of the stories will be exactly the same as yours: we are all different and our histories are also different. As you read through these stories you can think about what would be in your story if it were included in this chapter. Each story has three sections. First, the story as the person sees it. Second, things (thoughts, feelings, behaviours and past events) that make the story the way it is. Third, what a *kind* friend might say about the person.

The stories that follow are not accurate or full histories with loads of detail. You will notice that the first section of each story is about what the person feels or how they think about themselves and the world. It is important to notice this because the way we feel about ourselves may be a big part of the problem. It may be different from how other people see us. The second section of each story gives some ideas about why the person has the problem behaviours. These ideas help us view what is happening or has happened more clearly. There are a few technical terms, which you might recognise if you are having therapy (see also Glossary, page 347) but it does not matter if you are not having therapy. This book is designed to help you make sense of your own experiences. It will help you find ways to get your life back. This can also change the way you see yourself and the world.

The third section of each story shows what a *kind* friend might say about the person. Kind friends can see us differently from how we see ourselves. Noticing how a kind friend might see us helps us to be kind to ourselves. Their views can challenge our negative opinions about ourselves. Often our best friends do not know about some of the behaviours, thoughts or habits that we have. They would be surprised if we told them! Many of us have private behaviours or habits that we do not want others to know about, things we are ashamed of.

Some of the stories describe poor childhood care (neglect) or child abuse but not everyone has a childhood neglect or abuse story that affects his or her adult life. Your own story may involve childhood abuse or neglect, or it may not. We are all different.

As you read through the stories, start to think about *your* story. What is it that may have contributed to the way you think about yourself? Has it been over a long time or a short time? Months, years, or maybe your whole lifetime? When you think about what your kind friend might say about you, think of the most positive and loving things, no matter how big or small. Think about the kindest thing that your friend might say about you. At the end of the chapter you will be invited to write your story. You can write it in this book, or if you prefer, on a piece of paper or on your computer. Do not do this until you have read all the stories – they will give you ideas about how to do it. If you get stuck writing your story, do not worry. You can return to this task later on as you work through the book. There is no need to get it 'right' at this stage; there are no right answers and your story may change as your skills and ideas develop.

My story – Janet

Feels negative about herself, eats too much, has been shoplifting, feels angry.

Janet works in an insurance office, where she has been for fifteen years. Somehow she has not managed to get a promotion and feels she is not really popular with the other staff. The others seem to get on well, going to the pub together now and again after work. It is clear in Janet's mind that she is more skilled than most of her colleagues. She knows for a fact that Kelly only got a promotion because she flirted with the manager!

Janet is rather overweight and eats too many cakes and biscuits. It is a habit she got into when she was caring for her mum at home. She has decided that fashion is just not worth following and it merely shows how shallow people can be. Not many things seem to excite Janet but she does sometimes 'forget' to pay for things at the supermarket. Well, actually, she takes one or two packets of cakes or biscuits every time she shops. Janet is not sure why she does this, but her angry feelings about work seem to go away when she walks out of the supermarket with unpaid-for items.

Some things that may have contributed to Janet's story

Janet is not the sort of woman she would like to be. She feels she is treated as inferior to people at work, although she believes she is more skilled. This makes her feel angry. Janet feels angry when she believes people think that she is somehow sub-standard or even stupid. She thinks that people are laughing at her and not taking her seriously. When Janet eats cakes and biscuits she feels comforted and somehow warm inside. Then, later, she hates herself for being 'fat'. When Janet shoplifts, she feels less angry:

she feels in control when she shoplifts. She has never been caught so she knows she is more skilled than the shop staff or security people. This makes her feel really excited. Janet is at the top of her game when she is shoplifting.

What Janet's kind friend might say about her

'Janet is my next-door neighbour and we often have a cuppa together. I don't think Janet likes work too much. She had me in stitches the other day, telling me about some girl at work called Kelly. We both decided if flirting is the only way to get on we were both glad we have not been promoted! Janet is the salt of the earth. She does not dress fashionably, but she is always smart and more importantly, always there for me. When my mum died last year Janet came round and sorted out the house. I had left the cleaning and the kitchen was in a mess; I just stopped. But Janet came round and got stuck in and really pulled me back together again – thanks, Janet, I will never forget.'

My story – Tom

Gambling, lying, thinks he is addicted, avoiding therapy tasks.

Tom is a nice guy who is a solicitor at a local law firm. He has a gambling problem. He lost his marriage and contact with his two children because of his gambling. Now in a new relationship, Tom has come clean to Sarah about his problem. He is having Cognitive Behavioural Therapy (CBT) with a therapist he really likes. The gambling started when he visited a casino with his mates for his twenty-first birthday, and won £1,000 at roulette.

Now he loves betting shops, casinos, internet gambling and slot machines. Tom has vowed before to use 'willpower' to kick the habit. He managed OK for months, sometimes years. Then he went off on a gambling 'binge' that did not end until he had nothing left to bet. His previous marriage hit the rocks when his then wife found out he had taken loans on their house to fund his habit. He did this until there was no value left in the house. Their mortgage payments were funding his habit, but then the bank repossessed the house.

In therapy, Tom is beginning to understand that his gambling happens when he is upset. Sometimes he does not even know he is upset but when he looks back at a situation he can see that something upsetting had happened just before a gambling binge. He cannot imagine he is ever going to see the situation *before* it happens. It is no good looking back and understanding it if he cannot look forward and predict and prevent it happening! Also, his mind keeps telling him that it is a hopeless addiction and addictions cannot be cured, can they?

Tom's therapist asked him to keep a diary about his gambling 'urges'. Not just when he gambles but when he feels like gambling, and resists it. Tom is worried that if he thinks about gambling, he will be more likely to do it, so he is avoiding writing in his diary at the moment. He keeps making excuses to his therapist because he really wants her to like him.

Some things that may have contributed to Tom's story

Tom's gambling habit started when he won £1,000 at the casino. If Tom had lost £1,000 at the casino on his first visit he probably would not have a gambling problem now. We know that if a behaviour is rewarded *sometimes* it is very likely to keep going. This is known as 'intermittent reinforcement' and has been recognised by psychologists for many years. Tom has lost many times at gambling but his few wins convince him that winning is not only possible, but almost guaranteed. He never believed he would lose his money, his house and his family. Our personalities or the way we are made will also play a part in things. Tom started this behaviour after his big win. His friend Jack also won that night, yet Jack never went into a casino again. Jack had a good night out, but has no interest in gambling. Jack's personality is different from Tom's.

What Tom's kind friend might say about him

'Tom has friends who he has kept since school. Basically, Tom's a good mate and somebody whom you can rely on. He has had relationship problems, but he picked himself up again and found Sarah. Even though Tom has had some problems with gambling he's determined to sort it out and is seeing a therapist. I quite admire the way in which Tom has dealt with the many things that life has thrown at him.'

My story – Cheyenne

Self-neglect, lack of assertiveness, being overweight, not being sure who she is, binge eating.

As a child, Cheyenne was neglected. Her mother was self-obsessed and did not seem to notice the children. Her father was at work all day and out all evening. Cheyenne was not properly fed; food was unpredictable and poor-quality. She had school lunches, which were often her only meal of the day. Her clothes were dirty and did not fit properly, and often she was cold because she did not have enough clothes on. She could not bring any other children home as she was ashamed of where she lived. Anyway, her mother banned her from inviting friends home. Her best childhood memory was of going to a birthday party and being given a glass of lemonade by the birthday girl's mother – she had never had lemonade before.

Now grown-up, Cheyenne is a loving mum to her children. She does find it difficult to say no to anything they ask for. She has a steady job as a carer in a nursing home. Towards herself, however, she is very neglectful. She washes her hair in washing-up liquid as she feels she does not deserve shampoo. For the same reason she does not use hand cream or face cream. She struggles with her weight, craving calorie-rich food, resisting and then bingeing. Once she starts eating, she says to herself, 'You might as well carry on now, you have ruined the diet for the day again.' She has lost weight a few times in the past, but when she is slim, her mind tells her, 'You will slip back and put it on again, you always do.' Cheyenne cannot look at herself in a mirror; she finds it very difficult to wear make-up or to dress nicely. When she does lose weight, she finds it terrifying to buy a smaller dress size. Her mind says, 'That is not you, it is someone else.'

Some things that may have contributed to Cheyenne's story

Cheyenne was severely neglected as a child, which has had a great impact on her adult life. Children need good enough love and care to grow and to develop. When they do not get this, neglect can cause developmental damage. Developmental damage is long-term: it means the child lags behind other children, delaying the milestones of growing up. Thinking skills such as memory, concentration and problem solving can all be affected. We may be less able to calm ourselves down if we have such a background.

Cheyenne learned about herself as she grew up. She learned to believe 'I am not worth looking after'. When Cheyenne treats herself neglectfully, her anxiety goes down – she confirms her beliefs about herself. This is why she washes her hair in washing-up liquid. Such long-term beliefs are known as 'schemas' or 'core beliefs'. They are thoughts about ourselves, the world and other people, which can take many years to develop. Our schemas, or core beliefs about ourselves, are often different from how others see us.

When Cheyenne loses weight, we can see she looks good whereas she can only see the unwanted child (now her adult self) in the mirror.

What Cheyenne's kind friend might say about her

'The first thing you have to say about Cheyenne is that she is the most wonderful mum. The children never go without, they always come first. She cooks great puddings and the children are always ready for school. She is a bit overweight (aren't we all?) but she's lost a bit of weight recently and I know how she has had to fight to do it. If you want a good night out at the local, there is nobody better to go with than Cheyenne. I know she has a few problems but she is fun and feisty.'

My story – George

Hates the way he is, secretly smokes and drinks, feels excluded and guilty at home, feels depressed.

George is forty-three years old and he says he has been happily married to Jean for seventeen years. He works in a plumbing store on the counter. Jean is a primary school teacher. They have two children, Steve and Maisie, aged fifteen and twelve. Both children are doing well at school. They get lots of help with homework from their mum; after all, she is a teacher. Jean is a great mum and the kids love her. The family live in a nice semi-detached house that needs nothing doing to it, on a new estate. George is proud of his family but wishes they had a bit more interest in plumbing – or that they could at least ask about his day.

George largely 'gave up' smoking seven years ago, mainly due to pressure from Jean and the kids, but at work he smokes about three a day during his breaks. He has taken to a dram or two of whisky in the car on the way home. At work there is a secretary named Mary, who wears smart clothes. George can talk to her really easily. Nothing has ever happened, but you know it is nice to think (about what, George is not quite sure). Anyway, he feels depressed and a failure when he gets home each night. He hates lying about his smoking and drinking. He feels more like smoking and drinking when he feels depressed. When he feels depressed, he lacks energy and motivation – he sees everything around him as negative.

George has felt like this since the kids were small, especially when Jean was enjoying her teacher training. During the evenings at home George looks at Jean and the kids as though he is looking through a telescope: he observes his family but does not feel part of it. Sometimes he feels so detached he wonders if they are real. At times like this George feels more depressed. He goes out to the car on the drive and has another drink of whisky. This gives him a good feeling for just a few minutes but then he feels useless again, with no way forward.

Some things that may have contributed to George's story

George has an ideal picture of what his life should be like. He believes that Jean is more clever and talented than he is; that the children think she is more clever and talented too. Jean is a teacher and really tunes into the homework needs of the children. George does not control the house and his family as he believes a father and husband should. At work he is sure that Mary would appreciate him properly. He also knows that Mary is married and probably has no interest in him. This makes it safe to just wonder, if only ... George enjoys his smoking and whisky; no one can stop it. This high falls to a low when he gets home; it shows he is not the person he wants to be. It makes him feel depressed, as there seems no way forward but to just carry on. Sometimes depression can be a result of seeing no way forward or controlling things around us. This is sometimes known as 'learned helplessness'. It can mean a person gives up trying to change.

What George's kind friend might say about him

'I met George at the kids' football club about five years ago, when his son Steve started in the junior team. George is solid, he is a family man and family comes first. He's great with the kids and with Jean. He helps out at club events – driving, getting refreshments, that kind of thing. The club needs people like George to keep it going. Another thing is if you need any help or advice about plumbing, George is your man. He is a walking plumbing manual! We went round to George and Jean's a few weeks ago and their house is really smart, he is really skilled at DIY. Of course, the bathroom is stunning – now Trish is on at me to make ours like that.'

My story – Aleena

Experiencing loneliness, fearing abandonment, relationship problems.

Aleena was very close to her father, but he left the family when she was seven. She has not seen him since. When she grew up, she had a two-year arranged engagement to Ahmed. He pulled out of the engagement just a few months before the wedding. Now she finds she has relationship problems. Aleena is a very attractive woman, with an interesting personality. She lectures at a university and enjoys music and art. She has begun a few relationships, which have gone wrong. Recently, she has started using internet dating sites to find potential partners.

When Aleena discovers someone she is really attracted to, it is always the same old story. She works hard to please them . . . then she dumps them!

For example, she met Faraz on a dating site and found she had lots in common with him. They even live just 20 miles from each other. Faraz invited Aleena to a concert and they enjoyed an excellent meal, looking forward to the performance together. They were entranced by the music. Afterwards they discussed it excitedly. They found there was real chemistry between them. In the days that followed, Faraz texted Aleena every day. He told her how his feelings for her were very strong; he suggested times when they could meet. He even booked an evening of jazz for the following week.

As this day approached, Aleena found herself more and more agitated and anxious. Her mind told her that Faraz was suffering from 'rose-tinted spectacle syndrome'. If his specs fell off and he saw the real Aleena, he would be so disappointed. Her mind said she could never live up to the image she had created; he probably had another lover somewhere anyway … what was a handsome guy like Faraz doing being single? Aleena's mind became so provocative she had to shut it up. She texted Faraz and said she had changed her mind about the relationship: it was not really what she was looking for. Her work was very important at the moment and she really did not have time for such distractions. She said she was sorry and was sure he would find a good partner soon. Faraz was amazed at this. He texted, called and even turned up on Aleena's doorstep, asking for an explanation. She refused to answer him. Eventually, he gave up and went away so now Aleena suffers from loneliness.

Some things that may have contributed to Aleena's story

It seems Aleena believes she is not worth a relationship that is close and loving. We saw with Cheyenne that these beliefs can start from childhood experiences. However, this is not always the case. Aleena's father left her when she was young, and Aleena has had experiences of adult relationships going wrong as well. These experiences have made her feel that all men are bad and so you should not expect any to be good. Aleena has convinced herself that if any man shows an interest in her then he is a lying cheat who might abandon her like her dad did. After all, why would a man show an interest in her unless he was after something? She also believes that all he sees is a perfect image, not her true self, and he might discover the real her.

Aleena's mind keeps telling her these things and so she feels high levels of anxiety whenever she is in a relationship. When she gets in first and dumps the man, her anxiety levels come down. Then she feels a failure, convincing her again that she is never going to be worth a loving and caring relationship.

What Aleena's kind friend might say about her

'It's difficult to know where to start – Aleena is just so talented, she could be anything, an artist, a musician, anything. Aleena is super-intelligent, she works at the university teaching undergraduates and also does research. Aleena is so elegant and looks after her health. Aleena dresses in such a sophisticated way, blending eastern and western styles. She is so attractive, she always seems to have a date.'

My story – Pauline

Self-harms, has difficulties in forming relationships, feels ashamed and worthless.

Pauline hurts herself, by pulling out her hair. She also scratches her skin with her nails until it bleeds. She finds this very upsetting as people can see it. It makes her feel ashamed. She has tried to stop and her doctor has prescribed anti-anxiety pills, but these have not helped. She has done it for years, since she was eleven years old, and now she is thirty.

Pauline has a history of sexual abuse as a child, at the hands of an uncle. She told her parents but they did not believe her. Her mind has always told her it must have been her fault, and she hates herself for it. Pauline is looking for the right therapy to help her, but she found there is a long waiting list and she cannot afford private therapy. She has noticed that if she sees a programme on TV or hears a radio programme where sexual violence is involved, her hair-pulling and scratching gets worse. She has to wear long sleeves in summer and hats and headscarves, even inside. This affects her relationships with everyone at work and elsewhere. It is one of the reasons she steers clear of intimate relationships.

Pauline gets very angry with men who are sexual in their behaviour and she is terrified of men who appear aggressive; she needs a way out of the hole she is in. She has joined a website offering support to those who self-harm but many of the people on the site say she should not be ashamed of this and has a right to self-harm if it helps her through. She would person-ally like to stop, but it often happens without her noticing – that is, she has started scratching before she notices.

Some things that may have contributed to Pauline's story

Pauline was sexually abused when she was a child. This has had a great impact on her adult life. Sometimes it is difficult to work out how sexual abuse many years ago is so damaging now. When we are growing up we are developing and preparing ourselves for adult life. It is a time when we learn about ourselves and about relating to other people. Pauline told her parents about the abuse and they did not believe her so she learned that she was a liar; her voice was not worth listening to. She learned that close, intimate or sexual relationships are painful and can make you feel worthless. We know from her story that when she sees sexual violence on TV, this disturbs her and reminds her vividly of her own experiences. This is a 'trigger', which causes a 'flash-back'. When Pauline self-harms, she immediately feels better as her anxiety level drops, but later she feels ashamed and convinces herself that she is not worth looking after.

What Pauline's kind friend might say about her

'Hi, my name's Katrina. I've been out of work for two years now and I count Pauline as my only friend. She's never looked down on me and has never criticised me. I don't have a lot of money and Pauline often has me round for meals. A little while ago I harmed myself, cut my arm. I felt embarrassed when Pauline saw it, but she said she understood how I felt and said I could talk to her any time. Nobody's ever said anything like that to me before. I know Pauline hasn't got too much money but she did lend me £30 last week. She trusted me to pay her back. Thank you, Pauline, for all you are doing for me. I don't know where I would be without you.'

My story – Mandy

Feels she is a failure, hears voices; has problems walking.

Mandy likes cats, *Coronation Street*, collecting small knitted dolls, beef burgers, puzzle books and bingo. She does not like being confronted, green vegetables, walking or Barbara at the Jobcentre. Mandy also does not like the person who interviewed her for a job last week, or the person who asked her what her plans were to improve herself. Or her family doctor, who refused to sign her mobility forms. Things at the surgery were OK until Doctor Jones retired. Then that young girl took over (who knows nothing about real life – you do not learn that at the University of Wherever-it-was).

At school, Mandy was bullied. She got a GCSE in home economics, though. Her mum always told her that she was useless and just a burden. Mandy's mum often said she would have been better off if she had never met her dad. That is, of course, a dad who never materialised during Mandy's childhood, even at birthdays. Now, when Mandy tries anything that is challenging, she can hear her mum's voice telling her she is useless and a burden. At the job interview Mandy heard her mum as though she was in the room saying, 'You are just useless, Mandy – you will never be good for anything.' At least Fluffy (one of her cats) loves Mandy and never says a bad thing about her.

Some things that may have contributed to Mandy's story

As a child, Mandy learned from her mum that she had no skills and there was nothing special about her. This was confirmed by being bullied at school and, later, by a number of unsuccessful attempts to get a job. Mandy has learned that it is not worth trying and if you do, you just fail. This has resulted in lack of enthusiasm, energy and 'negative automatic thoughts' (NATs). Negative automatic thoughts are like mental chatter. In other words, your mind sends unhelpful thoughts into your head. This is like junk email arriving in your inbox. NATs can arrive in many everyday situations. For example, on Mandy's first day in a job at the local supermarket, her mind sent NATs into her head, saying that she could not get the right stuff into the right places on the shelves. This happened in the staff room before she had even started.

Mandy finds it difficult to explain, but she hears her mum's voice telling her that she is going to fail. She hears her mum's voice saying she is not clever enough to get it right. But her mum is not there, she died four years ago. Mandy is not willing to tell anybody that she hears her mum's voice just as though she is in the room. She is afraid that people will think she is mad. Many people hear voices, it is a common experience, yet only some of us need therapy or treatment.

Mandy is not good at walking any distance and gets out of breath easily. She thinks it's not fair that people expect her to have a job. When advisers talk to Mandy about job interviews she feels depressed and her walking problems get worse. The new family doctor has suggested that this is 'psychosomatic' because it happens when Mandy gets upset. Mandy does not accept this but she does realise that she does not get these problems when she is at bingo with her friends.

What Mandy's kind friend might say about her

'I like Mandy and she likes cats, and that is important to me. There is not much that Mandy does not know about cats. When my cat was poorly, Mandy came round and told me not to worry. Her cat had a similar thing and is OK now. We go down to the social club a couple of times a week, just for coffee and a piece of cake (or two). Mandy has a few problems getting about; I do not really understand it. I help her onto the bus and that sort of thing when we go out. It is difficult to explain, but I really feel good when I am with Mandy, helping her. We always have a good time together. Sometimes on a Sunday we go to a car boot sale and if anyone can spot a bargain, it's Mandy.'

My story – Rick

Has to look strong and be in control, gets impatient and angry with people; must get things right, feels inferior.

Rick is not a morning person and at 6.30 a.m. he does not want to be messed about by any of the family. He does not understand why Lisa just cannot get the children ready for school. Surely that must be her main job for the day? It is the same at work and indeed on the way to work. Some drivers are just stupid – cruising along at twenty-eight miles per hour, they make him feel like exploding. Last year, a cyclist cut him up at a roundabout. Rick got out of the car and shouted at him. Then the stupid cyclist called the police and they seemed to take the side of the cyclist!

By the time Rick gets to work he feels sweaty. His heart is beating fast and he is shaky. At work, he cannot believe just how rubbish many people are at their job. If they cannot do their job, they should get a different one. Rick shouted at one of his colleagues last month. He was given a final warning as he had also been rude and 'offhand' with two customers. On the way home, he gets angry again with other drivers: they are too slow and seem to have no driving skills. He hits the horn and shouts, but they do not bother to get out of the way. By the time Rick gets home he feels sweaty and tense. As he goes into the house the place is in a mess, the kids are arguing over the remote. It is just like turning up at work, and so the circle continues. Lisa is laughing and chatting on the phone to a friend. Rick feels like hitting her.

Some things that may have contributed to Rick's story

Rick remembers that when he was a child, things used to run like clockwork. His mum was a housewife and did not go out to work. Meals were always cooked well and on time. Washing was done every day and Rick and his brothers were looked after well. Rick remembers that his mum did all chores – his brothers and dad had little to do with the kitchen. Mum was always ready with a hug. This was different to his dad, who never physically touched the boys.

Rick wanted to join the army. He was in cadets for four successful years, but failed the entrance tests to be a soldier. This was a big shock for him. He had felt that his whole life and career was mapped out. His dad had been in the army and had been promoted to sergeant. Rick felt inferior and that he had let his dad down. In short, he felt like a failure. He was offered a job as a ticket clerk at the train station. It was a good job and gave security, a pension, five weeks' paid holiday and subsidised travel. For most of his day at work, Rick thought of what he could have been doing in the army. Customers with their questions made him feel annoyed and angry. Some customers seemed to feel they had a right to complain. He would mutter to himself, 'If you don't want to go on the train, catch a bus!' A customer once heard this and complained to the manager. When Rick was criticised it reminded him of failing the army entrance test, which made him angry. When he was angry he was also impulsive; he would say or shout things he later regretted.

What Rick's kind friend might say about him

'Rick is a bloke's bloke, he says it how it is. That is one of the things I like about him – you know where you are with him. Rick knows about cars. If there is a problem he can usually fix it. Rick's just an ordinary bloke, not up himself and not trying to be better than others. We often go out for a few drinks at the weekend, always to the same pub. He is a genuine friend and I would not be afraid of talking to him about anything.'

My story – Sally

Feels anxious, worried about how others see her, worried about her weight and looking old; feels guilty about secretly vomiting, zoning out.

International accountancy is the way forward. There is an excellent salary and a car allowance that covers almost any car. Not to mention an expense account that an international accountant can be most creative with. Sally has this post with Jones, Grabbit and Jones in the City. Successful in her education at a top school for girls, she has a first from Oxford in economics and management. At school Sally excelled in all subjects and was captain of the hockey team, as well as being head girl. She works hard and plays hard. Every evening, Sally goes to the gym on her way home then she goes on to a restaurant or bar to meet up with friends. This is a great way to keep up with everybody and also to network with the right people. When it comes to friends, Sally has masses – many from school and university. Sally's social life is full-on, with sports, parties and weekends away. Although Sally has not got a serious relationship at the moment she is more than popular. In short, she is successful, sporty and good-looking – no wonder she is so popular.

Although she is hugely popular, Sally has little sexual interest in men. She is gay, but coming out would be difficult for her. She thinks it would damage her professional image and credibility. Men often flirt with her and she joins in, but she feels like a fraud when she is flirting.

Sally usually gets home about eleven-ish each night. She kicks off her heels and takes off her designer suit, then she goes into the bathroom and makes herself vomit. Only at this point does her anxiety come down. She knows she has not put weight on, she is still looking young and she has got the toxins out of her body. If Sally did have a serious relationship, bringing someone home to her fifth-floor penthouse apartment would be a major problem. Nobody knows about the vomiting or the laxatives she also uses.

A couple of times a month, Sally cuts herself off from the world. She does not get out of bed all day, turns off her phone and loses contact with people. The next day she is ready to re-engage and goes into the office for 8 a.m.

Some things that may have contributed to Sally's story

Some of the previous stories described childhoods that were harsh and not rewarding. Sally's childhood was the opposite. She always had the best and succeeded at everything she did. Her parents were high achievers and successful in their professional careers. Sally knew that she had to be top of the class at her expensive boarding school. Anything else would have upset her parents; they gave the best and expected the best in return. Sally's parents were very proud of her when she went to Oxford. They constantly told all their friends about her progress. It was easy to get a job in the City with her first-class degree and her father's contacts.

Sally learned that only excellence is good enough, anything below that is unacceptable. This means she has to keep super-fit, be in the right places talking to the right people, wear the right designer clothes and not be gay. Sometimes she feels tired and overwhelmed; she cannot maintain all this excellence so she separates herself off from the world. She stays in bed with her phone off, keeping the blinds closed all day. At first it feels as though her head is about to burst with self-criticism. As she stays in bed in the dark, things calm down. Next day she can start over again. Nobody knows about this secret world that Sally lives in. Sally recalls that as her mum got older, she tried to look younger with too much make-up and too young clothes. She also remembers that her mum started drinking each evening at about 6 p.m. She would continue until her father came home from the City. Sally cannot stop thinking about her mum and is scared that she will turn out the same. These thoughts cause her to have high levels of anxiety and panic. Sally is secretly obsessed by how much food she eats; she hates feeling full and does not feel better until she vomits.

What Sally's kind friend might say about her

'I am Sally's best friend and, to be honest, I aspire to be like her at work. How much more successful can anybody be? Sally is my role model as well as my best friend. She has mentored me and helped me get my present job. When I say "helped me", I mean she practised interviews with me, she looked critically at my CV. She went through application form after application form. Sally really knows her stuff and she believed in me. That is what gave me the belief that I could do it.

'I met many of my friends through Sally. She is generous, sharing her social life, both at the gym and when we are out. Without Sally, I would still be in my old dead-end job. I know she worries about getting everything right all the time. We all make mistakes. If I could give her a gift it would be this: that she could be kinder to herself.'

Your story

Now it is time for you to write your story. It is much more productive to *write* your story and not just think about it. Writing it down makes us really think about what we are saying as we choose the words to use. Some of the stories may remind you of your own experiences and thoughts, but none of the stories that you have read will be exactly the same as yours. So, now is the time to start writing. Do not hold back or feel embarrassed. This is the time to be true to yourself and get our work together started.

Write in the space below, or use a separate piece of paper or your computer if you prefer. Follow the same structure as in the stories that you have read:

1. My story

_____

_____

_____

_____

_____

_____

_____

_____

_____

_____

2. Some things that may have contributed to my story.

_____

_____

_____

_____

3. Good things that your kind friend might say about you. If you cannot think of an actual kind friend, imagine one.

_____

_____

_____

_____

Well done! This is the first step towards changing. You have needed to be honest with yourself to complete this task. Before doing anything else, congratulate yourself. Notice any thoughts and feelings that you may have. You may have a feeling of achievement or some more negative thoughts, like, 'Well, nothing has changed yet.' Just notice these thoughts the way you might notice junk email.

Take a break if you like here, and give yourself a treat. Maybe have a cup of tea, listen to a piece of music you love, take a walk or call someone you would like to talk to.

Chapter 3

Success Stories

You have written a story of where you are now. The next step is to write a success story of where you want to be. First, let us look at the success stories of the people you have already met in this book. These success stories will help tune you in to decide *where* you want to be and give ideas of *how* you want your own life to be. None of these stories describes instant success; all of them are about hard work and challenges. The people in the stories have worked over weeks, months or years. At the end of this chapter you will be writing your own success story. Where do you want to be in your life, which things do you want to change? The rest of the book is about how to get there. Do not start writing your own success story until you have read these.

My success story – Janet

Problems: Feels negative about herself, eats too much, has been shoplifting, feels angry.

Goals: To stop shoplifting, manage her eating and anger better, feel less negative about herself, make more friends, be an honest person.

For three months Janet has been working on her problems, using a self-help book, and has made a lot of progress. She now appreciates her own skills at work and she has been working on whether people are in fact laughing at her as much as she thinks they are. It may be that people tend to be a bit flippant at work – they may be laughing at almost anything, just because they are bored.

Janet has taken time to think about what she really *values* in life, regardless of what other people may think. She has also spent time thinking about her friend Cindy next door. She has realised that she values her relationship with Cindy in many ways. If Cindy could like her, she thought, some people at work could like her too. She has made friends with some of her work colleagues.

Janet looked closely at her shoplifting behaviour and understood that it was connected to feeling angry. When she got less angry at work, she found that she could manage not to shoplift on the way home. In fact, she made friends with the cashier on the checkout. They now chat a little each time she shops.

Cakes and biscuits used to be a part of the angry shoplifting. Now they seem less attractive and she does not eat so many. She can manage not to shoplift and also to eat things she really likes, which turn out to be healthier things. Janet has lost a little weight. This makes her hopeful that over time she could lose more and she has treated herself to some new clothes. She accepts that she will never look like any of the catalogue models – she has realised that they are not real people anyway. Now, she can look in the catalogue and think about what would suit her own curvaceous figure. Janet is at a stage where she can appreciate herself more and she has begun to dress differently.

She has not yet reached all her goals but she can now allow herself to think that they are all achievable, given some more time. Janet's big goal for the future is to apply for promotion and be taken seriously – she knows she has the skills and feels that she could be ready to be open about saying so.

My success story – Tom

Problems: Gambling, lying, thinks he is addicted, avoiding therapy tasks.

Goals: To stop gambling, engage in therapy, be a reliable partner and provider, be a good dad and role model for his children, have more contact with his children.

It was Tom's family doctor who arranged for him to attend therapy at the local health centre. Tom believed that gambling was a hopeless addiction and there was no way to stop. His therapist seemed to acknowledge that he had this belief and asked him to keep an open mind about it. Tom did not really understand what she meant, but agreed to do his best. He started to understand that he gambled when he was upset but he could not tell when he was going to be upset in advance.

The therapist asked Tom to keep a diary of his gambling urges. This caused him to get upset and so he feared the therapy might even make things worse. The sessions continued and his therapist did not get angry about him not following instructions. Instead, she tried to work out with him what was holding him back from doing his diary. They spent time thinking about what he really valued in his life and whether gambling would help or hinder those things. Tom's therapist also spent time with him to understand how his gambling behaviour worked and make plans to deal with it: when was he likely to feel upset? What things could he do at those times instead of gambling? What would it be like to feel the gambling urge and yet not act on it?

As the sessions continued, Tom became more willing to fill in his diary and the sessions felt more focused. He told his therapist that he valued his relationship with his children and with Sarah more than anything else. It was difficult for him to say this to another person and he felt a small victory at being able to admit it. This in itself felt a little strange. Tom thought it should not be difficult to say that he values his relationship more than anything else without a problem. He has stopped trying to change the past; his house has gone and will not come back. Three people have believed in Tom: they are Sarah, John (his best friend) and his therapist.

Tom has not gambled for six months now. He has had many urges to do it. It has not been easy. Every time he wants to gamble, he has to think of the reasons he wants to stop. His relationship with Sarah and his children is so important. He knows his progress has to be protected. If he even has a small bet this might start the whole process off again but, if it did, he is aware that he has more skills to make the choice to stop again. Tom's next goal is to be confident that he can manage his urges to gamble. He feels it is time to increase his contact with the children. He has understood that he values this relationship more than winning at gambling.

My success story – Cheyenne

Problems: Self-neglect, lack of assertiveness, being overweight, not being sure who she is, binge eating.

Goals: To be a loving mum who can guide her children, feel that it is worth caring about herself, feel 'beautiful', have fewer negative thoughts.

Over the past few months Cheyenne has made a number of small achievements. These have added up to a big change. More than anything, she wants to feel that she is a good enough mum. She came to see that to do this she needed to be able to say 'no' to the children. Often she felt bad saying 'no', and thought she was a bad mum. Cheyenne wrote on a card that she was a good enough mum and the reasons why. She kept the card in her pocket. At these difficult times she took out the card and read it to herself. This reminded her that she is a good mum and that saying 'no' is a part of this.

The children continue to be demanding in terms of wanting things. This still plays on Cheyenne's emotions but now she is aware of it and can often choose not to be 'bullied' into giving in by her own feelings and thoughts. As she worked at being able to control the children, she began to think a bit more about her own mother's neglect of her. Cheyenne thought she found it difficult to be a mum partly because of her past experience. Cheyenne still sometimes feels like giving way to the children because her mind tells her she must not deprive them of things. When she is tired after work, it all slips a little.

Every morning Cheyenne says to herself, 'I am strong enough to manage today and I am worth looking after.' She used some of the children's shampoo in the shower and then went to work. She waited for people to say she looked nice, but in fact nobody did! Although she could not explain it, she felt a warm feeling inside. She began to feel more 'normal' and as good as anybody else at work. Whilst combing the hair of a resident (she is a careworker), Cheyenne looked quickly at herself in the mirror. This felt uncomfortable but it was the first step towards looking at herself fully in a mirror. Soon her mind was saying, 'Cheyenne, this really *is* you.' She is beginning to feel kinder towards herself.

Cheyenne is exploring new skincare products for sale at the supermarket. At first using the products felt awkward and she had all the usual thoughts about not deserving them. Now, occasionally, they feel good. When she has the negative thoughts often she can just let them be there whilst she continues to put the new skincare products on.

Cheyenne's next goal is to guide the children more instead of responding to their demands. She is working towards offering them things before they make demands and she has to say 'no'. An example of this is to have healthy food ready for snacks instead of the crisps and biscuits that the children prefer.

My success story – George

Problems: Hates the way he is, secretly smokes and drinks, feels excluded and guilty at home; depressed.

Goals: To be a supportive and loving husband and father, contribute to family life, stop drinking and smoking, be honest to his wife; not to feel depressed.

It has been crunch time for George. Jean knew full well that he smoked and drank and had known for a long time. He smelt of tobacco and whisky every day when he came home from work! One day, Jean was in a bad mood after some problems at work. She laid into George, saying she was fed up with his smoking, drinking and lying. This made George desperate. Now he did not just feel like a liar: he felt like a helpless, useless liar.

It was this event that made George go to the family doctor. During the appointment he asked for patches to help him stop smoking. As the appointment was ending, George became embarrassed. He said he was feeling depressed and thought that he needed some anti-depressant pills. George was surprised at the family doctor's attitude. The doctor said that low mood is often due to what is going on around us; pills may stop us from feeling the symptoms but will not change our life. He advised George to think about this and gave him some reading materials to get started. The doctor made depression sound normal, which annoyed George. He thought that the doctor could have been more sympathetic and might have seen things from his point of view. Secretly, he had hoped that he might agree that the family treats him badly.

George was left confused and ashamed of himself, thinking his life was in a mess but in fact, this was his first step towards changing. He had admitted to another person what was really happening in his life. And so George admitted to *himself* the position he was in.

George started working out what his values were and what he needed to accept. As far as he was concerned, his values were family, family and family. He wanted quality time with them all. It was scary to think of this slipping away. He thought that Jean must have no respect for him at all. He resolved to take some steps towards having quality time with the family.

At first George found it awkward and strange to behave differently but he accepted that his mind would send him unhelpful thoughts and feelings. He started developing his mindfulness skills, which helped him just notice the thoughts and feelings. Gradually, his thoughts and feelings stopped grabbing him. He learned to 'surf' his urges to drink and smoke; he noticed that if he just sat with them, they were like waves, which came and went. They went away when he did not act on them, he noticed. Then they came back, and he surfed them once again.

Six months after George's appointment with the family doctor things have changed a lot. He has got clearer on how he can contribute to the family as a dad. Jean is clever; she helps the children with their homework. George appreciates her gift for this when he watches her.

George gets on with the washing-up when it is homework time after supper. He has accepted that plumbing does not endlessly fascinate people. This has made room for him to listen more to other people. He is learning to talk about things other people enjoy, too. The low feelings of depression seem not so important. George has stopped trying to control things around him, which are actually impossible to control. Now he makes cups of tea for Jean and drinks for the kids as they do homework. He feels as though he is contributing and not helpless. It may seem a little change, to make tea and drinks, but the way he sees it and the meaning he gives it have changed a lot. The kids quite often smile and say 'Thanks' as they take their drinks.

George also thinks there was something useful in the family doctor's opinion, although it was irritating at the time. His interactions with the kids have changed because the way he sees things has also changed. Now family life feels more rewarding. Jean and the kids seem more relaxed and loving towards him. Six months ago George could see no way forward. Now he thinks the thoughts and feelings he was having about not being appreciated were just 'junk mail' his mind was sending him. He still has urges to smoke and drink, but most of the time he manages them. For the most part he has stopped drinking, smoking and lying, and yes, Jean knows that too.

My success story – Aleena

Problems: Experiencing loneliness, fearing abandonment, relationship problems.

Goals: To be an available and trusting friend and potential partner; to be able to be close to someone without huge amounts of anxiety.

Losing Faraz was a big blow for Aleena. She felt down for weeks, asking herself, 'How could I have been so stupid?' At this point Aleena started working on getting her life back. She attended a mindfulness class at the university, hoping this would help with her feelings about losing Faraz. Mindfulness classes were quite a surprise for Aleena. They provided a set of skills that she was not expecting. She learned how to watch her own thoughts, feelings, urges and sensations. She also learned how to choose whether she would follow them or just observe them and let them be. At the end of the six sessions Aleena *still* found that losing Faraz was one of dumbest things she had ever done but she was able to notice that this was a judgement.

Mindfulness is about letting go of judgements and developing a 'non-judgemental stance'. This is very helpful when we are 'beating ourselves up', psychologically. Aleena learnt to experience what is here and now, in the present moment. This may sound a little strange, but what is in the past has gone: Faraz will not suddenly come back. Aleena learnt that sometimes our internal world stops us getting our life back. Her mind kept telling her that men whom she is attracted to will always be 'after something'. This was a very unhelpful thought. It came along with feelings of mistrust and resentment; it did not help her to keep what she really wanted – a relationship. In fact, it had had the opposite effect: she had followed her urges and dumped Faraz.

Her mind still sends her these suspicious thoughts and feelings but now she is able to thank it for those thoughts. She calls these thoughts and feelings her 'Suspicious Mind' and imagines them being squawked by a parrot sitting on her shoulder. So now Aleena is talking to a man about marriage. She feels the anxiety and notices thoughts about the 'disaster' that her naughty parrot suspicious mind says is about to happen.

Aleena has now found Salim, a man she thinks she can grow to love. She is concentrating on moving towards that love. Another thing she does is to imagine how her kind friend would see this new man. She finds this gives her another perspective on the situation. She has written that her kind friend would say, 'Salim is a gentle and generous guy. He is genuine about his attraction to you. You are well matched in intellect and interests.'

Sometimes Aleena's thoughts urge her to constantly work hard to please her partner but she has noticed that doing this wears her out; it also stops her being herself. Working hard to please people was reassuring in the short term but it produced exhaustion and more anxiety in the long-term. In the past, this only disappeared when she finished the relationship and then she was unbearably lonely. We can do a lot of 'time travelling' to the past in our minds, or we can visit imaginary futures. What is important is what Aleena is experiencing *here and now*. Aleena is working to accept her thoughts and feelings without being bullied by them. When she uses her mindfulness skills she experiences the present (not the past or the future). She is learning to willingly accept the present, not to beat herself up about the past, and not to destroy her life for fear of the future.

My success story – Pauline

Problems: Self-harms, has difficulties in forming relationships; feels ashamed and worthless.

Goals: To stop harming herself, be free of anxiety and guilt; be a good friend, be able to trust in a relationship.

It is time to celebrate! Pauline has not scratched or hair-pulled to speak of for a year now. She can now go out without a hat or turban. Although she still feels like self-harming, she is recognising these urges and dealing with them. This started with Pauline sitting on her hands whenever she wanted to scratch – it makes her laugh when she recalls it now.

Pauline is thinking about her life and has looked at some dating sites. She is not ready to join, but she is able to think about it as a possibility. This has been a big move for her. She has reviewed her belief that 'all men are aggressive' and understood that it is far too general. If just one man were not aggressive this belief would be untrue, but she has got in touch with the fear she feels that any man she meets might be aggressive. She has realised that her life has been based on the *assumption* that he will be. Just think how any one of us would behave if we lived according to this rule. What a nightmare!

Pauline wrote down what she really values and in that list was being a good friend. She began talking to Katrina as a real friend, rather than somebody that she was 'rescuing'. Soon after this, therapy sessions were offered to Pauline at the local family doctor's surgery. The therapist showed Pauline how to keep a thought and behaviour diary so she asked her friend Katrina to keep a thought and behaviour diary too. Katrina joining in was a relief for Pauline: she had felt she might not have been able to do this by herself. During the diary keeping, Pauline noticed that Katrina's view of men was different from her own. Katrina was less suspicious and did not always assume the worst.

When Pauline recorded the behaviour of hair-pulling and scratching she found her mind had been full of thoughts about the sexual abuse she suffered. The hair-pulling and scratching her face and arms seemed to take the bad feelings away but this was just for a short time. Soon after she felt ashamed of these behaviours.

When Katrina saw Pauline's thoughts and feelings about the abuse she started shouting swear words about the uncle. This was shocking for Pauline. As she listened, she realised that it had never occurred to her that it was her uncle's fault: she had always been tied up in thoughts of self-blame and feelings of self-loathing. Katrina did not see that any blame could be attached to Pauline. This was the start of Pauline's journey to take a different view on what happened. At first she found she could understand logically that it was not her fault, but she still felt ashamed and to blame. She began to see these thoughts and feelings were not helpful and that she had to learn to handle them differently. She could not get rid of them but she could review them; she could also just let them be there without hooking her in. Gradually, her angry feelings changed and became directed against her uncle. She had to 'surf' waves of urges to go and confront him and then she had to recognise that thoughts of revenge were equally unhelpful.

It was time to stop being defined by the past. In the therapy sessions, Pauline was advised that the anger that she has felt about her uncle might not go away soon so she needs to feel the anger but not be imprisoned or driven by it. At first this made little sense but with new skills learnt in therapy, she began to 'get' how this works. Now, a year later, she can think about her uncle and about the anger she feels. The past no longer has such a hold over her. When she occasionally feels she is worthless she can see that this is a judgement sent by her mind; she really does know that it is not true. Pauline is more realistic about men in general. She believes it is important to start relationships cautiously and with appropriate levels of trust; she may soon be able to consider a relationship built on mutual respect and trust.

My success story – Mandy

Problems: Feels she is a failure, hears voices; has problems walking.

Goals: To have somewhere nice to live, to be able to earn some money, look after her health and love her cats; sort out her walking problems, stop hearing voices.

Mandy was stuck: she wanted to change. She could not think why she wanted to change right now, when she had not wanted to before – she thought it had something to do with her visit to the family doctor. When Mandy left the surgery, she felt like a child who had been told-off. She could hear her mum's voice, telling her off, just as though she was in the room.

Mandy's success story was not straightforward though. There were a few setbacks. Her family doctor suggested she keep a thoughts and feelings diary. She also recorded times when she had walking problems and noticed that her walking problems did not happen all the time: they did happen more when she felt depressed. When Mandy felt depressed she heard her mum telling her that she was useless. These experiences felt like a bowl of spaghetti – they needed to be untangled.

Mandy became aware that she sometimes had walking problems and sometimes did not. She began to start noticing these differences in her ability to walk. The family doctor arranged for her to go to the local gym. This seemed like a crazy idea but it did mean that Mandy could try out improving her walking. She was surprised at how supportive the staff at the gym were; they really wanted to help. They worked out programmes and exercises for her. Mandy thought that if she could get over her walking problems at the gym, perhaps she could do the same outside.

She made good progress in the gym, in spite of her mum's voice and her negative automatic thoughts (NATs). But walking outside was much more difficult. Without the gym staff to support and distract her, her mum's voice and her NATs became more powerful.

Mandy wrote out a list of what she really values in life and where she wants her life to go. Her real list was not cats, beef burgers, dolls, puzzle books and bingo. She wanted somewhere nice to live, to be able to earn some money, to look after her health and to love her cats.

Mandy began to do some work about her mum's voice. Her family doctor referred her to a voice hearing group. Here, she learned how normal it is to hear voices. She met some other nice people who heard voices too and learned that problems arise from how we *relate* to hearing voices. The group suggested she change her goal from stopping hearing the voice to handling it differently. If we let voices we hear bully us around or if we feel upset by them, they can become great problems. Mandy began to challenge what her mum's voice was saying and wrote down reasons why she was not a failure. She imagined her mum sitting in a chair opposite her. Then she spoke to her mum in the chair and said how much she disagreed with her. This made Mandy feel brave and stronger. Mandy also learned mindfulness skills. These helped her to focus on what she wanted to, not what her mum's voice was saying.

Now Mandy does not feel she has to listen to or agree with her mum's voice. When she hears the voice she can notice it is there but leave it chattering in the background. She can 'shine the torch of her attention' onto the job she is doing at the time. Mandy is doing a similar thing with her NATs – she is aware that they still come along, but she does not have to listen to them or believe them.

A year after that family doctor appointment, Mandy has started a job in the local flower shop and is saving up for a deposit on a new flat.

My success story – Rick

Problems: Has to look strong and be in control, gets impatient and angry with people; must get things right, feels inferior.

Goals: To be a loving and supportive husband and father, control and understand anger, have more self-respect; contribute to society.

The decision to change came about when Rick got his final warning for being rude to customers. This final warning caused him to have feelings of out-of-control panic, which made him sweaty and shaky. He no longer felt strong and in control – Rick had just become like a rabbit caught in front of car headlights.

Rick kept thinking about losing his job and his house. What if he could not provide for his family? This was his worst nightmare. That night he went home and cried. He could no longer look strong and be angry. To his surprise, Lisa was able to help and understand. Sometimes things happen in life which have the same effect as a starting pistol. Rick and Lisa went out together and got a self-help book. The book helped him get clear about his true values. It also helped him become more aware of his thoughts and feelings. He read about some simple self-control techniques.

Rick realised that if he lost his job and the family lost their house, all that he valued would be lost. This made him take a new look at what was really important to him. When Rick thought he might lose his house and family he found this more upsetting than his feelings about not being in the army. In fact, being constantly upset about not being in the army was causing huge problems. With the help of the book Rick got clearer about his values. They were about being a loving and supportive husband and father. Also, he wanted to contribute something to society.

Rick read about how to become more aware of his thoughts and emotions. Actually, his thoughts and feelings were not necessarily 'true', they were simply things going on in his head. He began to think about how he could steer his life the way he wanted it to go.

At first Rick observed his anger. He noticed it was connected with strong urges to do impulsive things – things like shouting at people. He decided that shouting at people would lead him *away from* rather than *towards* his goals so he got better at noticing his urges. Eventually, when Rick wanted to shout at somebody, he managed to say out loud 'STOP! THINK!' Then he would take two deep breaths and count to five. The urge to shout would lose its strength. He would do this as many times as he needed to.

The more Rick practised simple anger-control techniques, the less he relied on them. He began to be able to turn his attention away from himself and to check out the world around him. Now he is in a position to see that being 'right and strong' was a shield that protected him from the rest of the world. Many people were afraid to challenge Rick as they were afraid of him, but he now accepts that he is not in the army and does not need to act like a commando! The army was his identity; he accepts this is in the past. More importantly, he can make his own life: he does not have to be what he thinks his dad would want him to be.

Six months after Rick's final warning a number of things have changed. At home he is able to get closer to the kids with a cuddle before they go to bed. Joint jobs around the house with Lisa are now a part of everyday life. These things move him towards his values every day.

Rick's mind still sends him judgements that some customers and drivers are just 'stupid' or 'arrogant'. At times like this he thanks his mind for that observation. Then he looks on with curiosity. Rick has thought about his job in a new way. He sees that it involves helping the public and he can make a difference to each person's day just by how he deals with them. He is contributing to the running of a huge transport system, a system absolutely essential for the country to function.

Though this process of change started out of panic, Rick is now doing it for himself. He has some new life goals and each day he steps towards them; he is not constantly thinking about the army and how he failed to get in it. This has left room to think about other things. He might even apply for a management post. Rick can now be in charge of his own life.

My success story – Sally

Problem: Feels anxious, worried about how others see her, focused on her weight and appearance; feels guilty about secretly vomiting, zoning out.

Goals: To be a loving partner, be honestly herself, stop vomiting and using laxatives; manage her anxiety.

One day, in bed during a 'zone-out day', Sally decided she wanted to change. The night before she had been at the wine bar, talking to Rosemary, a school teacher. During their conversation Sally felt that Rosemary really connected with her. This was difficult to explain. Was Rosemary gay? Anyway, it caused Sally to panic. She broke away from the conversation, went home to vomit and then she felt completely hopeless. After very little sleep, Sally zoned out in bed all day. She found herself wishing that she could have invited Rosemary back. Also, she found herself thinking she was going to spend the rest of her life alone. She said to herself, 'That's it – I'm going to change!'

Sally researched her issues on the internet and found some CBT, DBT, CFT and ACT sites which helped her (see also page 347). She decided to start with 'exposure'. Meaning, she would resist taking laxatives and vomiting and learn to tolerate whatever feelings came along. It was too much to stop in one go, so she limited herself to both vomiting and laxatives only once per week. At work her anxiety levels rose as her mind told her she looked bigger and older. In fact, nobody commented or seemed to notice. It was the same at the wine bar so she 'sat with the anxiety' and kept going.

After a couple of weeks Sally weighed herself and she was a little heavier. She had feelings of sheer panic. All her urges to vomit and use laxatives grew greater. This made it really difficult to stick to her once-a-week routine and she wondered whether she could be successful. Yet at work nobody seemed to notice. The men at work still flirted but now Sally did not feel obliged to flirt back. The fear and anxiety that she felt at this time started to include some joy and excitement. It was like being on a roller coaster. With the help of the internet sites and some social-media connections, Sally began to practise mindfulness. She also allowed herself to notice her attraction to women; she was now able to tell herself that what she really wanted was to be a loving partner to a woman.

About a month after this Sally met Rosemary again at the wine bar. As it was a 'non-vomit' night, Rosemary was invited back to the penthouse. Sally and Rosemary became friends. This gave Sally the final strength and confidence to stop vomiting and using laxatives altogether. She realised that she had listened too much to her own mind's judgements. It was the way in which *she* had seen *herself* that was the problem. Rosie (yes, it is 'Rosie' now, not Rosemary) had seen Sally very differently to how she saw herself. When Rosie told Sally she loved her, Sally was able to feel the fear and go for it anyway.

Six months later, Rosie said she would like to grow old with Sally in a little cottage somewhere. This really challenged Sally: she still had the image of her mum growing old ungracefully but her mindfulness skills helped her just observe this image and her own thoughts. She did not have to buy into them. She was able to visualise other images and think differently about her own future with Rosie.

Sally's mum and dad have met Rosie but still pretend Sally is straight. Sally feels OK about this, as she does not need their total approval. Her mind still tells her she should have a perfect body (she calls this her 'Miss Strict' mind). She has understood that perfection is a monkey trap. When monkeys grab hold of a handful of seeds inside a pumpkin, they become trapped: their hand is now too full to come out of the hole in the pumpkin and they are unwilling to let go of the seeds. Sally had been unwilling to let go of the need to be perfect. Now she does not have to follow Miss Strict's instructions all the time. She has come out at work, which interestingly has not changed the flirting or the sexist jokes, which she sees as childish and immature. Sally will soon have the strength and confidence to make an official complaint and take control of the situation.

Your success story

Generally, something happens to make us want to change. It can be as small a thing as walking down the high street and meeting a person who has made a change in their own life since you last met. Sometimes, there is no recognisable event or experience that makes us finally decide to change. In the stories above, Jean confronted George about his drinking, smoking and lying; Aleena lost a relationship because she could not manage her fear; Rick got a final warning; Mandy became angry with her new family doctor, who would not support her 'illness identity' and Sally met Rosemary, which made her review many of her beliefs and habits.

Before writing your success story, think about why you have decided to change now. Do not focus on previous attempts or reasons why it can never work. Most of us have tried to change and not succeeded, with our minds reminding us of this every time we attempt to start again. Be truthful to yourself – why do you want to change now? Think about the cost of your current behaviour, how it affects your life negatively, drains your energy, hurts your loved ones, etc. Think about whether it is stopping you from getting the things you want in your life.

Write down why you want to change now:

_____

_____

Now that you have read some success stories it is time to write your own. The task might seem difficult: you are being asked to describe where you would like to get to, just as you are starting the journey. Generally, we all know inside ourselves how we would really like to live our lives. As you continue through the book you will learn how to achieve your own success. The task here and now is to think about how you want to live your life in your success story. Write down how you would like your success story to be. We can return to it later on and change it, if we need to. As you move away from troublesome behaviours you may see new opportunities and so your success story may change, but this is your starting place. As we have said, you will not find an exact match for your story in this book. The stories are here as a guide to help you build your own ideas and story.

Now, write down what you want your own success story to look like. Obviously, you cannot describe the struggles you will have as you are only just starting out, but try to describe what your success will look like. For example, Janet wrote, 'I'll be an honest person, less angry and with no shoplifting habit.' Tom wrote, 'I'll be a good father and reliable provider for the family, with no gambling habit.' Write your own success story here:

_____

_____

_____

_____

We will work some more on what your success will look like later in the book. You have a rough idea of where you want to go so now you need to know how to get there. The following chapters will guide you towards reaching your goals. In the next chapter we will get clearer about your values and goals, then you will be invited to learn a range of skills. These will help you to understand why you do things and what to do about changing. There will be a number of steps you need to follow. These will be laid out in the chapters to come.

Now, you might like to take a break and do something different. Come back later or tomorrow and we can talk again.

Chapter 4

Why Change? Values and Goals

At this stage you may be asking yourself, 'Why change, why bother?' Why not just carry on living as you are right now and not put in all the effort, discomfort and hard work that making changes is going to take? You have had a first go at answering this question at the end of Chapter 3. This chapter will help you to think more about your answer, about why you want to change and what success will look like when you get your life back.

Things I want to stop doing

We all have repeated patterns where we act in ways we would not be proud of. Or sometimes others treat us in ways we do not want to be treated. Identifying these habits and patterns helps us build our motivation. When things begin to change we might forget this previous unhappiness and lapse back into old habits. Or we might get stuck and just feel like giving up. Reminding ourselves of the reasons we wanted to change in the first place can help to keep us going.

Things I want to start doing

It is fine to want to stop doing things but the question is, 'What will I be doing when I'm not doing these things?' We need to identify what we really want in our lives. Once we know how we want our life to be, we can start taking baby steps towards our goals. Ask yourself, 'Five years from now, for example, how would I like my life to be?' Most of us would answer something like this: 'To feel good about myself; have someone to love; somewhere comfortable to live; to be healthy; to make a contribution to my community; perhaps to have the job that I want.'

You may notice your mind saying, 'But I can never manage this. Heaven knows, I've tried so many times.' Life is not always kind so you need to identify your own personal values and the directions you want to go in your life. Here is another way to get clearer about your values. Imagine you are now eighty years old. Imagine you overhear someone talking about you. They are talking about the kind of person you are and what you have done with your life. What would you like to hear? What kind of person would you like them to say you have been? How will you have treated others around you and how will you have looked after your own needs? What will your achievements have been?

The reason you need to know your values and goals at the outset is to give meaning and motivation as you work through the rest of the book. You would not volunteer to do uncomfortable and challenging things without good reasons. If I had a bed of nails to offer you and asked you to lie down on it, you would probably say 'No!' But if I said to you, 'Here is a bed of nails, lie on it for two minutes and your life will be transformed' or even, 'Here is a bed of nails, lie on it for two minutes and your pet/child/lover/ parent will be saved from a painful death', you may say 'Yes'. Being clear about your own personal reasons is an important part of guiding your work and building and keeping up commitment. We will need to be willing to experience some discomfort in order to get to where we want to be.

What are values, goals and actions?

Values are about what is really important to you: how you want to live your life. Our values are what make us feel good about ourselves. They show us the way towards the identity that we want. Values can guide our choices so that we do the things that we see as important or desirable. There is no correct or incorrect value or goal: it is personal to each of us, ranging from looking good to wanting a meaningful job. The way in which we relate to others – loved ones, family, people we meet at work – can be dependent on our values. Your values are your reasons to work towards your goals.

It is quite tricky to tell the difference between a value and a goal. One way of looking at it is to say that values are about *how* we want to be and goals about *what* we want to do. In fact, it does not really matter. What we are aiming to do here is to:

a. Get clear about believing in something/wanting something in our life (value/goal)
b. Imagine how this is going to look in our own life (imagine how this value/goal would look in reality)
c. Plan to take a small action in this direction (baby step)

For example, I could have a value about my relationships. I could say:

a. I want to be someone who is respectful towards other people (value/goal)
b. I would like to show my respect for my mother (imagine how this value would look in reality)
c. I'm going to thank her for the cake she made (action/baby step)

Remember Janet? She has problems with eating and shoplifting and angry relationships at work in the insurance office; she dislikes herself. She wants to stop these things. But what does she want instead? What floats her boat? What gets her up in the morning? In Janet's success story (page 39), we saw her personal answer to 'Why?' She wants to stop shoplifting, manage her eating and anger better, feel less negative about herself, make more friends and be an honest person. She might say:

a. I want to be an honest person (value/goal)
b. I would like to pay for everything I get from the shops (imagine how this would look in reality)
c. I'm going to the supermarket to choose and pay for three small things (action/baby step)

Looking at how she wants to be in terms of her health, she might say:

a. I want to be someone who looks after my health (value/goal)
b. I want to eat healthy food (imagine how this would look in reality)
c. At the supermarket I'm going to choose fruit and muesli to buy (action/baby step)

Looking at how she wants to be with her work colleagues, she might say:

a. I want to be a person who understands and forgives other people (value/goal)
b. I want to be understanding and forgiving towards my work colleagues (imagine how this would look in reality)
c. This morning, I'm going to look at things from Celia's (work colleague) point of view (action/baby step)

You can see from this that it is useful to get clear on your values and goals in various areas of your life. Four useful life areas are Relationships, Health, How I Occupy My Day and Leisure/Growth. Notice that Janet is starting to make baby steps towards her goals. Baby steps are small steps that work towards your goal, not one huge step that lands at your goal immediately. Taking baby steps makes it easier to succeed. We will go on to look at these four life areas and learn some more about baby steps.

In the previous chapters your story showed that you are not living your life as you really want to. This means that you are not living your life according to the values you think are important. The task now is to work out what are your own personal values and goals and how you want to live your life.

What values and goals are not

Wishes about other people changing

For example, I might say, 'I want my husband to listen to me more.' Janet might say, 'I value other people being nice to me,' or, 'I want to be respected by other people.' We cannot control what other people do, so there is no point having these on our values and goals list. But sometimes we can translate these wishes into useful values or goals. For example, I could say, 'I value doing things that make it likely my husband will listen to me,' and set a goal of choosing to talk about a topic I know he is interested in. Or Janet might say, 'I want to be worthy of respect from other people,' and set a goal of doing an act of kindness once a week.

Wanting to feel happy, or pain-free

There can be huge problems chasing happiness. Often, to achieve something worthwhile, we need to be willing to feel discomfort, sadness, anger, doubt, even despair, along the road to our goal. For example, suppose you decide to climb Mount Everest. Even with good training and fitness, as you set off you expect to feel: fear of falling and of avalanches; exhaustion; shortness of breath; strong urges to give up; anger with yourself, with colleagues, the mountain, or the weather. Your skills in managing all these emotions and urges will be a big part of your chances of success. If you give in to each impulse, you are very likely to turn back and never finish the climb. So, if you judge each moment or day according to whether you are happy or not, you will never get anywhere you want to be. Then it is pretty certain you are going to be sad. It is natural to avoid uncomfortable painful feelings and to chase feeling better in the short term, we all do it. But training ourselves to work for the long-term is the key to getting our life back. Having a life worth living can bring its own contentment so fixing our eyes on the middle distance and focusing on our values and goals is essential to overcoming short-term-ism. Short-term-ism is what leads to our problems in the first place, as we will see later.

Values and goals bull's eye exercise

Swedish ACT therapist Tobias Lundgren originally developed this exercise, but we have changed it a bit. Here, it involves:

1. Identifying your values in four key life areas
2. Boiling down your values into three or four key words
3. Checking out how near or far your life is from your values

4. Recognising which actions are in line and which are out of line with your values

5. Taking a baby step towards a value

1. Identifying your values

Here are the four key life areas to think about and fill in:

- *Relationships*

In my relationships with my friends I want to be (some examples could be trustworthy, likeable, supportive, reliable, etc.):

_____

_____

In my relationship with myself I want to be (things like calm, soothing, confident, satisfied, etc.):

_____

_____

In my relationship with my colleagues and people I meet in everyday life I want to be (some examples could be worthy of respect, skilled, reliable, etc.):

_____

_____

In my relationship with my partner I want to be (some examples could be loving, supportive, loyal, reliable, attractive, etc.):

_____

_____

Even if you do not have a partner or colleagues at the moment, imagine if you did: what kind of person would you want to be when relating to them? In any other relationships you can think of (perhaps family, people on the bus, pets, people at the clinic, etc.), how do you want to be?

_____

_____

- *Health*

In terms of my physical health I want to be (fit, active, as healthy as possible, to feel OK with my body, etc.):

_____

_____

In my mental health I want to be (some examples could be having a positive attitude, calm, emotionally under control, able to manage sadness, anxiety or fear, etc.):

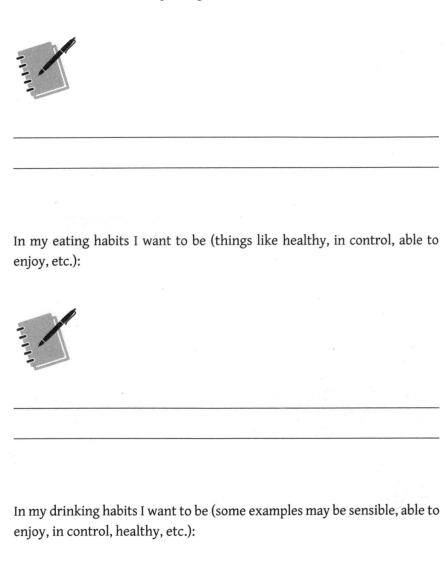

In my eating habits I want to be (things like healthy, in control, able to enjoy, etc.):

_____

_____

In my drinking habits I want to be (some examples may be sensible, able to enjoy, in control, healthy, etc.):

_____

_____

Other health assets you can think of (things like fit, not worn down, having as much energy as possible, managing long-term health issues, etc.). How do you want to be?

_____

_____

- *How I occupy my day*

In terms of how I occupy my day, I would like to be (some examples could be meaningful, making a difference, successful, careful, enthusiastic, helpful, friendly, creative, quiet, outside, physically active, thoughtful, highly skilled, interesting, etc.):

_____

_____

- *Leisure/Growth*

For relaxation and pleasure, as well as to develop myself in new ways, I would like to be (some examples could be adventurous, open, calm, sociable, fun to be with, challenged, etc.):

_____

_____

2. Boiling down your values into three or four key words

Now you have written down your values, let us simplify them. Stand back a bit in your mind and come up with three or four words for each value area that sums it up for you. For example, Janet could say, in her relationships area, 'Understanding and forgiving', Aleena could say, 'Trusting, brave and close', Mandy could say, 'Confident and caring', whilst Rick could say, 'Managing my anger and appreciating people'.

Boil down your values statements here into a few key words:

- Relationships

_____

• Health

• How I Occupy My Day

• Leisure/Growth

Your values diagram

Fill in the following four areas in the values diagram below with your key words. You might notice that some of the areas are more important to you than others. Most people find that this is the case.

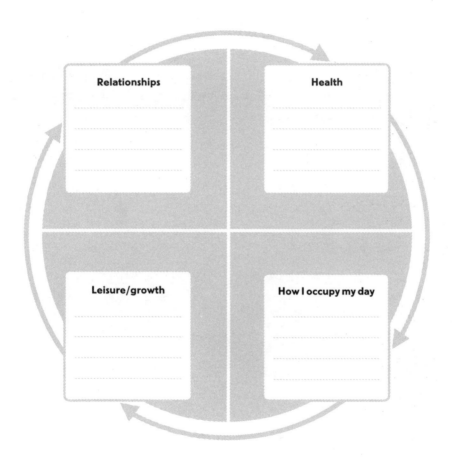

You might want to make a note of the key words from your most important values area and put it in your purse or pocket or on your phone or computer so you can look at it when you need to. This might be quite often during your everyday life at work, home or when you are out and about.

3. Checking out how near or far your life is from your values

Here is a bull's eye diagram. The idea is to step back and really take a look at each area that you have thought about. Look at your key words, then look at how your life is right now in each area. If you are living close to your ideal life, put a cross close to the bull's eye. If you are not living so close to your ideals, put a cross further out towards the edge. You can then look at the bull's eye and see how you are living in each area right now. For example, Janet has stated that she wishes to be understanding and forgiving towards her work colleagues, but right now she is feeling angry and judgemental. But she also stated she would like to be approachable for advice; right now she is doing this. Janet puts a cross halfway to sum up the situation in her relationships area.

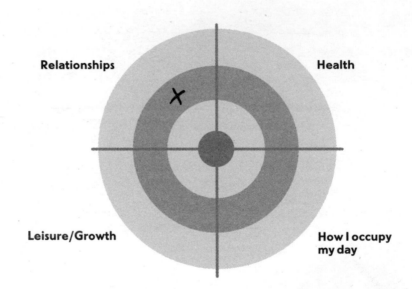

Have a go yourself below by putting a cross in each of the four areas:

My Bull's Eye

Date: _____

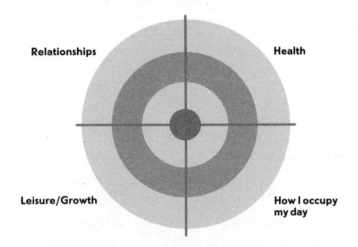

Relationships

Health

Leisure/Growth

How I occupy my day

If you notice anything about your bull's eye, write it here:

_____

_____

Which of these four areas do you think is most important to you right now? This might change from time to time as you go along. Write down which area(s) is/are most important here:

_____

_____

Excellent, well done! You can come back to this bull's eye and see how your progress is going later.

4. Recognising which actions are in line and which are out of line with your values

Just take a moment to consider last week. Look at the four areas again (these are the same as in the bull's eye). Do not think too long or hard, just see if you can grab hold of one or two actions you did which were *in line* with your values and one or two which were *out of line*. For example, Janet wrote her key words for each value area then she thought about her actions last week. She noticed some were in line and others were out of line and noted them here:

My values	My actions last week
Relationships being understanding being forgiving being approachable for advice	• **In line** *looked at work from Celia's point of view* • **Out of line** *scowled at Mary when I heard her talking*
How I occupy my day using my skills at work being honest	• **In line** *worked at a high skill level on the accounts* • **Out of line** *stole a packet of biscuits*
Leisure/growth have a hobby meet new people apply for promotion	• **In line** *can't think of anything at the moment* • **Out of line** *didn't go out in the evenings*
Health take exercise eat more healthy food lose weight	• **In line** *made a plan to walk into town twice a week* • **Out of line** *ate almost a packet of biscuits every day*

Have a go yourself. Write down your key words under each value area heading like Janet did. Then just notice how your actions have been last week. Notice any judgements you are making and see if you can just describe your actions, without any judgement words. Write down examples of actions that were in line and actions that were out of line in your life last week.

My values	My actions last week
Relationships _____ _____ _____	• In line _____ • Out of line _____
How I occupy my day _____ _____ _____	• In line _____ • Out of line _____
Leisure/growth _____ _____ _____	• In line _____ • Out of line _____
Health _____ _____ _____	• In line _____ • Out of line _____

You may notice that many actions we take in life can be seen as steps towards or steps away from our values. For example, Janet scowling at her colleagues is a step away from her values of being understanding and forgiving. Looking at things from her colleague Celia's point of view is a step towards this value. Now we are becoming aware that we have many choices, many times each day to work towards or away from our values and goals. We can actively plan to take steps towards our values each day.

5. Taking a baby step towards a value

Choose one life area from the bull's eye. For example, Janet chose the relationships area. She planned to try to see things from Celia's point of view. This made it much more likely that she would actually do it. Janet had to remember her ABC:

a. I want to be a person who understands and forgives other people (value/goal)

b. I want to be understanding and forgiving towards my work colleagues (imagine how this would look in reality)

c. This morning, I'm going to look at things from Celia's (work colleague) point of view (action/baby step)

This was how Janet planned it out. Now it is your turn to fill in your own ABC. Start at (a) with your values words from one area. Then at (b) imagine what this will look like. What would I see if I could be a fly on the wall, watching you acting out this value? Where would you be? Who with? How would you look? What kind of things would you be doing? Write down next to (c) one action you can do in the next day or so to take a baby step towards your value.

a. I want to be _____

_____ (values words)

b. I want to be _____

_____ (imagine how this would look in reality)

c. This morning/today/tonight/this week I'm going to _____

_____ (action/baby step)

Congratulations on trying this technique, which may look easy but it is not. Do not worry about whether you have got it exactly right or not. Like all skills, it takes practice. The most important thing is to have a go.

Homework

For the coming week, do this exercise so that you choose to take one baby step each day. It might be the same baby step or it could be different ones. Write down in your Baby Steps Diary how this goes. Also, make a note of things that get in your way and stop you or almost stop you from taking your baby steps. These could be practical problems (lack of time, money, etc.) or messages from your mind ('What's the point?' or 'This is silly' or even 'I'll fail', etc.). Things that help are important too so make sure they are also written down. For example, remember my value about my relationships (see page 61). I said:

a. I want to be someone who is respectful towards other people (value/goal)
b. I would like to show my respect for my mother (imagine how this would look in reality)
c. I'm going to thank her for the cake she made (action/baby step)

The italics in the diary show my recording of taking this step.

Keep this diary going as you do other exercises in the book. Good luck and remember, we all started walking with baby steps.

My Baby Steps Diary

Day	Baby step	Did I do it? Yes/No	Things that got in the way	Things that helped
Example	Thank Mum for cake	Yes	Thought she'd think I've gone soft	Practised saying thank you first before I did it with Mum
Monday				
Tuesday				
Wednesday				
Thursday				
Friday				
Saturday				
Sunday				

Chapter 5

Acceptance and Mindfulness

What is mindfulness and why do I need it?

Mindfulness is focusing on the present moment with awareness and acceptance, without judging. Why do we need to do this? Because we have language, our thoughts come in words as well as images. Human minds are very good at 'time travel'. Our minds spend a lot of time visiting the past, with thoughts like this:

> 'If only . . . (I had chosen differently/done something else/said something, etc.)'

> 'I wish . . . (I had done X/given my kids more time/worked harder in school, etc.)'

> 'That was a bad thing s/he did'

These words in our thoughts are called 'ruminations'. They are often at the centre of low mood and depression; there may also be images in our minds of the events or situations we remember. Our minds also spend a lot of time visiting the future. We can easily imagine the worst happening, in words and images, like this:

> 'What if . . . (I lose my job/run out of money/get ill/my child gets run over, etc.)'

We also make predictions in our minds and then believe them:

'She will laugh at me'

These thoughts are connected with anxiety. There may also be vivid images of what might happen. We can spend a lot of time problem-solving them in advance:

'I'll take sandwiches in case the car breaks down'

'I'll take my teenager to school in case she gets run over'

As well as time travelling, human minds are very good at judgements, saying things like 'X is bad, Y is good'. But sometimes this ability works against us:

'I'm a bad person' (bad)

'My life is not good enough' (bad)

'It is good to always clean my teeth after eating' (good)

'She is a terrible mother' (bad)

'I can't do that' (usually bad)

'It's good to exercise every day to keep fit' (good)

Many of these judgements can lead us to feel awful – about ourselves, the world and other people. They can also affect how we see the future:

'It's hopeless'

'There's no point'

'It won't work'

'I can't keep up with my expectations'

Here, our minds are making predictions (judgements about what will happen). Then we make them come true, because we believe them!

Because we are doing all this time travelling and judging, we often miss what is around us right now. We are too tangled up with our thoughts. Life can slip by and we can miss it. In order to squeeze the most juice out of life, we need to get hold of the life lemon right here and right now. This is where mindfulness comes in.

Mindfulness is mind training

It trains our minds to stay in the here and now, the present moment. That way we can really experience life. Because mindfulness is mind training, it takes practice. If you go to the gym, you need to go regularly to feel the benefit. If you do mind training, you need to do it regularly to build up your 'mindfulness muscles'.

Mindfulness is the opposite of problem solving

That is why it is part of acceptance work. It might seem strange, but sometimes our efforts to solve problems actually make things worse. For example, think about Sally. She was vomiting to solve her problem of feeling fat. This worked in the short term but in the long-term it made her feel ashamed and unable to share her life with a loved one. For Sally, an alternative to solving the problem by vomiting might be to learn skills to *accept* her feelings and thoughts about fatness and toxins. This might sound impossible but let us imagine she manages it. Let us imagine she becomes able to observe and describe feeling fat, without judging it and without trying to change it. She might observe the sensations in her body when she has this feeling (discomfort, bloating), or her emotions (fear, frustration). Or her thoughts ('I need to get rid of these calories and toxins'). Or her urges (strong urge to go to the bathroom and vomit). She does not have to *like* the feeling or *want* to have it, but if she is able to 'sit with' the feeling, she does not need to vomit to get rid of it. This opens up all kinds of new possibilities for her life.

Mindfulness is about experiencing things directly, doing things with awareness

This is instead of avoiding or changing them. An image which may help here is the 'quicksand' example often used in Acceptance and Commitment Therapy (ACT). If you get stuck in quicksand, you will start sinking. The more you struggle, the quicker you will sink. The thing to do is to give up the urge to struggle, and instead stretch out your arms and get in contact with the quicksand as much as you can. This is your best way of surviving. Mindfulness is a way of getting in contact with your feelings and the world. Using mindfulness, Sally has 'stretched out her arms' and got in touch with the feeling of fatness she has been struggling to avoid. This allows her to experience a new way forward.

Mindfulness is being non-judgemental

Making judgements is another very useful human skill. We need to make judgements to learn how to improve things, do better next time, plan ahead, etc. But you will notice that a lot of the troublesome thoughts listed above involve judgements, for example:

'S/he will laugh at me'

'That was a bad thing s/he did'

Giving up judgements and simply observing and describing what is in front of us takes a lot of practice but it also frees us up. For example, one woman on a mindfulness course was given a task to do something mindfully over lunch.

She noticed that she always chose a ham sandwich because she likes ham the best. She had a judgement: 'ham sandwiches good, other sandwiches bad'. She did not even usually think about this. Over lunch, she decided to *notice* all the sandwiches available, put aside her automatic judgement, and make a *conscious choice*. She chose egg and cress. She enjoyed it; she was surprised.

In summary, mindfulness is:

- Mind training
- The *opposite* of problem solving
- About experiencing things directly, doing things with awareness
- Being non-judgemental

Mindfulness is *not*:

- Relaxation
- Feeling better
- Pushing away thoughts (they always come back)
- Emptying your mind (there's always something going on in there)

Sometimes when we practice mindfulness we will feel relaxed, other times we will feel restless. Sometimes it will be easy, other times it will be hard. We are working to *accept* whatever it is, however it is at the time. The next section will show you how to develop mindfulness skills.

Mindfulness skills

Mindfulness 1: Get off automatic

Think of something you usually do automatically, without thinking. This might be driving, eating, taking a shower or drinking coffee. Now make up your mind to do this thing today with awareness. Doing something with awareness means that you:

- Notice it (pay attention to what you are doing)
- Notice any judgements which come into your mind, let them be there and then bring your mind back to what you are doing
- Do this thing with care, do it carefully
- Do not do anything else at the same time

So, if you are walking, just walk. Turn off your headphones. If you are showering, just shower. If you are eating, just eat. Do not mess with your computer, your phone, or watch TV whilst you are doing it; leave the radio off too. If you are chopping carrots, just chop carrots. If you are playing with the kids, just play with the kids. Pay attention to all the sensations you feel whilst doing this. For example, if you are showering, notice the temperature of the water, the feel of the water on your skin. Notice the texture and smell of the soap, the bubbles from the shampoo. Notice your own body in the shower, the shapes and textures of it. Notice what your feet can feel on the shower floor. Whilst you do this, your thoughts will run off somewhere. Thoughts are like untrained puppies, they are always wandering off and getting distracted.

You cannot do much about this. But, when you notice your thoughts have wandered, you can make a choice to leave them be and bring your mind back to the sensations (smell of the soap, bubbles, shapes, textures, etc.). Make sure you do this when you are doing your activity.

Write down here the thing you have chosen. Something you normally do on 'automatic pilot', something you can take a break and go and do right now.

_____

_____

Now write here how you imagine it will be to do this with awareness, like in the shower example above. This may be something like 'I will really think about the fragrance of the soap and how many bubbles it makes' or 'How many tastes are there in this cup of coffee, how hot is it, how long does it stay on my tongue before swallowing?'

_____

_____

Now go and do it. Maybe you need to time it. If so, five minutes is a good length of time. Then come back and write down your observations about the experience:

_____

_____

_____

What did you learn from this?

_____

You might want to take a break now and do something else and come back later. If you want to continue, here is another mindfulness exercise.

Mindfulness 2: Eat a raisin

First, read the instructions below. There are also free recordings of these exercises available to download at www.getyourlifeback.global. You could also make a recording of the following instructions to listen to as you go along. Or just read it, then do whatever you remember. It does not really matter if you miss anything out.

- Go and find a raisin or another dried fruit or nut
- Sit down with this food object near to you
- Pay attention to how you are sitting
- Sit with your feet on the floor and your hands in your lap
- Make sure your neck is supported on your shoulders and your back is straight
- You can use the chair for your back or sit away from the back of the chair if you prefer
- Put the food object in the palm of your hand

LOOK: Lift your hand so you can take a close, mindful look at the object. Check out the colours, textures and shadows. Turn it over and study the other side.

SMELL: Lift the object to just below your nose. Observe what you can smell, if anything.

LISTEN: Take the object around to your ear. Rub or squeeze it and be aware of what you can hear.

TASTE: Put the object in your mouth and leave it on your tongue. Resist the urge to move it around for a moment. Notice your mouth salivating. Notice any thoughts or judgements that come. Now, move the object around your mouth a little, maybe pressing it against the roof of your mouth. When you are ready, slowly bite the object, and bite again. Notice the changes in taste and texture. Resist the urge to swallow for a moment. When you are ready, chew and swallow until most of the object has gone from your mouth. Notice what remains after the object has gone. Maybe small pieces are there in your mouth, a lingering taste, perhaps. Perhaps an urge to pick your teeth, or to have some water.

EXPAND: Now let your awareness grow, expanding from the inside of your mouth to your whole body. Then to the whole room and the world around you. Keeping this awareness in this moment, write down your observations about this experience:

What did you learn from this?

_____

When we take feedback on mindfulness exercises, people often say 'I liked that one' or 'That one was hard' or 'That was relaxing' or even 'I hate raisins'. You will notice that a lot of these statements are judgements, about the exercise or about our ability to do it. Our minds love to make rules about what is good and bad. We could mindfully notice these judgements and carry on.

You might want to take a break now and do something else and come back later. If you want to continue, here's another mindfulness exercise.

Mindfulness 3: Breath

Read these instructions then have a go. It does not matter if you forget any of the instructions.

> Get a timer (egg timer, phone, alarm clock, radio, etc.).
>
> Set the timer for five minutes.
>
> Sit down, straight back and neck.
>
> Close or half-close your eyes, or focus on a point on the floor in front of you, about a metre away.
>
> Bring the spotlight of your attention to your breath. Do not change your breath.

Notice:

> AIR IN – Notice the air travelling over your upper lip and in through your nostrils. Perhaps it is cool as it comes in and warm as it comes out again. Notice how your chest and tummy rise as your lungs fill with air. Notice how your ribcage expands. Perhaps there is a little pause at the top of the breath, or maybe a smooth transition to breathing out.
>
> AIR OUT – Observe the shrinking of the tummy and ribs as the air leaves your body. Do not change your breath, just observe. Notice the air leaving your nostrils.

As you sit and do this exercise, the untrained puppy thoughts will arrive again. There may be judgements such as wondering if your breath is OK or not. Or whether you are doing the exercise right, or whether the exercise will help at all. You may be distracted by body sensations, like an ache in your back or a tickle in your throat. When these happen you can decide to 'fix' them by moving or coughing. Or you can decide to resist the urges and see what happens. In either case, make the decision with awareness. Remember, it's normal to get distracted. When you notice you have left your breath, be kind to yourself. Gently bring your mind back to the breath. When the alarm goes off, bring your mind back to the room, keeping the present moment awareness of yourself and the world around you.

Write down your observations about this experience:

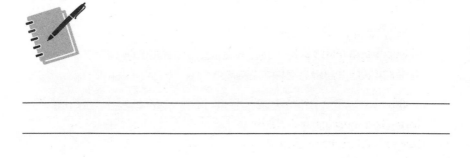

_____

_____

_____

What did you learn from this?

You might want to take a break now, do something else and come back later. Or if you want, you could try another mindfulness exercise.

Mindfulness 4: Mindful stretch

Stand up and lift your arms high above your head. Really stretch out your arm muscles, feeling the stretch throughout the arms. Look up at the ceiling and try to touch it. Let your head fall back and stand on tiptoes, really stretching for the ceiling. Feel this through your whole body.

Next, plant your feet on the floor firmly and fold your upper body forward from the hips as far as you comfortably can. Just dangle there. Shake your head gently and let your arms flop forward. Just hang out here for a moment. Notice any discomfort or pleasure, or warmth or stiffness in your muscles.

Uncurl slowly back to standing upright.

Place your palms in the small of your back, push your hips forwards and lean back from the hips, squeezing your shoulder blades together, as if you are worn out after gardening.

Straighten up. Put your hands on your hips and lean to the right. Notice the muscles down the left-hand side of your body. Then lean to the left, noticing the muscles on the right side.

Straighten up and shake out each arm and each leg. Notice the whole of your body. Now notice three things about the room or environment around you.

Do all this with as much awareness and acceptance as you can manage today.

Mindfulness 5: Thoughts

This exercise also helps us gain more awareness of our thoughts. There will be much more about this when we look at 'thought catching' in later chapters.

> Set your timer for five minutes.
>
> Sit (or stand) with your back and neck straight and your feet on the floor. Imagine a row of soldiers marching through your head. Picture them if you can. If you cannot (not everybody can), just imagine them as clearly as possible. Imagine them marching through your head and out of your ear. They are marching down your arm and across the floor, then back up your other arm and back into your head.
>
> Now notice thoughts that come into your head. As you notice each thought, give it to a soldier to carry out of your ear. When you notice another thought, give it to another soldier, and so on.

> When your mind wanders and you notice you have stopped doing this, gently bring your mind back to the task.

Write down your observations about this experience:

_____

_____

_____

What did you learn from this?

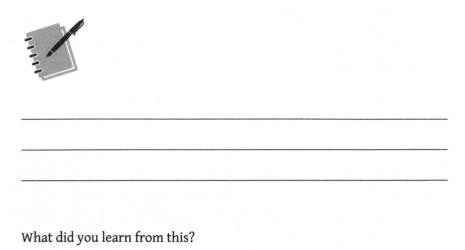

_____

Mindfulness 6: Feelings

This exercise was developed by ACT therapists and is great for getting hold of painful emotions and also for physical pain. It is known as the 'physicalising exercise'.

Sit (or stand) with your back and neck straight and your feet on the floor.

Bring to mind an emotion which is painful for you. It may be associated with a recent or past event, or with thoughts which upset you. Or you might want to work with a physical pain in your body.

Ask yourself, 'Where in my body do I feel this pain or painful emotion?'

Once you have located the pain, take both of your hands and place them on that part of your body. Then (really do this) use your hands to take the pain out of your body and hold it in your hands in front of you.

Observe and describe this pain:

LOOK – what colour is it, shape, size, transparent or opaque, still or moving? Is it solid or liquid or gas?

FEEL – how heavy is it, what texture (rough, smooth, prickly). Is it sticky or hairy, or something else; is it warm or cold?

LISTEN – is this pain silent or noisy? What noise is it making, loud or quiet, high or low?

SMELL – does this object smell of anything or not? What kind of smell, strong or weak?

Once you have thoroughly observed and described the pain, lift it with your hands and place it back inside your body.

Take a breath.

Then, once again, use your hands to take out the pain. Check it out again – what it looks like, feels like, sounds like, smells like. Has it changed in any way, or is it just the same?

When you have finished observing and describing the pain, place it back in your body using your hands again. Leave it there.

Write down your observations about this experience:

_____

_____

_____

What did you learn from this?

_____

Often, people feed back that they feel strongly that they do not want to put the pain back in. Of course, this is quite normal – who would want to? But the putting back in is important too, because we are learning to be with the pain.

Mindfulness 7: Grounding

When we are using mindfulness to bring ourselves back into the present moment it is often referred to as 'grounding'. This is very helpful for dealing with spacing out or time-travelling worry about the future or the past. One way to do this is as follows:

- Use a 'reminder' (smell a lavender roll-on, flick an elastic band on your wrist, squeeze a stress ball)
- Look around you. Name three things in the room

- What is the time and date?
- What is your name?
- What colour is the carpet?

Once you get good at mindfulness you can 'ground' yourself quite quickly by just bringing your attention briefly to your breath, taking a quick look around the room or by paying attention to the soles of your feet. Eventually, your 'reminder' will work to ground you without you having to do anything else.

In summary, mindfulness work will develop our mindfulness muscles just like going to the gym develops our physical muscles. Using our mindfulness muscles we will become skilled at taming our unruly puppy thoughts. We will change our relationship with these thoughts so that we can be the ones in charge.

How do I use mindfulness to help with my problems?

A lot of our problems are to do with thoughts, feelings and sensations we understandably do not want to have. Most of us have tried for many years to rid ourselves of these thoughts and feelings but, like naughty puppies, they just will not go away. So then we get involved in behaviours which have the effect of getting rid of these thoughts and feelings. We might drink ourselves into oblivion or stuff ourselves with food. Or become focused on gambling or pornography. We might self-harm or become obsessed with cleanliness or checking things. This is the trap: the very behaviours that work to get rid of unwanted thoughts and feelings become problems in themselves.

Mindfulness teaches us to relate differently to our thoughts and feelings. We can stop fighting them and trying to rid ourselves of them, which occupies a lot of time and effort and does not work long-term. We can observe and describe them non-judgementally; also practice re-stating our thoughts more mindfully. That is, just *observing and describing* the situation and stating the facts. So, instead of saying, 'I'll never manage to get a job', for example, I might say, 'I have not got the jobs I've tried for so far. It seems getting a job is difficult'. Instead of saying, 'This meat is disgusting', I might say, 'This meat smells as if it is rotting and I can see mould growing on its surface'. Instead of saying, 'You have betrayed me and let me down', you might say, 'You made me a promise and you did not keep it'.

We can also use mindfulness observing in the following way. When our mind sends us a thought like 'I'm not worth loving', we just note that this is a message our mind is sending us. So it now becomes 'I'm noticing that my mind is sending me a thought which says I'm not worth loving'. That way we get the chance to decide whether to get hooked up by the thought or not. The basic idea is to stay in the present moment without judging, and being willing to experience. When you notice you have left the present moment just gently come back to it. So, if you are having a boring time in a meeting, at a family event or even waiting at the bus stop, instead of staring out of the window and dreaming about what else you could be doing, throw yourself into the meeting or the event. Pay close attention to the people around you. Take an interest in what they are saying. Give up being right or needing to get your opinion heard. Just listen and notice what is going on, inside you and out. We can call this *participating*. The main reason to be mindful is so that you can progress towards getting your life back. When you know your values clearly, mindfulness will help you focus on them and take daily steps towards them, even when this is uncomfortable and difficult.

If you have decided you want to be a loving and supportive parent, for example, then that is great. But perhaps your kids start to behave in that old infuriating way. Mindfulness can help here. You can notice the bodily sensations, feelings, thoughts and urges to snap at the children without having to act on them. You can decide to still act exactly as a loving and supportive parent would, no matter how you feel.

If you are having trouble sleeping and waking up with unwanted thoughts going round in your head, or if they come along during the day, you can observe them and describe them. Then turn the focus of your mind to where you want it to be. During the day, it may be an activity. During the night, you might want to watch your breath or practice the 'thought soldiers'. If you find thoughts like, 'Oh no, I'm never going to get enough sleep now!', give that thought to a soldier to carry on the march through your head, down your arm, across your tummy, up the other arm, back inside your head and out of your ear again.

If you are having an urge to self-harm, notice this. Observe it and describe it. Choose to 'surf' the wave of it. Do this as many times as you need to.

Do I need to practise mindfulness?

Yes! Ideally, do at least one exercise every day. But there is also the aim that you get to be able to access a mindful stance as you go through your normal day. Once you have practised the exercises for a while, just try grounding yourself whenever you need to. In schools, some students are using 'FOFBOS' (Feet On Floor Bottom On Seat) to ground themselves just before an exam or to help deal with stress. So, we just let our mind focus on our feet on the floor, and then turn our attention to our bottom on the seat. This takes less than a minute, but puts us in the here and now and in the right frame of mind to be effective. Another version of this, which we use in work with business people, is 'Breath Feet'. Just notice, 'Where is my breath?' and notice, 'Where are my feet?' Then continue your task, keeping your focus in the present moment.

What might go wrong with mindfulness?

Very often people say to us, 'I've tried it, but it doesn't work.' The question we ask then is, 'What do you mean by work?' Usually, what people reply is, 'Well, it hasn't made me feel better.' Then we need to chat about how tricky constantly seeking to feel better can be. The more we chase it, the more we monitor 'Do I feel better or worse today?' and the more feeling better eludes us. One thing that mindfulness teaches us is to 'hold things lightly'. This means to let go of struggling to fix all the problems we have all the time. Holding things lightly means we have them in our awareness but they are not dominating our existence. If we really want to get our lives back, we need to shift our focus away from feeling better and onto moving towards our goals and values.

Bring to mind someone who has achieved something. Maybe someone you know or someone in the media or a figure from history. Someone you genuinely admire. Now consider their journey towards that achievement. Would you guess it was always pleasant and easy? Sometimes they will have had to struggle to keep going. Usually, getting your life back involves quite a lot of discomfort, difficulty, being afraid, uncertainty and doubt.

Let us think about George. You may remember that the life he wanted was about being a loving and supportive father and husband. After working hard on his thoughts, sometimes he still finds himself being judgemental about Jean and the kids but now he is able to notice that his mind is sending these thoughts to him. Most of the time he just lets the unruly puppies in his mind bark at him and continues to behave as he really wants to, helping with the washing-up, etc.

Developing a mindful attitude

Although we practise exercises to train up our mindfulness muscles, we also try to develop a mindful attitude. This means living life as much as possible in the present moment, being aware non-judgementally of every experience and actively participating in the world. To do this, we need to drop coping by avoiding things and learn to accept what is happening. Because George developed this attitude he was able to notice what his thought puppies were up to and take some action. If he had tried to just shut the thoughts out, he would not have been able to do this. Being open and aware like this is a lifetime's practice – we need to keep at it whenever we remember and whatever we are doing. It is a key to getting your life back.

Make up your mind now to do something mindfully in the next few minutes. Then after you have done it, take a break and do something different, other than reading this book.

Chapter 6

Compassionate Self-validation

Do not let this chapter title worry you, as it sounds rather complex. By the end of it you will be able to apply compassionate self-validation to your-self. You will also be able to offer compassionate validation to others. This chapter builds on the skills that you learned in the previous chapter on mindfulness. Validation will increase your listening skills. This may sound a little strange as you probably feel you have been listening to people all your life. But validation is another tool in your life skills tool belt that will help you to reach your life goals. Sometimes our minds tell us things about ourselves in a negative, judgemental way. Mindfulness is a new way to handle what our minds send us. It is helpful to thank your mind for its messages and not act on them.

We now need to take these skills a step further. Telling ourselves constantly that we are not good enough and need to change (our weight, appearance, drinking habits, job, relationships, negative thoughts, etc.) is a recipe for despair. Being compassionate towards yourself is being kind and caring to yourself, as a kind friend might be towards you. Constantly reminding ourselves that we should be able to do better is like a cooking pot for despair.

Acceptance comes about when we are able to validate and be compassionate towards ourselves. This can give us an accepting attitude: 'I am as I am, and it is understandable that I am this way'. Genuinely, there is a way of understanding every person's way of being in the world. This understanding can be found in their history, in their inner world and in their outer world, as we saw in Chapter 2: My Story. For example, if you have been criticised as a child, it is understandable that you would have learned to be self-critical or defensive as an adult. Compassionate self-validation says, 'Given how things were, how else could I possibly be – many people who experienced similar things are like me'.

Sometimes, it is easier to learn to validate others before trying it on yourself. We will start with validation towards others and then move on to compassionate self-validation.

Validation

Simple steps to learning validation: mindful listening

1. *Listening:* have you ever had a phone call from a friend with a problem? Do you find that soon into the conversation you stop listening because your mind is searching for a good response? 'What am I going to say when she stops talking?' Mindful listening involves becoming aware of how our minds keep looking for answers, and then bringing our minds back to what the person is actually saying.
2. *Not judging:* as you are listening, you may notice your mind sending you some judgements. 'I don't think she should have been with this person in the first place, I think she is doing the wrong thing'. When we are being non-judgemental we notice our minds making these judgements and just let them be, bringing our attention back to what the person is actually saying.
3. *Reflecting:* in response to what is said to you, one thing you can do is to sum up what you have heard and check that you have really heard the person accurately. You might say, 'So what you're saying is . . . Is that right?'

4. *Guessing how the person might be feeling:* as well as listening carefully and reflecting back, you might try guessing how the person is or was feeling. You might say, 'Did you feel really sad about that?'

An example:

Your friend Stacy rings up. She is very upset, as she has had a big row with her partner Steve over his friendship with another woman. Stacy is your friend and, to be honest, you have never really liked Steve and think he is a waste of space. After Stacy has told you this on the phone, there are a number of ways in which you can reply. Your replies can be validating or not validating. The two examples start with how *not to use* validation when you reply.

How not to use validation

- You – 'I just knew this would happen – he's a waste of space and you should never have got together with him, you know you are too good for him'
- Stacy – 'Yes, I know'

Now Stacy will probably not want to continue this conversation – she feels worse and told off for getting in a mess. Stacy will feel better if she stops talking to you and you have not helped your friend. This is not using validation with Stacy.

How to use validation

- You – 'Oh Stacy, you sound really upset, you've had a big row with Steve?'
- Stacy – 'Yes, it was awful. I feel like it's time to break up'
- You – 'Gosh, break up. It's that bad?'
- Stacy – 'Yes, it is. He's too friendly with that woman at the club'
- You – 'Oh, that must really hurt you so much'
- Stacy – 'Yes, it does. I feel like I can't stop crying'
- You – 'You know, Stacy, if that was me I would feel the same'

What was gained from using validation?

The first conversation stopped very quickly and excluded Stacy. She was made to feel responsible for the whole mess. Stacy is unlikely to ring again or to continue talking as she got told off. You may have been trying to help but she heard you telling her off.

When you used validation, you were not judgemental. Stacy felt understood and was starting to continue talking in that safe conversation. It may sound as though you were just repeating what Stacy had said, yet you were in fact telling her that you understood the seriousness of the situation and that you were ready to support her. You used your mindfulness skills and did not act on the judgement thoughts about Steve. In your opinion, Steve is, was and always will be useless. This would not be helpful to Stacy. Not judging allowed you to see that your friend was hurting and needed you to help her. Validation does not mean that you agree with or condone a situation. It means you are able to listen and understand what you are being told. You can validate Stacy's distress even though you feel that she should never have got together with Steve. Your focus needs to be on your friend, who needs your help, and on your wish to give her comfort.

FAQs

Q – Is validation just repeating?

A – No, it is not just repeating, it is making the person feel heard. You can see from the example that Stacy relaxed, felt supported and continued to talk.

Q – Is this just parroting?

A – You do not have to say the exact words that you hear. Just sum up and reflect back in your own natural words and check with the person that you have understood correctly.

Q – Is it agreeing or approving?

A – You do not have to agree or approve to validate. You need to understand and validate the person's distress even if you do not agree.

Q – Is it giving reassurance?

A – No, it is just accepting things as they are without an easy 'It'll all be fine'.

Q – Won't I just annoy people?

A – No, validation really does work – try it out on a friend.

Q – But I won't solve my friend's problem by validation

A – Validation is about understanding and supporting, not solving problems. Your friend is more likely to find her own solution if you help her in this way.

This little story is real and was feedback from a validation course we taught. A young man told us what happened when he went home afterwards. When he got home his mother said that she had had a bad day. He validated his mother's feelings by reflecting back what she had said and guessing how she might have felt. His mum looked very worried and said, 'Are you ill or something? You *never* normally listen to me!'

Validation with compassion

We can take validation to another level by adding some compassion. Adding compassion means to add loving-kindness and caring. When validation was used with Stacy a powerful statement was made in a very accepting way. 'You know, Stacy, if that was me I would feel just the same.' It was the start of adding some compassion to the conversation. This very simple statement told Stacy that you are not telling her off or criticising her, but you are feeling and understanding her pain. In a way you are 'normalising' Stacy's feelings. You are letting her know her feelings are normal, given the situation. You are telling Stacy that in her situation we might all feel the same. She is distressed, but is still your precious friend. Compassion with validation allowed you to provide a safe place for Stacy where she could start to accept and hold her very raw emotions.

Compassionate self-validation

Using validation and compassion sometimes feels more comfortable when we apply it to other people. A key skill at this time is to learn to apply both validation and compassion to yourself. If we criticise, blame or tell ourselves off, we will feel worse and unable to move on. Compassion is often used in therapy (for example, in Compassion Focused Therapy) to free us from negative and damaging judgements about ourselves. Listening to other people and to ourselves with compassion and acceptance has endless benefits.

Compassion involves empathy, which means being able to understand one's own and other people's feelings. We can be caring, accepting and tolerant of distress in ourselves and others. By not judging ourselves or other people, we can take a more compassionate view. Our brains have evolved over hundreds of thousands of years to have feelings and thoughts, which help us survive and make us human (see also Chapter 9, page 132). Anxiety, anger and depression are natural experiences, which are not 'our fault'. Experiences such as neglect, bullying and abuse may lead to ongoing fears like being afraid of rejection or behaviours such as staying in abusive relationships. We can try to cope and control negative feelings, for example by avoiding social events, showing submissive behaviour or drinking too much. But these avoiding behaviours can become big problems themselves. Validation and compassion help when we feel anxious, threatened and self-critical. We can talk to (validate) ourselves with compassion, to change our focus of attention, so that we can take a non-judgemental and caring approach to ourselves. Here are some short examples of compassionate self-validation from the earlier stories:

Janet

'Stopping shoplifting is very hard. I know other people struggle with it too but I am making progress.'

Tom

'Most dads have doubts about whether they are good enough. I know I can be a good dad so I have to work hard to gain my children's trust and get contact started again.'

Cheyenne

'I find it difficult to feel good about myself because I have had many years during my childhood of being taught that I was not wanted.'

George

'I've been feeling left out and not as useful as Jean and this has been making me feel bad, but these are just my thoughts. Many people struggle with drinking and smoking, I'm not the only one.'

Aleena

'I know my anxiety about being abandoned is natural, and it has led to me dumping potential partners. I have to start trusting men more.'

Pauline

'I panic when I am near men. I guess anybody who was abused as a child like I was would have these sort of problems.'

Mandy

'I can understand how anyone who listens to a critical voice will feel terrible. People who hear voices usually listen to them; I am learning not to.'

Rick

'I find it tiring, getting angry at other people. It is hard to change but this is now a lot less than it was.'

Sally

'At last, I am understanding why I have to be best at everything and also when I can relax and do not have to do quite as well.'

Compassionate self-validation exercise

Now it is time to apply all this to yourself. Think of a situation that is difficult for you at the moment. This might be at work, with a friend, thoughts you are having, a behaviour that you are doing. Here is an example of the way we tend to talk to ourselves about difficult situations:

> 'I went to that job interview today. I knew it was a waste of time – I'm not clever enough to do that work. I've never been any good at office work. I should have worked harder at school instead of messing about all the time. There's just no way forward.'

This person's unruly mind has gone crazy on the judgements! Put a ring around any judgement words you can recognise here. Examples are 'a waste of time' and 'never been any good'. Obviously, this is just an example, it is not your own situation. Write here your own difficult situation, thoughts, feelings or behaviour. Feel free to be as judgemental as you normally would be:

_____

_____

_____

Before you start the next step, compassionate self-validation, do the following mindfulness exercise. Pay attention to your breath. Notice the breath in and the breath out. Do this for three breaths, then take these steps:

- Notice your judgemental thoughts. You can notice them by looking for judgement words like 'should', 'never', 'always', 'good' and 'bad'. Go back and put a ring around your own judgemental thoughts.

- Step into your kind friend's shoes for a minute. How would s/he see your difficult situation? What might they say?

- Re-state your difficult situation without any judgement words, just observing and describing it.

With compassionate self-validation the job interview experience could be re-stated like this:

> 'I went for a job interview today. I didn't get the job. It was a complex job, which I may have found difficult. It's not surprising I was upset and I guess the other people who didn't get the job were also upset. I thought I might be upset as I've tried for a few jobs before and been upset then. Well done for getting shortlisted'.

Now re-state your difficult situation, thoughts, feelings or behaviour using compassion and self-validation. Just observe and describe. Do not forget that judgements are banned from this description. Be kind, loving and supportive to yourself, just as a kind friend would be:

_____

_____

_____

Take a few moments to compare your first description with this one. The content has not really changed, but the way in which you see it may have. Sometimes, we have to accept that we are as we are. This is not making excuses or approving, simply accepting. Many people have similar problems after similar experiences. We can stay compassionate towards ourselves whilst we are working towards changing. There is more about this in Chapter 8, What Needs to Change? (page 121). Here, you are starting to reframe your thoughts and what your unruly mind is telling you. The content has not changed but the way in which you see it is changing.

Now take a break. Show yourself some loving kindness before reading the next chapter. You could give yourself a compliment (write it down if you wish) or buy yourself some flowers.

Chapter 7

My Strengths and Resources

Your strengths and resources are important for the journey ahead. If you plan to climb a mountain you do not go unequipped, unfit or without backup support. In order to prepare yourself for the next chapters, let us take a look at who and what you have to help you.

Make a list of all the talents and skills you have (some examples may be musical ability, running, spelling, maths, nail art, knitting, etc.) even if you have not used them in a while. Include in this list any daft things you might think are of no use to anyone, so long as you love doing them. So, worm-collecting, cloud-watching or carpet-throwing are all fine here. So long as it floats your boat. You may find, if you are in a negative place right now, that you have not done some of these things for a while. When you think about doing them again, your mind may send you some obstacle thoughts like 'Well, I'll have to go right back to the beginning and I'll be so frustrated' or 'What's the point of starting all over again?' If this happens, thank your mind for the thought and gently bring your mind back to making the list.

My talents

Any ability or interest you possess or have ever possessed can go in here. You might want to ask a friend if there are any other things you have missed. For example:

* *Playing the piano*
* *Singing*
* *Understanding algebra*
* *Mechanics for cars*
* *Hair-cutting*

Write your own list here:

_____

_____

_____

_____

_____

_____

_____

_____

_____

_____

My social support network

Next, let us look at your social support network. This could be your family, friends, work colleagues and neighbours. Only include people if you think they can be helpful to you. For example:

* *Sylvia next door*
* *My brother*
* *My tennis partner*
* *My friends on Facebook*
* *My social worker*

Write your own list here:

_____

_____

_____

_____

_____

_____

_____

_____

_____

_____

_____

My ways of occupying my day

Next, how do you occupy your day or how did you in the past when you enjoyed it? For example:

- *Looking after the children*
- *Volunteering, for example at the charity shop*
- *Going to work*
- *Meeting my friends*
- *Going to college*
- *Doing exercise*

Write your own list here:

_____

_____

_____

_____

_____

_____

_____

_____

_____

_____

My ways of supporting myself financially

Now think about how you support yourself financially. For example:

- *Going to work*
- *Partner or family member*
- *Inheritance*

_____

_____

_____

_____

_____

_____

_____

_____

_____

_____

My personal strengths

Now think about your personal strengths. For example, being a good listener, empathy for others, able to stand up for yourself, etc. Here is a list of ideas:

- *Kindness and generosity*
- *Being a good listener*
- *Keep myself fit*
- *Able to stand up for myself*
- *Give to charity*
- *Look after my animals*

_____

_____

_____

_____

_____

_____

_____

_____

_____

My achievements so far

Write here any achievements you have made in your life so far, things you are proud of. If you find this hard, step back and look at yourself as your kind friend would look at you. What would s/he say? For example:

- *Looked after my dog even when I was ill*
- *Qualified as a mechanic/supervisor/gardener/fireman/secretary/florist, etc.*
- *Raised money for research into cancer*
- *Completed a Duke of Edinburgh Award*
- *Raised two children*
- *Learned to cook nice meals*

Write your own list here:

_____

_____

_____

_____

_____

_____

_____

_____

_____

_____

Fill in the lists for yourself in this chapter. If you struggle, ask a friend or partner to help. Recognise that you may not have thought of these things as strengths and resources before. You will need these lists later when we are thinking of what to do instead of our unwanted behaviours. Looking through your own lists, is there one activity that you would like to re-start, or maybe use in new areas of your life? Or build on it in some way? You could have a look at the examples below if you are stuck. If so, make a plan to re-start or re-use at least one strength or resource. For example, 'I plan to go to the gym for an hour on Wednesday evening after work'. Write your plan here:

_____

_____

Add this to your Baby Steps Diary (see page 79). Here are some examples from the stories:

Janet . . .

Remembered that she used to go to the gym, as she made her lists. Because she wanted to get fitter and manage her eating, she decided to add going to the gym to her Baby Steps Diary.

Tom . . .

Noticed that he used to write little stories for the children, which they liked. He decided to start doing this again.

Cheyenne . . .

Realised that she was a great pudding cook. She decided to cook healthy puddings for herself and the children.

George . . .

Wrote down that he was good at doing things in the kitchen like washing-up and putting away. He decided that he would do this regularly and wrote it in his Baby Steps Diary.

Aleena . . .

Had never thought that being clever was a strength and resource. She is spending some time getting used to this idea now. She did not feel she needed to re-start more resources just now.

Pauline . . .

Did not realise that being kind and understanding what people need is actually a great resource. She did not need to re-start it but she decided that she would recognise it when she was using this strength and feel proud.

Mandy . . .

Chose to use the skill of bargain spotting. She used to sell the stuff she bought at car boot sales. She thought she would start this again.

Rick . . .

Remembered he used to go mountain biking, but he sold his bike five years ago. He decided to get another and go mountain biking for more de-stressing and to get fit.

Sally...

Has been a role model and mentor before for her best friend. When Sally realised that this was a strength of hers, she decided to join the company mentoring scheme for young accountants.

As we come to the end of this chapter, take a moment of self-compassion and validation. Notice the lovely things about yourself.

Homework

Keep practising mindfulness and filling in your Baby Steps Diary this week. Be proud of your strengths and resources.

Chapter 8

What Needs to Change?

We have been spending time focusing on our strengths and resources. Also, we have been looking at what we have in our lives already that we value. And we are getting clearer on the directions we really want to travel in our lives. To travel in our chosen direction, we need to change a few things. We have outlined some of what we need to change in the problems list right at the beginning of the book. In this chapter, we will think about other things we need to change too. Before we start, let us look at an attitude of mind, which might help us to be open and non-judgemental (yes, mindful!) as we go about doing this.

Dialectics

'Dialectics' is the idea that everything is relative and everything is constantly changing. For example, you may have heard the saying 'You can't step into the same river twice'. The water will be different water. In this way of looking at things, instead of Truth, there are only Truths. Every Truth has an opposite, which is also true. To make this clearer, take a look at this example:

- Truth One: money is the root of all evil
- Truth Two: money is a very good thing

In the dialectical view of things both Truths One and Two can be true at the same time. Our task is to search for another truth which includes both these two. For example:

- Truth Three: money can be used for both good and evil purposes

Of course, we can come up with a statement opposite to that, too. For example:

- Truth Four: money corrupts all those who have it.

So, in the world of dialectics we have to hold opposite views in our minds at the same time. We can stay aware of our own point of view and still practise seeing another point of view. You may remember that our best friend saw things differently to us in Chapter 2: My Story. We can practise being aware of opposites and dilemmas without trying to resolve them. We can be aware of the naughty puppy thoughts rushing around in our minds and *yet still* take steps towards change.

In dialectical language, all human beings are wonderful just as they are *and* they need to change. Try to hold this dialectical attitude as we go through this chapter. We will be inviting you to look closer at all the behaviours you need to change, and you are still wonderful.

Often when people describe themselves they use a lot of negatives, but there is always an alternative, compassionate, best-friend view. When people make a list of all their unwanted behaviours they usually find it depressing and you may too. Dialectics helps to balance this depression by letting you hold in your mind the opposite, which is acceptance. Values and goals are the key to moving forward.

Things I need to change: steps away from getting my life back

Each day we can take steps towards the life we want or steps away from it. You are invited to identify the exact behaviours, thoughts and feelings you want to change. In other words, the times you step away. As you do this, try to have a mindful and dialectical approach. 'Things I need to change' come under three headings:

1. *Things I do which harm myself or others, for example:*

- Hitting my partner
- Drinking myself into oblivion
- Binge eating
- Vomiting
- Over-exercising
- Cutting myself
- Pulling my hair out

2. *Things I do which stop me from changing, for example:*

- Refusing to talk about the problem
- Pretending it does not exist
- Thinking I can never change
- Minimising the effects of the problem
- Arguing back with people trying to help me
- Apologising profusely and then doing it again
- Not asking for help when I need it
- Being afraid to change

3. *Things I do which mess up my life or stop me from reaching my goals and values, for example:*

- Thinking I cannot do anything worthwhile
- Dumping promising partners before they dump me
- Having negative, hopeless thoughts
- Staying up late playing video games so I cannot get up in the morning

- Avoiding applying for jobs
- Not going out because I am anxious
- Lying awake at night thinking what a bad person I am
- Doing things to please other people so my needs never get met
- Reacting really fast before I have had time to think
- Worrying about bad things that might happen
- Getting so angry that I shout at people

You may not have found your own exact problem behaviours, thoughts and feelings in this list. These are just examples. Here is a 'Behaviours to Change' list made by Tom, whose main problem was gambling.

My Things to Change (Tom)

1. *Things I do which harm myself or others*

- Gambling

Tom thought some more about how he dealt with his gambling by lying about it, and other things that stopped him from making the changes he needed to make. He wrote this list under section 2:

2. *Things I do which stop me from changing*

- Lying about gambling
- Minimising the effects of gambling
- Not filling in my gambling diary for my therapy
- Apologising profusely and then doing it again
- Not asking for help when I need it
- Thinking 'I'm addicted to gambling so it's not worth trying to stop'

Tom boiled down key words for his values and goals including: reliable partner, available dad. When Tom planned a 'Baby Step' of calling his estranged children, he found he could not do it. His puppy thoughts kept barking that his kids would reject him and sent him images of this happening. He added this to the list below of things which were messing up his life:

3. *Things I do which mess up my life or stop me from reaching my goals and values*

- Gambling
- Having hopeless thoughts about being a gambling addict
- Getting upset and not being able to manage the upset without gambling
- Not contacting my children because I'm anxious they'll reject me
- Lying awake at night thinking what a mess I've made of everything
- Arguing with my ex-wife about the children
- Lying to my new partner in case she rejects me

My things to change

To help with completing section 1, *Things I do which harm myself or others*, go back to Chapter 1: How and Why to Use this Book. Some of your things to change will come from your problem list in Chapter 1 (page 3). You may want to add others or the problems from Chapter 1 might be enough. Write your list here:

1. *Things I do which harm myself or others*

_____

_____

_____

_____

Section 2, *Things I do which stop me from changing*, is often new to people. You may not have thought before about things you do which stop you from changing. Most of us do some of these. Think about a specific time when you have tried to change but something you have done or thought or felt has stopped you. Let us take the example of not asking for help. Try to think of a time when you have needed help but not got it. Perhaps your mind puppies were barking 'Nobody cares anyway'. This might have the effect of stopping you from even asking so you did not get help. Another way to do this is to look at your Baby Steps Diary from Chapter 4. Here is the example again:

In the Baby Steps Diary example, my thinking that Mum would think I've gone soft could have stopped me from going ahead with saying thank you for the cake. I can put this in section 2. I would write 'Having thoughts that Mum will think I've gone soft'. Copy your own Baby Steps Diary from Chapter 4 in the spaces on page 127 then use the 'Things that got in the way' column to add to your section 2 list. Write your own list here:

2. *Things I do which stop me from changing*

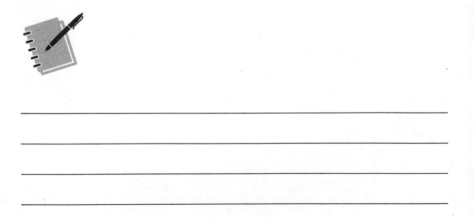

_____

_____

_____

_____

In section 3 we write things which generally mess up our lives – Tom wrote about lying awake, being anxious and not contacting his children,

My Baby Steps Diary

Day	Baby step	Did I do it? Yes/No	Things that got in the way	Things that helped
Example	*Thank Mum for cake*	*Yes*	*Thought she'd think I've gone soft*	*Practised saying 'Thank you' first before I did it with Mum*
Monday				
Tuesday				
Wednesday				
Thursday				
Friday				
Saturday				
Sunday				

(please see page 126)

for example. Think about things you do, feel or think which really stop you from getting your life back. Write them here:

3. *Things I do which mess up my life or stop me from reaching my goals and values*

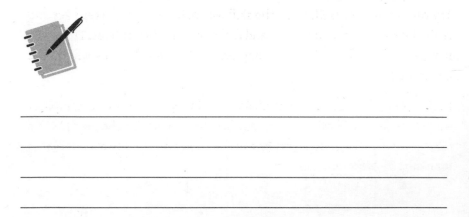

_____

_____

_____

_____

Well done! We know this may have triggered off some naughty puppy thoughts in your head. Just observe and describe these then turn your attention to the achievement you just made. You can now *stand back* enough to really see these behaviours, thoughts and feelings clearly. You have met the monster on the road and instead of screaming and running, you have taken a good long look at it. Now you see it clearly you will have some new options for dealing with it. This is not a one-off shot – we need to get into the habit of being willing and able to stand back and look at our behaviour regularly. We need to do this without beating ourselves up, but with awareness of what takes us towards our values and what takes us away.

Now you know the things you need to change, the steps you take away from the life you want. It is important to start keeping a close track of them as they pop up in your life each day. A diary sheet to start recording your 'steps away' behaviours from sections 1, 2 and 3 in 'My Things to Change

List' is overleaf. It is very important to fill it in every day. My Things to Change Diary can also be downloaded from www.getyourlifeback.global. The italics are example entries from Tom. Tom could not possibly record all of his things to change, so he chose the most serious ones. These are in section 1 (gambling) and section 2 (lying).

Try this out for yourself. Here, the skill we are learning is to step back and really look at what we do, think and feel most days in our lives. This is the material we need for the next chapters, which will show us what to do about it all.

Decide now where to keep your diary – in your pocket, on your computer – and when you will fill it in each day. It is a good idea to choose the same time each day. Or else to link filling in the diary with a daily event, such as immediately after dinner.

Write your plan here:

I will keep my diary in _____

I will fill it in at (time) _____

Great! Now you may need a break. Go and do something different for a little while.

My Things to Change Diary

DAY	BEHAVIOUR	WHAT WAS HAPPENING BEFORE?	WHAT HAPPENED AFTER?	THOUGHTS AND FEELINGS	HOW BAD WAS IT? (1–10)
Monday	Gambling 11 p.m.–2 a.m. online	Kids did not turn up for contact after school	Went to bed	I'll never be able to stop. Felt rejected and alone	7
Tuesday	Lied about this to Sarah	She asked what I'd been doing	Could not sleep	What a heel I am. Sarah could do better. Hate myself	6

Chapter 9

The Wheel of Experience

Each experience we have can be broken down into the aspects that we are about to look at. An event (inside or outside our bodies) is responded to with thoughts, feelings, body sensations and behaviours. We call this the 'Wheel of Experience'. This chapter looks at our experiences and spends some time looking at feelings too. It ends with hints and tips on how to handle feelings. Advice on handling thoughts and behaviour comes in later chapters.

What are feelings?

Feelings are things like anger, sadness, love, etc. and are a part of everyone's experience. They are important because they often drive our behaviour. For example, Cheyenne has thoughts of being worthless and undeserving. She feels numb and ashamed so she washes her hair in washing-up liquid and gives *all* of her time to her children, neglecting herself. Cheyenne is doing this because she feels she does not deserve nice shampoo or time for herself. When Cheyenne tries to use things like a nice shampoo she feels more strongly that she is not worth it and more ashamed. On the other hand, when she uses washing-up liquid she feels at one with her shame. Cheyenne does not really understand or think about this – she just feels the feelings that drive her behaviour. We will look at Cheyenne's hair-washing behaviour some more in a moment.

Many of us have learned that we cannot bear our feelings. Extreme feelings are often very unpleasant and they come along as a package with thoughts, behavioural urges and body sensations.

The Wheel of Experience

We can think of our experiences as in the diagram. An event happens outside or inside our bodies and we have this whole 'Wheel of Experience' response to it. Some examples of outside events are somebody shouting, being stung by a wasp, winning the lottery or eating lunch. Examples of inside events are having a stomach ache, thought puppies barking, having a memory, or seeing an image of past abuse. In the Wheel of Experience diagram below you can see that each event triggers:

- *Thoughts*, such as 'I'm worthless', 'This is dangerous' or 'This is great'
- *Feelings* such as fear, sadness, anger or joy
- *Behaviours* such as running away, shouting, crying, hugging someone, opening champagne; also, *urges* to do things, which we might resist actually doing
- *Body sensations* such as getting tense in the jaw, shaking, having butterflies in the tummy, or headaches

Looking at our own experience using this wheel can help us to understand in more detail what is going on in our inner world.

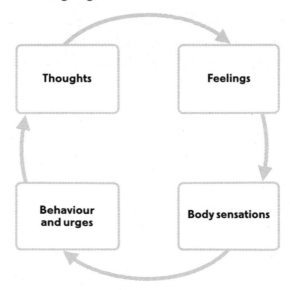

When Cheyenne takes a shower and washes her hair in shampoo, her Wheel of Experience looks like this:

If Cheyenne could take a snapshot of her inner world whilst having a shower, the words in the diagram are the words she would use to describe her thoughts, feelings, behaviour and body sensations at the time. You will notice that having a shower is not a big event; it is just an ordinary, every-day happening. Many trigger events are just like this, normal, everyday things. This book is about learning to describe our own experience in the same way.

An exciting email!

You may have received an email before now, from someone in a foreign land. He or she says they want to give you a million pounds. All you have to do is just send your bank details so they can put the money into your bank. We are guessing you did not believe this email, but we would like you to really imagine you *did* believe it. Close your eyes and imagine getting this email and really buying it. We know you are not so gullible, but just for a moment let yourself imagine you really believe you are going to get a million pounds. Now fill in the segments below about what body reactions, thoughts, feelings and behaviour and urges you have.

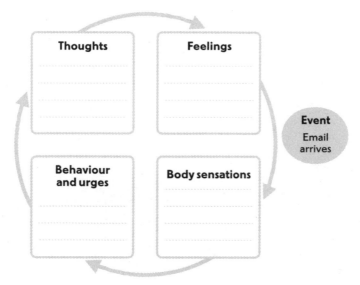

What have you noticed? Sometimes it can be difficult to identify feelings and what goes on in our bodies when they happen. We'll work on this further on in this chapter. Now repeat the exercise for how this Wheel of Experience would look if you did your usual thing and did not believe the email:

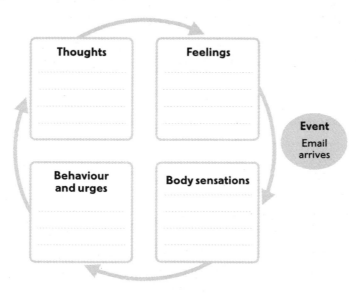

Notice the big difference between how you react if you believe the email compared with if you did not. Only the thought is different, but your whole inner world changes. A lot of our thoughts are like the email: junk! But we tend to believe them, just because they have arrived in our heads. Beginning to observe your own thoughts, feelings, body sensations and behaviour can give you a 'helicopter view' of how you react to the world around you. We can also react to inside events like body sensations and memories. For example, Pauline was sexually abused when she was a child. As an adult she gets images in her head and unwanted, horrible memories. These are inside events that connect with a whole Wheel of Experience that looks like this:

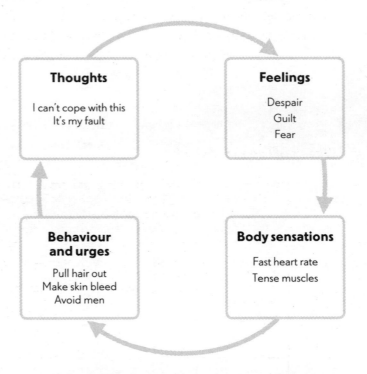

Thoughts

I can't cope with this
It's my fault

Feelings

Despair
Guilt
Fear

Behaviour and urges

Pull hair out
Make skin bleed
Avoid men

Body sensations

Fast heart rate
Tense muscles

Recognising our feelings

Identifying each part of a Wheel of Experience is a skill. Many of the things in a Wheel of Experience come automatically and are outside of our awareness. We are learning to bring them more clearly into our awareness so that we can understand and work on them. Here is a table of things that tend to go together inside Wheels of Experience. For example, if we are aware we are *feeling* angry, it is likely that we will have an *urge* to attack (physically or verbally), which we may or may not *act* on (behaviour). We are also likely to feel *body sensations* of increased tension, heart rate and breathing. We will probably have blaming-type *thoughts*. You can see this in the first row of the table. Each row has a set of things that tend to happen together. Sometimes it is easier to notice the body sensations first, sometimes we might notice a thought first or even a behaviour we are doing. These can be seen as clues to the rest of the parts of our wheel at the time.

Typical Wheels of Experience table

Feelings	Thoughts	Behaviour (including urges to do stuff)	Body sensations
Anger	It's his/her fault I'm going to get him/her	Attack (verbal, physical)	Muscle tension Fast heart rate Breathing fast
Guilt	It's my fault, I'm to blame	Say sorry, put it right (some people do things to get punished)	Squirmy, restless, tense Looking away

Feelings	Thoughts	Behaviour (including urges to do stuff)	Body sensations
Fear	Something bad is going to happen S/he/it's going to get me	Run away Avoid Escape (very high fear can lead to being frozen)	Fast heart rate, muscle tension, sick stomach, dizziness (very high fear can lead to shutting down)
Shame	I'm worthless I don't deserve good things	Hide Avoid Pretend Neglect self	Blushing Tension Not looking at people
Joy/Happiness	This is great I love this	Laugh Jump about Do it again	Alert Body upright Pleasure
Disgust	Yeeuch! Get this away from me	Avoid Be sick Retching	Stomach churning
Sadness	I've lost a loved one I'll never be happy again	Cry Look for what is lost	Muscles shaking Feeling weak Body not responding

Feelings	Thoughts	Behaviour (including urges to do stuff)	Body sensations
Excitement	It's great, I can do it, I want to find out more	Perform	Alert

Raised heartbeat

Flushed face |
| Surprise | I didn't expect that, wow! | Find out what's new

Turn towards the new thing | Depending on good or bad, surprise could be elation or panic |
| Interest | I need to know about this, this is important | Learn things, gather information | Alert

Other things that are going on around may be excluded

Attention focused |
| Love | I want to be with X all the time

Kind thoughts | Seeking out and being with the loved one

Showing care and acts of kindness | Eyes dilated and sexual arousal (for sexual love)

Warmth, comfort, safety (for friendship love) |

What are feelings for?

Our feelings may be in the driving seat when it comes to problem behaviours. Sometimes feelings happen at the wrong time or with a strength that makes them difficult to control. You may have had a 'panic attack' at a time when you did not expect it. Panic attacks happen when your body responds dramatically to fear messages coming from your mind. If these messages come at the wrong time or with great force, we can have a strong reaction to danger that is not there or is not very great, so we need to recognise our feelings to help understand our thoughts, urges and body sensations. We also need to take this a stage further and think about what our feelings are for. Take a look at the following chart and think about what your feelings are for:

Feelings	What they are for
Anger	Achieving goals/getting needs met, protecting our rights
Guilt	Repairing relationships, righting wrongs
Fear	Protection from harm

Feelings	What they are for
Shame	Preserving social relationships/rules
Joy/Happiness	Built-in reward for achieving goals and getting our needs met
Disgust	Preserving health and protecting us from disease
Sadness	Getting back what's lost Accepting that things have gone
Excitement	Improving performance
Surprise	Refocusing attention, getting us ready for anything

Feelings	What they are for
Interest	Getting important information
Love	Relationship glue

When you think about your problem behaviours you will probably be able to recognise feelings that go with them. Write down what feelings come along with your behaviours. As we have already seen, Cheyenne had feelings of shame, which made her be unkind to herself. Rick had feelings of anger, which made him shout at other road users. Some of our feelings produce good outcomes but they can also increase our problems.

What are the feelings that come with your problem behaviours? Write them down here:

Problem behaviour

_____

_____

Feelings

_____

Problem behaviour

_____

_____

Feelings

_____

How to handle feelings

When our feelings are extreme and intense, the first thing we need to do is to disentangle ourselves from them. This means being able to stand back and observe them mindfully. The 'physicalising' exercise in Chapter 5 (page 93) is very helpful for this. Here is another version of this exercise.

My feeling as a painting

- Name the feeling you are planning to deal with (e.g. fear, anger, sadness)
- Imagine that this feeling is a painting
- Describe the painting:

  ◊ How big is it?
  ◊ What paints have been used to make it?
  ◊ What colours are in it?
  ◊ Are the colours pale or strong?
  ◊ Is there landscape, buildings, people, or is it abstract art?
  ◊ If there are people, what are they doing?
  ◊ What thoughts do you have about this painting?
  ◊ What feelings do you have about this painting?

Feelings come along with urges

As we learned earlier, feelings often come along with a behaviour or an urge to behave in some way. When Rick got angry he sometimes wanted to give his wife a push. He knew this would be terrible and had never done it, but he worried about it all the same. Instead of worrying about it, he could use urge surfing. Science shows us that urges are like waves – they build up to a high point and then get less and less and fade away. The whole process takes just a few minutes. Fretting about urges and having desperate or critical thoughts about them will keep them going much longer. Urge surfing is a very useful technique where we mindfully observe the urge to do something without acting on the urge. For example, when we have an itchy nose, we want to scratch it. We guess you may have an itchy nose now and want to scratch it. If you do, just observe the urge without scratching. It will build up a bit then fade away, like a wave. You can surf the wave like a surfer on the beach. Just hold steady, keep your balance and you will glide gracefully onto the sand as the wave disappears.

Urge surfing exercise

- Name the feeling you are having
- Name the urge that comes along with it
- Make a picture of yourself surfing the wave of this urge
- Just observe and describe your feeling and urge
- Rate how strong your feeling is every now and then, using 1 as the least and 10 as the strongest feeling
- Every now and then rate how strong your urge to act is
- Keep observing and describing your feeling and urge until your ratings come down to 3 or 4 out of 10

We have thoughts and feelings about our feelings

This may sound strange, but you might have noticed that Rick worried about his angry feelings and about his urges to push his wife. He had thoughts like 'I must be a closet wife beater'. He also had beliefs about his feelings and urges, such as 'I can never change this' and 'I have angry feelings so I'm just a totally angry person'. He felt guilty about feeling angry! Pauline had thoughts like 'I can't bear feeling like this' and 'I must do something to get rid of these feelings'. You can see that such thoughts and feelings about feelings and urges only serve to tangle us up even more.

Write down here any thoughts, beliefs or feelings you have about your own feelings and urges:

_____

_____

You can challenge these thoughts by asking yourself what your kind friend might say about your feelings and urges. Or you can use some of the techniques you will learn in later chapters.

Some feelings are just not deserved

Pauline felt ashamed and guilty about having been abused as a child. She did not deserve these feelings, yet she still had them. If she had stolen someone's purse, she would have deserved to feel ashamed and guilty. The feelings might have helped her to return the purse or make it up to the person in some way. Try to take a look at your own feelings: are they more extreme than they should be? Sometimes it is hard to tell whether your feelings are appropriate or not. A kind friend may give you a more realistic opinion than you have yourself.

Some feelings are just not helpful

Regardless of whether we think our feelings are deserved or appropriate or not, some feelings are just not helpful. Hating yourself, for example, will never help you get your life back. Endlessly dwelling on things you 'should' have done differently in the past will not help you either. So leaving aside the question of whether our thoughts, feelings and urges are deserved or not, appropriate or not, a good question to ask is, are they helpful?

Write down here whether your feelings are helpful right now:

_____

If the answer is no, it is time to disentangle and leave the feelings, thoughts and urges in the background as you work towards getting your life back.

We also need to leave behind wrestling with questions about whether our thoughts and feelings are 'right' or 'wrong'. Try this mindfulness exercise:

- Sit in the usual mindfulness position, with your back straight and your hands resting in your lap
- Bring your attention to your breath, without changing it, for three breaths
- Open your mind and observe what is going on in it from moment to moment, labelling thoughts, feelings, urges and body sensations as they come and go
- Try not to let your attention be hijacked by any one particular thought, feeling, urge or body sensation; just label them and let them pass by
- When your attention does get hijacked or wanders off somewhere, notice this and gently bring your mind back to observing and labelling
- Do this for five minutes

Write your observations about this exercise here:

_____

Opposite to feeling action

In order to change how you feel, or reduce the strength of the feelings, you can practise acting opposite to the urge that comes along with the feelings. For example, when you feel sad, smile. Your face will send a message to your brain that you are feeling happy. When you feel angry, practise a 'half-smile'. This is almost but not quite a smile and will send an opposing message to your brain to counteract the anger.

Willing hands

Willing hands is a mindfulness exercise that works well with feelings. It is an acceptance exercise and helps us to stop avoiding our feelings. Try this mindfulness exercise:

- Sit or stand in your mindfulness position as before
- Hold your hands out to the sides, elbows bent, palms up
- Use this gesture to express your willingness to experience and accept painful feelings
- Allow the feelings to come and go whilst mindfully observing and describing them without judging or getting tangled up in them
- If you find yourself judging, getting tangled up in the feeling, or wandering off in your mind, know that this is normal and bring your mind back to the feelings

Summary

To sum up, we have learned how to view our experience as wheels of thoughts, feelings, body sensations and behaviour, which happen in response to events outside and inside our bodies. We have learned that thoughts, feelings, body sensations and behaviour go together and are connected. Feelings come along for a reason and have evolved over a long time to help us survive and thrive in the world, but extreme feelings can be very painful, can be undeserved, and can also be unhelpful. When we recognise our feelings are not helping us we can take steps to manage them so that they do not prevent us from getting our life back.

Write down here what you personally will take away from this chapter:

_____

_____

Well done for reaching another stage! You may need to have a little rest from this book, do something else and come back later. Maybe it is time for a cup of tea.

Chapter 10

How to Understand Behaviour

Explaining behaviour

This chapter shows you how to understand your out-of-control behaviours and what keeps them going. Mindfulness is important as we do this task (see Chapter 5). We need to be able to step back and look at our behaviours without judging them or ourselves. This is not to say we approve of our behaviours or agree with them. If we get stuck in judgements then we end up just saying things like 'It's all my fault' or 'It's their fault' or 'I'm a bad person'. Judgements can feel like some sort of explanation but they are not the same as explanations. Judgements do not help us understand our behaviours and what keeps them going. An *explanation* will help us to understand our behaviours and will put us in a position to choose to change. Explanations are not the same as excuses. That is, explanations do not make it fine to just carry on as we are. But they do allow us to be kind to ourselves and empower us to choose to be different. It is difficult to *approach* thinking about our own out-of-control behaviours, rather than *avoiding* thinking about them. We are often ashamed of these behaviours. As discussed in the previous chapter, shame is associated with an urge to hide, from others and from ourselves.

What does my behaviour do for me?
My behaviour solves problems for me and causes more

Often, out-of-control behaviours solve a problem of living for us in the *short-term.* For example, getting blotto removes all awareness of our debt problems for a short time. Long-term, however, these behaviours cost us dearly, as we worked out before. Getting blotto on a regular basis causes long-term problems in our relationships, in our jobs, in our social reputation. It seriously damages our health, taking years off our lives. So, the same behaviours that solve problems in the short-term cause problems in the long-term. We need to learn to shine the torch of our attention on the long-term. To do this, we need to understand (a) what problems our out-of-control behaviours are solving in the short-term, and (b) do something different to solve those problems. This chapter is about (a). We will discuss (b) later in the book.

This chapter takes us through the stages of understanding our behaviour as follows:

- *Observing* behaviour (collecting data): taking a close look at what happens before and after specific problem behaviours and our thoughts and feelings during the behaviour

- *Describing* behaviour: drawing a Wheel of Experience for the specific problem behaviour

- *Understanding* the behaviour: drawing the chain of events, thoughts, feelings and body sensations that leads up to the problem behaviour and past it to what happens after

- Getting an idea of how the problem behaviour works for you short-term as well as the long-term consequences

Observing behaviour (collecting data)

The key question is, what does my problem behaviour do for me? We can approach this question by first collecting information, like scientists collect data. Then we can study it further. The good news is, you have already collected information in your My Things to Change Diary from Chapter 8 (page 125). On the next page is Tom's My Things to Change Diary from his gambling days. He was focusing on his gambling and lying behaviours. Have a look at this now.

Describing behaviour: drawing Wheels of Experience

Now we have started collecting some data like this we can begin to work out the Wheel of Experience of our behaviour. What thoughts, feelings and body sensations go along with the problem behaviour? Let us choose the time when Tom lost £500 at the casino. In his My Behaviours to Change List (page 153) gambling is at the top. In his diary this was a serious behaviour with a high score on 'How Bad Was It?' We are choosing this because it is the most severe behaviour in his diary, and also because he can remember it quite well. Let us ask Tom to describe this behaviour. He might say: 'Despite promising Sarah that I would never gamble again, like the loser I am I find myself in the casino, losing a lot of money. Whilst I'm there, I'm totally focused on the game and I'm sure I can win. What an idiot! But I lose £500 and have to go home and lie. I'm a heel.'

If we work hard, we might persuade Tom to leave out all the judgement words and just observe and describe the facts of exactly what he did. He then might say: 'I went for a walk and started thinking about the casino. I went in that direction without really noticing I was going towards the casino. I stopped outside it and went in. I started gambling. At first I had thoughts and feelings about winning and I felt good. Later on, as I kept losing, my thoughts and feelings got more negative and panicky. I kept on gambling to try to win the money back, but I lost £500.'

As Tom gets better at talking about gambling without judgement words, it seems to get clearer that there are two phases to the evening. At first he feels great (short-term gain); later, he feels terrible (long-term pain). The

My Behaviours to Change Diary (Tom)

DAY	BEHAVIOUR	WHAT WAS HAPPENING BEFORE?	WHAT HAPPENED AFTER?	THOUGHTS	FEELINGS	HOW BAD WAS IT? (1–10)
Monday	Gambling 11 p.m.–2 a.m. online	Kids did not turn up for contact after school	Went to bed	I'll never be able to stop	Rejected and alone	7
Tuesday	Lied about this to Sarah	She asked what I'd been doing	Could not sleep	What a heel I am Sarah could do better	Ashamed	6
Wednesday	Gambling at casino for four hours Lost £500	Bad day at the office Sarah moaning about bills	Went home, snuck into bed Lied to Sarah	Worry thoughts about money It's hopeless I'm an idiot	Anxious Felt terrible Despair Hated myself	9
Thursday	Lied to Sarah again	She asked where I was last night I said I went for a walk	Sarah not speaking to me	She does not believe me	Ashamed Rejected Hopeless Anxious	7

judgement words were clouding the facts of what was really happening. We could make two Wheels of Experience, one for each part of the evening.

Tom's Wheel of Experience for feeling good and escaping when gambling – early evening

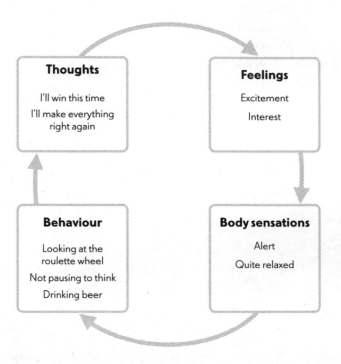

Thoughts

I'll win this time

I'll make everything right again

Feelings

Excitement

Interest

Behaviour

Looking at the roulette wheel

Not pausing to think

Drinking beer

Body sensations

Alert

Quite relaxed

We could notice here that at this early stage of the evening, Tom is *feeling good*. His whole mind is focused on the roulette game. His body is alert but relaxed and he has positive thoughts and feelings. So the gambling activity has *solved his problems* of feeling worried and helpless about work and money, but this is only for the *short-term*. Let us notice that when we say 'short-term' we really mean short-term, a few hours or even minutes of escaping from feeling bad.

As the evening goes by, Tom keeps losing. As this happens he is unable to ignore the losses and his anxiety begins to get higher and higher. Now he feels he has to play to win back his losses, otherwise how can he go home? But he keeps on losing and eventually he cannot afford to buy more chips. So he is faced with going home feeling worse than when he started.

Tom's Wheel of Experience for feeling terrible when gambling – later in the evening

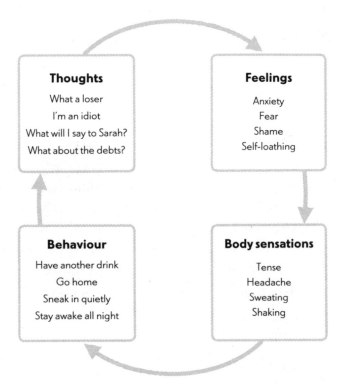

We could notice here that Tom feels even worse than before he gambled that evening. He has accidentally created more *long-term problems*. These are going to weigh him down for months to come, and make him want to escape more. This wish to escape will probably be felt by him as a strong urge to gamble again.

Understanding behaviour: drawing the chain

A further step towards understanding our problem behaviour is to tell the story of it. We will string out the Wheels of Experience into overlapping circles just like a chain. The links of the chain will contain events, thoughts, feelings, body sensations and behaviours, which will change as the story goes on. This is called 'drawing the chain'. It is done after the problem behaviour, not during it. Drawing the chain like this allows us to see how the same behaviour has different short- and long-term effects. We are going to do this for the same example as above, Tom gambling and losing £500 in the casino.

The vulnerability cloud

Above the chain diagram is a cloud. In this cloud we can put anything which makes us more *vulnerable* to feeling bad and upset – things such as lack of sleep, not eating properly, events during the day, as well as generally being under stress. Looking in his My Things to Change Diary, Tom saw that he had had a bad day at the office and that Sarah had been 'moaning' about the bills. These were entries in the 'What Was Happening Before?' column. The bad day at the office was a whole set of complicated and difficult things which just made Tom feel bad and *vulnerable* so he put having a bad day at the office in his vulnerability cloud (see opposite). He remembered that his colleagues had been making fun of him and criticising him.

Triggers and the chain

We can often find a *trigger* which sets off the whole chain reaction. In Tom's case it was Sarah mentioning money problems: Tom felt responsible and helpless to fix them. We can feel his frustration and anger when we read his diary where he says she was 'moaning' about the bills. This is a big judgement word and suggests he is blaming himself when she said it. We are going to start with this trigger event then we will look at each thought, feeling, body sensation, behaviour and further events as the story goes on. We will continue right up until after the problem behaviour has been done, so that we can see the short-term gain and long-term pain caused by the problem behaviour. Here is Tom's example:

Tom draws his behaviour chain

Tom's Vulnerability Cloud

Bad day at the office, colleagues making fun of me, criticising me.

Trigger Event

Getting home to find Sarah complaining about not enough money for bills

Feelings

Sad, angry, guilty

Thoughts

It's hopeless
It's all my fault

Body Sensations

Tense jaw and shoulders
Head throbbing

Behaviour

Urge to get out of the house
Urge to gamble

Problem behaviour

Gambling

Thought

I'll just nip in for a drink

Behaviour

Went for a walk, to the casino!

Body Sensations

Energetic, alert

Thought

Mind focused on game

Short-term gain

Event

Losing games

Thought

Oh no!
This is a disaster

Behaviour

Keep gambling

Feelings

Despair, self-loathing, shame

Body Sensations

Tense jaw and shoulders, felt sick

Behaviour

Left, went home

Long-term pain

Feelings

Felt terrible
Hated self
Despair, worry

Behaviour

Lied to Sarah

Here, we can see that gambling successfully got rid of difficult-to-bear feelings, replacing them with positive ones (alert, excited, hopeful), but *for a short time only*, resulting in a *long-term worsening* of the situation.

Getting an idea of how the problem behaviour works for Tom: The short-term as well as the long-term consequences

In summary, Tom's gambling behaviour works for him in two ways. First, it makes him feel good, excited, buzzy, alert, interested, relaxed (*reward*). He does not get this from other areas of his life. Second, it provides *escape* from his problems with Sarah, money and the kids, by powerfully distracting him.[2] Until now, Tom has not known this explanation for his gambling. We are not usually fully aware of why we do things (in other words, how our behaviour works for us). Noticing how it works is important – it will give us and Tom some ideas about how to get his life back. For example, he needs a source of excitement in his life other than gambling. This would help with feeling good (*reward*). He needs to learn skills to solve problems with Sarah, money and the kids, so that he does not need to *escape* by gambling.

Your turn to understand your problem behaviour

At the beginning of this chapter we described the process to go through to get to an understanding of our behaviour. Then we showed how Tom did this. The steps are:

- Observing (diary – collecting data) and describing (Wheels of Experience) behaviour

- Drawing the behaviour chain and understanding the behaviour (short- and long-term)

---

2   These two things, feeling good (*reward*) and escape from negative things are usually the two ways problem behaviours work for all of us. Feeling good (reward) is known technically as 'positive reinforcement'. Escaping from or avoiding negative things is known technically as 'negative reinforcement'. Reinforcement is anything that strengthens a behaviour, including problem behaviours making them more likely to happen again.

Observing (diary – collecting data) and describing (Wheels of Experience) behaviour

Here, we take a close look at what happens before and after your specific problem behaviour and your thoughts, feelings and body sensations during the behaviour – in your 'My Things to Change Diary'. Follow these steps:

1. Look at your My Things to Change diary (see page 130).
2. Find a good example of a problem behaviour. A good example is a time when the behaviour happened that you can remember quite well and that was quite serious.
3. Copy your chosen example of your problem behaviour into the boxes in the table overleaf.
4. Thinking back to this example, when it happened, can you notice any time during or after the behaviour that you felt good, or you felt relief (*escape*) from something like emotional pain, even very briefly? Sometimes this can be difficult, as it feels like there are no good feelings (*rewards*) or no escape from things in your problem behaviour. You may have to think hard. For example, if I stay in bed all day being depressed with negative thoughts, it seems like there is no reward or escape here. Yet I may be escaping from the pain of going out and facing people when I stay in bed all day, even though I do not think of it like that at the time. Search for any good feelings (*rewards*) or escapes from things in your own behaviour and write them here if you can find them:

_____

_____

My Problem Behaviour Example

DAY	BEHAVIOUR	WHAT WAS HAPPENING BEFORE?	WHAT HAPPENED AFTER?	THOUGHTS	FEELINGS	HOW BAD WAS IT? (1–10)

5. Now fill in the Wheel of Experience for the good feelings (*rewards*) or escape from things you have identified in your chosen behaviour, if you have managed to find them:

My Wheel of Experience for feeling good and/or escaping from things in my behaviour

Just sit back and notice the benefits (including escaping from things) of the behaviour. This is why you keep on doing it!

6. Write down any long-term problems caused in your life for yourself or others by this behaviour:

_____

_____

7. Now fill in the Wheel of Experience for after the behaviour, focusing on the long-term problems it caused for you and/or others.

My Wheel of Experience for long-term problems caused in my life for myself or others by this behaviour

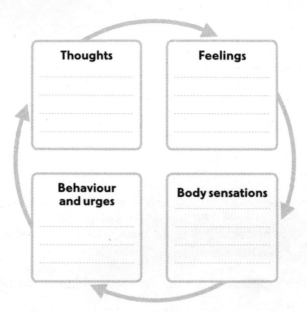

Just sit back and notice the cost of the behaviour.

8. Write down here the benefits and costs of your behaviour that you have noticed:

Benefits (short-term)

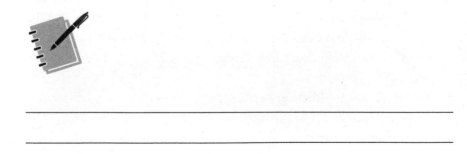

_____

_____

_____

Costs (long-term)

_____

_____

_____

Filling in your behaviour chain and understanding your behaviour

Follow the steps below and fill in the empty chain links (see page 165) to work out your own behaviour chain:

a. Start with your chosen problem behaviour again, in the My Problem Behaviour Example.

b. If your mind tells you that you do not want to look at this, say, 'Thanks, Mind,' and bring your thoughts back to this task using mindfulness.

c. In the vulnerability cloud write anything you can think of that might have increased your vulnerability to doing your problem behaviour. Things like lack of sleep, having a hangover, lack of exercise, getting bullied at work, etc.

d. Now look for a trigger – the thing that set you off doing the behaviour. This could be in the 'What Was Happening Before' column. Put the trigger in the first link of the chain as an Event (this can be an outside event or an inside event like a naughty puppy thought or hearing a voice).

e. Use your My Problem Behaviour Example entry and your Wheels of Experience to fill in the chain links. Just go round and round the Wheels of Experience to string out the chain of your thoughts, feelings, behaviour (including urges to behave) and body sensations. You are trying to tell the story of the behaviour by describing the chain. Unpack this into the chain links. You can use:

    E for events (these can happen in the middle of the chain too)

    F for feelings

    T for thoughts

    B for behaviour (including urges to do things which you might act on or you might resist)

    BS for body sensations

f.   Continue the chain until you get to the problem behaviour itself.

g.   Once you get to the behaviour, try to think of the immediate short-term benefit, which may be good feelings or relief (*escape*) or both.

h.   Continue the chain to the long-term effects (e.g. *despair* and *shame* in the Tom example we did earlier).

My behaviour chain

Follow the instructions in (a) to (h) above to fill in your links. You do not have to fill in all of the links, or you may even want to add one or two more.

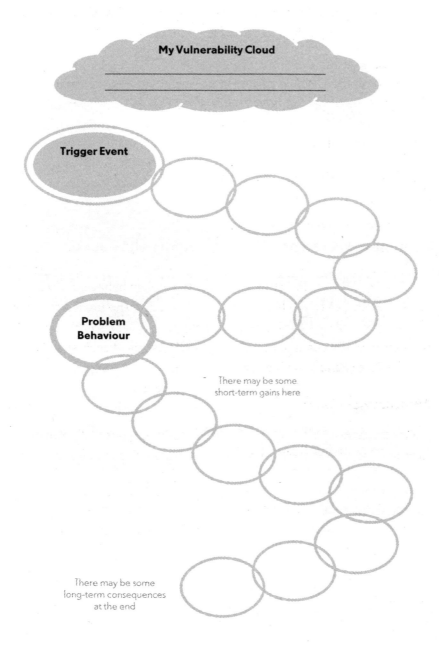

My Vulnerability Cloud

_____

_____

Trigger Event

Problem
Behaviour

There may be some
short-term gains here

There may be some
long-term consequences
at the end

Understanding my behaviour

Notice whether the problem behaviour is helping you *change* bad feelings like escaping from emotional pain. Maybe it is also having short-term reward effects like Tom's excitement when gambling. Or perhaps it is doing something like pulling people towards you to rescue or take care of you, at least in the short-term. For example, when Pauline self-harms, her family often panic and come over to her place and take her to hospital. This distracts her from seemingly impossible problems and also pulls some care out of her family, even if they are cross with her at the time.

What have we learned about problem behaviours?

We have done all these exercises: the My Things to Change List and Diary; the Wheels of Experience and filling in the behaviour chain. What have we found out about how problem behaviours work? Here are some things people often learn from this:

- It is important to use mindfulness and be non-judgemental when thinking and talking about problem behaviours
- As well as long-term pain there is often short-term gain
- Problem behaviours involve thoughts, feelings and body sensations as well as behaviour and urges
- Problem behaviours are more likely to happen when vulnerabilities are around
- Often there are triggers to problem behaviours
- There are a number of links in the chain leading up to and past a problem behaviour

What have we learned about your own problem behaviour?

Let us consider how you think your problem behaviour works for you in the short term. Tom might write 'Gambling makes me feel alert, focused, hopeful, excited and buzzing, instead of helpless and frustrated. It also takes my mind off all the problems we have'. So, we can see Tom gets pleasure (*reward*) from gambling, however short-term this is, and he gets short-term relief (*escape*) from bad and hopeless feelings.

After filling in your behaviour chain, can you summarise how you think your chosen problem behaviour can work for you? Try to talk about pleasure (*reward*) and *escape* like Tom has above. If this is too difficult, just copy the 'benefits' from point 8 in *Benefits and costs of your behaviour* (see page 162).

Write your summary here:

_____

_____

We can use what we have learned about your problem behaviour to make a plan to change it that will work. It is important to stay mindful and non-judgemental about all this, increasing our awareness without judging. If you notice your mind beating you up in any way, just observe this, say to your mind, 'You may be right, you may be wrong, let us just put that to one side for the time being,' and bring your mind back to this book.

The next chapters will show how to use our understanding of the problem behaviour to reduce it, and replace it with new behaviours. The new behaviours will need to give the same short-term gains without the nasty long-term effects. Now you have reached this part of the chapter, it is certain that you have been very brave. Go away and have a reward: do something you love doing, see someone you love, take a walk outside or listen to some music. See you later for the next chapter.

Chapter 11

Practical Ways to Accept Yourself

Accepting yourself

Let us take a moment to go back to why you started this journey. It was because of the terrible costs of the out-of-control behaviours that you did not want in your life. We looked at getting clear on your values and goals. Then we came to understand how your feelings, especially avoiding negative feelings, can be in charge of your behaviour and stop you getting your life back. In previous chapters we spent time building up skills to stand back and observe your mind. Do you remember the naughty puppy thoughts and feelings that seemed to be in control of your life? With your new skills you can stand back and observe the puppy thoughts and feelings and not always act on them.

When you validate yourself with compassion, you become more able to describe your problem behaviour clearly, without judgement, and to resist urges to act on thoughts and feelings. You are able to see yourself in a different light. Seeing yourself compassionately means you do not have to beat yourself up. This brings us on to the idea of a 'perfect nurturer'. The Perfect Nurturer idea was originally developed by Deborah Lee and Paul Gilbert as a part of Compassion Focused Therapy. Some of this chapter will be based on that work.

The Perfect Nurturer

We can now look at what a perfect nurturer is and how you can form an image of a perfect nurturer which will be able to meet your emotional needs. A perfect nurturer is an image of someone, or something, maybe an animal, a spirit or even a tree, you can go to and be safe and feel nurtured, often hearing compassionate, caring advice. You need to form an image of your perfect nurturer in your mind's eye. If this is difficult, try some mindfulness exercises so that you can focus on this task. There are some examples coming up which may also help you if you are getting stuck.

- Make a picture of this (real or imagined) perfect nurturer in your mind's eye
- Tell them about your struggles with your problem behaviour so far and about your new understanding of how it works
- If your perfect nurturer is able to speak to you then listen to its reply

In the examples coming up you may notice that Mandy has three perfect nurturers and they are her three cats. When Mandy forms an image of her three cats they often speak to her, but sometimes they just purr and smooth themselves against her arm. Mandy's image is not true to life, but she takes great comfort from it; her image of her cats feels compassionate and is meeting her emotional needs. Some of us do not readily have a perfect nurturer so we may have to stop for a while to think of one. Your perfect nurturer may be real and close to you or may be a person, thing, place or a situation from the past. If you get stuck here and cannot think of a perfect nurturer, read the examples and try again. Here are some examples from the stories in chapters 2 and 3:

Janet imagines herself in a cosy office at work. She has her own desk and coffee machine. When Janet imagines this, she feels safe and warm. Janet's image takes another step as she imagines the area director standing at her desk, talking to her. The area director is talking compassionately to Janet, being kind and understanding as well as giving her wise advice.

Cheyenne is at home in her kitchen with her best friend, cooking puddings – chocolate, jam and then, yes, treacle! She is feeling safe and happy; her best friend is able to talk to her as they cook. Cheyenne chose this image as she enjoys and is skilled at cooking puddings. Everybody likes Cheyenne's puddings. With her best friend there too, the combination of the two made a strong positive image.

George is at the junior football club. He chose this as he is respected there. At the junior football club George feels like a hero. He never gets the urge to drink or smoke at the club. George has an image of a Premier League football star talking to him. They can talk about many things: they can talk tactics for an upcoming game and they can talk about George and how he is working hard towards his life goals. Also, George can use his new skills to be able to understand the football star's own past issues with life problems.

Aleena has an image of herself leaving work, with Salim waiting for her outside. Aleena allowed herself a little extra treat here, as she usually leaves by the fire escape door at the back of the building, not down a flight of stone steps outside of the prestigious university building. Salim understands how hard Aleena has been working and is congratulating her on her progress. He understands her new ways of looking at her behaviours and says he loves her and to him she will always be beautiful.

Pauline goes to a big tree in the park and sits on the grass underneath it with her back leaning on it. She has known this tree since she was a girl. It has always been there; it is strong and unmovable. Pauline does not know why but she has always felt safe under this tree so her choice for a perfect nurturer was easy for her. When there is no one in the park, she does give it a hug. Pauline has an image of this huge tree having a mouth and being able to speak. This tree is absolute strength and is able to see strength in Pauline. It is very patient and never moves or wavers in the wind. Pauline's tree has been with her since childhood and completely understands her new way of looking at her thoughts. Not only that, the tree encourages her new skills.

Tom imagines himself having a picnic on the riverside in the summer. He is with Sarah and his children. Some of this is from his past as it is the same riverside that Tom's parents used to take him to when he was a child. Tom is not quite sure who he is speaking to in this image. The whole image seems able to reassure him that he is doing well. Tom imagines himself talking out loud during the picnic and feeling at peace as the water continues to babble past, the children continue playing and Sarah continues to get out food. Nothing has stopped as Tom talks about his problems and his progress, not the river, the birds, the children or Sarah. He feels that this is the way in which his whole life is listening to him with compassion and being at one with him.

Mandy has an image that is her perfect nurturer. Her image is sort of real. She imagines herself in the bingo hall, all ready for calling. You may think that this is in fact real and not an image but Mandy has added a little to it. Mandy also imagines that she has her three cats with her, just sitting there purring, ready for the game to start. Sometimes when she talks to her cats they just purr and smooth against her with their soft fur. Other times she is able to have conversations with them and they give good advice as well as understanding Mandy's struggles.

Rick immediately knew where his perfect nurturer was. He walks along the beach at low tide, just where the waves reach the sand. It is about half a mile out from the beach path. Rick is alone with the sounds of the sea and oyster catchers echoing in the air. Here, he is at peace, with no one to shout at, no one annoying him. Rick feels his breathing slowing and imagines his anxiety being washed out to sea on the gentle waves. He is able to talk to the sea as he walks along. The sea does not talk back to Rick but does wash away thoughts, feelings and emotions. Rick imagines his mind sending him unhelpful messages which can somehow fall onto the waves and be washed away. When they are washed away he feels that some of the obstacles that stop him getting near to his values are also washed away.

If Rick is not on the beach, which is his perfect nurturer, he is able to form an image of the sea and waves, taking away his negative thoughts. With practice he can do this when he is at work in the ticket office.

Sally is at home with Rosie. They are about to have supper; it is warm, candles are lit and she feels like a little bird in a nest. Soon another little bird joins her in the nest. This little bird always arrives when Sally wants to talk to her. Sally is able to talk to the other little bird in the nest. They can just get their heads over the side of the nest and see Rosie. As they are watching Rosie, they are able to talk about how things are going and how well Sally is doing. The other little bird does not have a name but understands Sally and is able to tell her how well she is progressing even when she feels like giving up. At the end of their conversation the other little bird flies away. Rosie does not know about Sally's little bird.

There will be times when we need to have an image of a perfect nurturer. Your perfect nurturer is like a port in a storm. The journey towards reaching our goals will not be smooth and there will be times when we fail to live as we would want to. Sometimes things are going well then all of a sudden disaster strikes and we slip back and feel a failure. Maybe our baby steps are too big and we have to make them even smaller. All of these hurdles and many more are waiting to trip us up. When we feel tripped up we need a place to go. This is the time for our perfect nurturer to start working. It does not matter whether our image is real or imagined. When we are with our perfect nurturer we can stop, rest, regroup and get ready to move back to the journey towards our values and goals. Your perfect nurturer will help you stay compassionate, clear, strong and non-judgemental as you steer your boat and sail the seas towards getting your life back.

Well done! Please have a break and we will speak soon.

Chapter 12

Practical Ways to Handle Your Thoughts

Handling your thoughts

Our brains are just another part of our bodies, though magical in their complexity. They evolved as part of our bodies over thousands of years to keep us from harm and help us get on in a scary and dangerous world. Back in the early days of mankind, it was very important to be on the lookout for danger and to be ready to avoid or fight the danger. You probably know this as 'fight or flight'. It was also important to compete with others as part of the 'survival of the fittest'. We needed to gather information and gather things for ourselves, defending them from other people for the survival of our family. Other things like sharing and self-sacrifice can also be seen to have evolved to protect our genetic material, if not ourselves. So it is natural for our minds to be constantly evaluating the world around us. This makes us alert for danger and driven to do better than others. We know that everyone's minds do this.

Human beings have the gift and the curse of language. This allows us to build cities, societies, share knowledge, create the internet and even go to the moon. It also means we can time travel, think about the past, and worry about the future. Think of this example:

One day Cheyenne and her dog were walking along in the park when they were attacked by a guy with a stick, who stole Cheyenne's purse and ran off. Both Cheyenne and her dog were traumatised and both would be terrified if they met the man again. But Cheyenne was the one who had nightmares about the attack and who started taking strong painkillers to try to block out the memory, not the dog! The dog will only worry when things remind him, like meeting a guy with a stick. But Cheyenne can travel back in time and ruminate about this event and also travel forward in time and worry, 'What if it happens again?'

This time travelling can be a source of great pleasure or great anguish in our lives and it has been found to underlie many mental health problems. In mental health settings worrying about the past is known as 'rumination'. Rumination is generally about the past whereas 'worry' is generally about the future. The problem is that this can run out of control so we end up believing all the naughty puppy thoughts our minds send us as if they are true. Let us suppose that I am a nurse with twenty years' experience and my mind tells me that I know nothing about nursing. I may believe it is true or a fact, just because I thought it. If I *think* I'm rubbish, I *feel* rubbish and this can affect my performance. My naughty puppies may notice my reduced performance and start to say, 'Look, I told you, you are hopeless,' and before I know it, I may believe it. Thoughts and feelings are like emails – they can be helpful or unhelpful, useful or potentially destructive.

How to catch a thought and see it for what it really is

This skill is very important for what comes next in this book so give it a chunk of your time – it will be worth it. Imagine a yard full of puppies. They all have different personalities. Some are friendly and fluffy and affection-ate; some are timid and unsure. Others kind of skulk in the background and look miserable. Then there are the ones that snarl and bare their teeth. The yard is your mind and the pup-pies are your thoughts. Your task is to catch a puppy and take a good look at it. You will need a net to do this.

Positive thoughts

The warm friendly puppies are the easiest to catch. These are the thoughts we do not mind having. And we do not mind catching and looking at them either. Thoughts like these might say things like 'I'm a nice person' and 'This is going to be easy'. So they are easy to catch, even pick up and cuddle. Yet, even though they look nice and cheerful and attractive, they can lead us astray: the thoughts can be too optimistic, too unrealistic. We can start off underestimating the effort a project is going to take – for example, by assuming it will be easy. Then we can get fed up pretty soon when we find it is harder than our thought puppies had told us.

Miserable thoughts

The miserable-looking thought puppies are less attractive. Generally, we can still catch them in our net. These thought puppies may bark things like 'It's all hopeless', 'What's the point?' and even 'You're a complete loser'. We may spend a lot of time with these miserable thought puppies and find it difficult to leave them alone as they seem so right about us. Yet doing this means we lose all of our hope and motivation and feel like just giving up. If we really listen to these thought puppies and buy into what they bark at us, we can actually give up. This will make us feel better in the short-term but terrible in the longer term. In the longer term, because we have given up and lost our motivation, there will be no sources of joy in our lives: we will not have any challenges, stimulation or anything interesting to do.

Anxious thoughts

The timid, anxious thought puppies are not so attractive either. Usually we can catch them if we try. These thoughts may say things like 'It's too scary, don't do that' and 'What if you have a panic attack?' and even 'You're having a heart attack' (when you are not). Sometimes it is not clear exactly what they are barking; we just know they are generally saying, 'Be afraid!' We can give these puppies a lot of our time. For example, we might not want to ignore them in case they are saying important things about how to keep safe and out of danger. We can put a lot of effort into reassuring them that everything will be OK and making plans to deal with all of the 'What ifs' the anxious thought puppies come up with. The trouble is, every time we make a plan they come up with a new 'What if' and off we go again. These anxious and timid puppy thoughts can really take up all our available time and energy so that we spend all of it trying to get safe and have no time left for getting our lives back.

Angry thoughts

The fierce, snarly, angry, teeth-baring puppies are often the trickiest. It is not easy to catch them. In fact, we may wish they were not in our yard at all. These thoughts may blame us, saying things like 'You are an idiot' and 'Why the heck did you do that?' Or they may blame others, saying, 'How dare she', 'He's out to get me' or even 'I'll make her suffer for that'. We have to be brave to catch these puppies. They look like they will attack and hurt us, or make us attack and hurt other people. Once we do catch them and pick them up, we will find that they cannot actually hurt anyone. All bark and no bite, they just *look* scary. It is only if we *act* on them that harm may be done.

So why do I need to catch my thoughts?

One of the big skills to learn when handling thoughts is how to get some perspective on them. That is, to see them from a little way off. Instead of just acting as if all our thoughts were true, we can then decide whether we would like to follow their advice or not. After all, if you got an email from a remote country saying, 'Deer Freind, I have two million dollars for yoo', you would not believe it, would you? Thoughts can be like emails too. There is a famous example often used in CBT of 'The Cat in the Night', which goes like this:

You hear a noise downstairs in the middle of the night. Your unruly puppy thoughts tell you, 'It's the cat.' How do you feel? Write your answer here

_____

You hear a noise downstairs in the middle of the night. Your unruly puppy thoughts tell you, 'It's a burglar!' How do you feel? Write your answer here

_____

You hear a noise downstairs in the middle of the night. Your unruly puppy thoughts tell you, 'It's my partner staggering home drunk again!' How do you feel? Write your answer here

_____

The thing to notice is that the noise stays the same in each example. Only the thoughts change. It is the thoughts which give meaning to the event and link up to our feelings. So if we change our thoughts, we can change our feelings too.

How do I catch my thoughts?

Well, first you need the net we mentioned earlier, a thought catcher. If you are doing CBT, this is known as a 'Thought Record'. The thought catcher is the net in which you can catch your naughty puppy thoughts and then take a good look at them. It does take a bit of practice to catch thoughts. Here is a basic thought catcher, which George filled in:

George's Thought Catcher

Situation	Thought	Feeling
• At home with family • Kids ignore me	• No one really needs me • They are bad kids	• Sad, lonely • Angry

You can see the first thought, 'No one really needs me', is a miserable-looking puppy. The second one, 'They are bad kids', is more snarly and fierce. You can also see that each thought has a feeling that goes with it. The thoughts each happen in a situation; the thoughts are the meaning we give to the situation, like the 'Cat in the Night' example.

Have a go at catching one or two of your own puppies (thoughts) here:

Situation	Thought	Feeling

These thoughts and feelings are like untrained, unruly puppies – they just run around, causing havoc. We will learn how to tame them. Eventually, they will have collars and leads. We can take them along with us to where *we* want to go, along the road towards getting our lives back.

How can I handle unhelpful thoughts?

There is a lot of scientific knowledge about thoughts and how they work. Based on this evidence, there are two basic approaches to dealing with unhelpful thoughts:

a. Get a perspective on them, review them, challenge them and change them.
b. Get a perspective on them and leave them be, without letting them control you.

(a) Reviewing, challenging and changing thoughts

The CBT word for negative thoughts is NATs (Negative Automatic Thoughts). Negative thoughts have negative feelings associated with them. One of the ways we can learn to handle NATs is to review and challenge them. A key question to ask ourselves is 'How do I know?' That is, to look at what actual evidence there is for the truth or accuracy of the thought. Another key question is 'What would someone who disagreed with this thought say?' In other words, what is the evidence against my thought? This second question is often hard to answer. We all have a bias towards gathering up evidence that supports our own beliefs. Sometimes, asking a friend to point out evidence against a thought can help.

Cheyenne had a NAT or naughty puppy thought that she did not deserve to use shampoo. She reviewed and challenged her NAT using this table:

Thought	Evidence for	Evidence against
I don't deserve to use shampoo	I feel bad when I use shampoo	My best friend says I deserve to use shampoo
	My mum used to wash my hair in washing-up liquid	Every human being deserves to use shampoo

Looking at her table, Cheyenne came up with a more realistic thought. It went like this: 'I know I do deserve to use shampoo, just like everyone else'. Even though she did not feel this to be true when she was actually washing her hair, she read it out loud before she went into the shower as if she did believe it. With practice this helped her to tame her naughty puppy thought and get it on a lead, so she could take a shower and use shampoo.

Write your own NAT in the table below. You can copy it from the 'thought' column you filled in earlier, if you like:

Thought	Evidence for	Evidence against

Write your 'realistic' or 'balanced' thought here. This should be what you think is a realistic statement based on all the evidence above (you might need to ask your perfect nurturer or best friend for help with this):

Well done! We will come back to this later.

CBT encourages us to look at our thoughts and see whether they contain any errors. Aaron T. Beck, the founder of CBT, first proposed the theory behind thinking errors. The author David Burns, who helped make CBT popular, gave us simpler names and examples for the errors.

Here are some common errors we all make in our thinking. Tick 'yes' if it is something you do yourself, 'no' if you do not:

My thinking errors

Negative bias

We take the negative details and magnify them. We filter out positive aspects of a situation. For instance, a person may pick out a single unpleasant detail and dwell on it.

Do I do this? YES/NO

Black and white thinking

Things are either 'black' or 'white' with no shades of grey. We have to be perfect or we are a failure, there is no middle ground. People and situations go into either good or bad boxes, not allowing for how complicated most things are.

Do I do this? YES/NO

Over-generalising

We jump to a general conclusion based just on one single thing. If something bad happens only once, we expect it to happen over and over again. For example, if someone lets us down once, we decide they can never be trusted.

Do I do this? YES/NO

Mind reading

We are sure we know how other people are feeling and why

they act the way they do. For example, we may decide that someone else does not like us even though they have said and done nothing nasty.

Do I do this? YES/NO

Expecting disaster

We expect disaster to strike, no matter what. We use *what if* questions – for example, 'What if tragedy strikes?' or 'What if it happens to me?' We see even small things as disasters. We make mountains out of molehills.

Do I do this? YES/NO

Personalising

We believe that everything other people do or say is some kind of direct personal reaction to us. We compare ourselves to other people to see who is smarter, better-looking, etc. We may also see ourselves as responsible for bad things happening.

Do I do this? YES/NO

Too little or too much control

We can see ourselves as helpless victims. For example, 'I can't help it if the dinner is burned, you asked me to cook it for half an hour and that was too long'. Or we can take responsibility for the pain and happiness of everyone around us. For example, 'Why aren't you happy? Is it because of something I did?'

Do I do this? YES/NO

It's not fair

We feel resentful because we think we know what is fair, but other people will not agree with us. You probably remember that our parents told us 'Life isn't always fair'. Some people go through life making judgements about whether or not things are fair and getting angry when they decide they are not fair.

Do I do this? YES/NO

Blaming

We blame other people for our pain, or blame ourselves for every problem. For example, 'Stop making me feel bad about myself!' No one can *make* us feel things; only we can develop control over our own thoughts and feelings.

Do I do this? YES/NO

Shoulds

We have a list of rules about how we and other people should behave. People who break the rules make us angry, and we feel guilty when we break these rules ourselves. A person may often believe they are trying to motivate themselves with 'shoulds' and 'should nots'. For example, 'I really should exercise, I shouldn't be so lazy'. 'Musts' and 'oughts' are also offenders.

Do I do this? YES/NO

Believing our feelings

We believe that what we feel must be true automatically. If we *feel* guilty, then we must *be* guilty. We assume our unhelpful feelings tell us about how things really are. 'I feel it, so it must be true'.

Do I do this? YES/NO

Forcing others to change

We expect that other people will change to suit us if we just pressure or nag them enough. We need to change other people to make ourselves feel better.

Do I do this? YES/NO

Labelling

We put labels on ourselves and others which are too general. Making a small error can lead to us attaching a big global label to our whole self. For example, I may say, 'I'm a loser' in a situation where I failed to remember all the shopping. A small positive gesture from someone else might lead us to idolise them forever as 'The Best Person in the World'. When someone else's behaviour rubs us up the wrong way, we may attach a negative label to the whole person, such as 'He's a total waste of space'.

Do I do this? YES/NO

Always being right

We feel continually on trial to prove that our opinions and actions are correct. Being wrong makes us feel terrible, so we will go to any length to demonstrate our rightness. For example, 'I don't care how badly arguing with me makes you feel, I'm going to win this argument no matter what because I'm right'. Being right often is more important than the feelings of others around us, even loved ones.

Do I do this? YES/NO

Expecting rewards

We expect our sacrifice and self-denial to pay off, as if someone is keeping score. We feel bitter when the reward does not come.

Do I do this? YES/NO

Take a moment to find examples from your own thinking of some of these errors. Our NATs generally have one or more of these errors in them. What might be a more realistic way of describing the situation? For example, Janet noticed a lot of 'personalising' in her NATs. She used to think that most of what other people said or did was all about her. She began to think of other reasons why someone in the office might be yawning, frowning or looking at her, reasons which might have nothing to do with her at all. Cheyenne had a lot of 'labelling' thinking errors. Every time she forgot to put biscuits in the kids' lunch boxes, she believed she was a terrible mother. She learned to spot this and counter-act with 'I know I'm a good enough mother'. The first stage in changing is to become aware of our own thought patterns, then we can move on to challenging them.

Have a go at completing the table below for your own NATs. These might involve some of the thinking errors in the list above. Try to write down all the NATs you can think of that often pop into your mind, then have a go at filling in the last column. A good way to do this is to stand back and look at evidence for and against and see what you really think is realistic or balanced. You might need help from a friend to do this, as it can be difficult. There is an example to get you started:

Challenging my NATs

My NAT	Evidence for	Evidence against	Realistic or balanced thought
Today has been a total disaster	*Lots of bad things have happened today*	*A couple of good things happened too*	*Today has been difficult, with bad and good things happening*

Did you notice that as you filled in the table you could get some distance from your NATs just by writing them down? Some people find that doing this immediately helps. Others find that actually thinking about thoughts in order to write them down makes them feel worse. If feeling worse is your reaction, you probably usually cope by not thinking about things. You could be an 'avoidant thinker' and here we are asking you to do the exact opposite! Please keep going – it gets easier and it will help in the end if you can just hang on in there for some time.

Some people find that though they know their realistic or balanced thoughts are more accurate, they do not really feel this. Their feelings stay negative and do not change. If this is happening to you, read your realistic thought from the table and pretend you really feel it is true. For example, Pauline wrote that the sexual abuse she suffered was not her fault. This was her realistic thought. Yet she still felt guilty. She acted as if she did not feel guilty and this helped her to sit on her hands when she had the urge to harm herself. When you are in the middle of a crisis of negative think-ing, it is really hard to remember and believe your new realistic thoughts. Because of this we advise writing them down and keeping them handy. In a crisis get them out, read them (aloud, if possible) and even if you do not believe them, pretend you do. Act as if you do believe them – this will take you forward towards your values and goals.

Write down your plan for where you will keep your realistic balanced thoughts here (e.g. in your pocket, on your phone):

_____

_____

(b) Mindfully leaving thoughts be, without letting them control you

Mindfulness approaches to handling thoughts are a bit different. Yet they also involve getting a perspective on our thoughts. As in standard CBT, we need to stop avoiding our thoughts and feelings and start observing them. But in mindfulness approaches we do not engage with our thoughts: we let the puppies bark away but we have them on leads and train them to walk behind us. Mindfulness approaches are described in ACT, for example, as ways to 'unhook' ourselves from our thoughts, ways not to 'buy into' them. We do not fight them or try to change them as this takes our energy away from where we want it to be: we want our energy to be used in taking steps towards getting our life back.

Mindfulness teaches us that we are not our thoughts. I am the person who is observing my thoughts. It can help us learn to observe our thoughts from a bit of a distance. With practice, we can get a perspective on what is going on in our minds without being judgemental, then we can decide whether or not these thoughts are helpful. If they are not helpful, we can use mindfulness to allow them to be on the edge of our awareness, but not in focus and certainly not in the driving seat. Mindfulness is used in several therapies, including mindfulness-based CBT, ACT, DBT and CFT.

Images are very helpful when we are working on being mindful, without judging, and staying in the present moment. One image from ACT is of Passengers on a Bus.

You can download this video from www.getyourlifeback.global.

Here, we imagine we are driving our Bus of Life. We should be in charge and deciding where to go, but our thoughts are like out-of-control passengers who keep taking charge by telling us we cannot do things. It feels hopeless or that things are too scary, etc. Our job is not to fight with the passenger thoughts, as this will just take up all our time and energy. We cannot push them off the bus as they keep jumping back on at the next stop, so we keep our focus on our values and goals and leave the passengers to get on with all their chatter. Then we can decide where we drive our Bus of Life, towards the destination of our goals.

Naughty puppies in the yards of our minds often bark a lot of judgements at us. They can bark all the things in the thinking errors list earlier. A mindfulness approach gets these puppies on a lead and trains them so that they walk just behind us without dragging us along and pulling us where they want to go. This frees us up to follow our values and goals and get our lives back.

More ideas to handle thoughts

Here are some exercises that you may find useful. As we are all different, you may find some are more helpful than others.

Marching soldiers

This is a mindfulness-to-thoughts exercise similar to the one earlier in the book (see page 92). Remember the soldiers marching through your head and down your shoulders? During this exercise the soldiers are going to sing your thoughts.

- Bring the focus of your attention to your breath
- Take two or three breaths
- Bring your attention to your thoughts
- Notice as your thoughts come up

191

- As each one comes up, a soldier is going to sing it. You can watch thoughts being marched away out of your mind as the soldiers sing each one and march down your shoulders

Singing or dancing your thoughts

This is a good exercise if you like music or dancing. When negative or unhelpful messages are arriving from your mind, sing the words to your favourite tune. It could sound like this: 'I can't do that, I can't do that, I can't even try, I can't even try', or even 'Stupid, stupid, stupid, stupid'. You can also dance to the messages, maybe when cooking or doing housework. This might sound a little ridiculous at first. However, there is a more serious side to this exercise. Your mind is sending you unhelpful messages that are usually negative. When you sing or dance as a 'reply', this is not the response that your mind is expecting. Your singing or dancing response is not as serious as your mind expects it to be. Two things are happening. First, you are responding in a different way than before. With practice, you can change your response from one of panic, despair, worry, etc. to singing and dancing. Second, it is difficult for your mind to hold onto the seriousness of the message. Many people say their thoughts suddenly sound not nearly so important or distressing. Some people find that a mocking tone comes out when they sing their thoughts. If this happens to you, ask your perfect nurturer (see page 168) to sing the words for you in a lighter tone.

The Demon Chest

For this exercise you will need a box, some paper and a pencil or pen. A cardboard box will be fine, any size will do. When you have unhelpful or negative automatic thoughts (NATs), write them down on a piece of paper, thank your mind for them and put them in the box. Soon you will have a chest full of demons. This exercise is helpful because when negative thoughts come along, it is difficult to know what to do with them. If we do not do something with them and we start worrying about them, they may stay with us and become more powerful. You may notice that the demons in the chest make a lot of scary noises but they cannot actually harm you.

Yes, but . . .

'Yes, but . . .' involves talking to your thoughts. As you have worked through this book you have gathered a lot of information about yourself. Some information has come from people like best friends. You can use this information to reply to your negative thoughts. So if your mind tells you that you will never get a loving partner because you are not attractive, you can reply, saying, 'Yes, but my best friend thinks I am attractive.'

Another approach is to ask your mind what evidence it has for making that statement. If your mind does not answer this question, ask it again. This exercise disrupts the process of your naughty puppies bombarding you with negative messages.

Stand back and step up

This is the idea that when our naughty puppy thoughts threaten to take over our life we can always stop. When you have the feeling that things are getting out of control again, try this:

- Take a deep breath
- Stand right back and take a long, cool look at what is happening. It will usually be similar to the behaviour chain you worked out in the last chapter. You might be at the beginning of the chain or halfway through, or nearly at the end but you can still stop
- Next, step up. Decide what you really want to do (your values) and then step up and do it

Helicoptering

When you fly up in a helicopter and look down at the ground below you can see more than just where you live. You can see the park, the road, the shops, the whole scene – you can get a bigger perspective. You can see where you fit in.

When you use helicoptering as a thought-handling skill, you:

- Stop
- Take a deep breath
- 'Helicopter up' above the situation and look down at it
- Get in touch with the bigger picture and ask yourself, 'How do I want to behave in this situation?' (values)
- Decide what to do
- Helicopter back down and do it

Some people use reminders like smells or tastes or squeezing a stress ball to make the move to helicopter up. For example, George decided to use an elastic band around his wrist as his reminder. When he noticed his naughty puppy thoughts about not being valued in the family, he would gently ping the elastic band on his wrist. This would remind him to helicopter up above the situation. From here he could look down and see himself below, having the negative thoughts that threatened to take control. He could get the bigger picture by getting outside of himself; he could also get in touch with his values and remember he wanted to contribute to family life. This allowed *him* to be in charge, not his thoughts. He could helicopter back down and get on with the washing-up, staying aware of why he was doing this.

Being the stage

This exercise uses the idea that we are not the actors, nor the audience, nor even the play. If we want to be mindful and in touch with our values, we can do this by becoming the stage. From here, we can watch our thoughts as if they are actors acting out a play. We are not involved with them, we are just the place where the drama happens. Make a picture in your mind of yourself as a stage, with your thoughts as the actors in a play. You can sit solid and still while the drama goes on.

The bully in the chair

This exercise is great for dealing with self-blaming thoughts and feelings:

- Sit near an empty chair and imagine there is a person in the chair called 'The Bully'. This bully is your own mind, when it sends you messages about what a loser you are, how you can never get anything right, how terrible a parent you are, etc.

- Next, change seats and actually become The Bully, really using a bully voice to give your other 'self' in the other chair what for. Really go for it.
- Now, return to the first chair and ask yourself how it has made you feel being bullied in this way by your own mind. Is it helpful? Do you want to carry on being bullied like this?
- If the answer is no, answer The Bully back. Tell The Bully what you think of it and how things really are. If you find this difficult, imagine The Bully has been bullying someone you love and speak out in defence of that person. You can also get your perfect nurturer to sit with you as you answer The Bully back.
- As you go through your day, practise spotting The Bully when it gets active and say, 'Thanks, but no thanks.'

Make friends with your behaviour

Another skill to learn for times that are difficult is to make friends with your behaviour. Although it may be difficult to understand, your behaviour has come along to try to protect you in some way or to meet your needs. It is trying to be your friend, but going about it in a way that ends up destructive. In a similar way in which you learned to thank your mind for its naughty puppy messages, you can learn to thank your behaviour for trying to help.

Explain to your behaviour that you appreciate its efforts but need to find another way to achieve a longer-term good outcome without the destructive 'help'. Ask yourself what you would say to your friend if they were struggling with a behaviour like drinking, self-harming or binge eating. Would you blame them or would you give some other advice? Accepting your behaviour is not the same as approving of it or wanting to justify it: acceptance says simply 'It is what it is'.

Take a moment to look back over the exercises you have just read and circle one or two that appeal to you. Try them out right now.

Summary

Your naughty puppy thoughts can be tamed by being challenged. They can also be tamed using mindfulness to let them be, but not let them be in charge. These thought-handling skills will help you stay at the wheel and in control for the whole voyage, or let you seize the wheel back when you lose it. Both your perfect nurturer and your thought-handling skills will act as ports in a storm when things get rough. Congratulations, you have again reached the end of a chapter, so it is time to take a break. Maybe have a cup of tea and try out a couple of the exercises. See you later for the next chapter.

Chapter 13

Learning New Skills for Self-control

In this chapter we learn tried and tested techniques for self-control. Loss of self-control causes a barrier, which stops you from living your values and reaching your goals. This chapter has a list of skills that will help you gain and keep self-control. You will not be able to use all of these skills, so look through and decide which skill would help you best. You may select more than one skill depending on your individual needs.

The mind-body road

The road between your mind and body has two-way traffic. Your mind (or your brain) is constantly telling your body to do things such as move, walk, breathe, run away from danger, etc. This is not a one-way street. Going in the other direction are constant messages from your body to your mind and brain. The simple diagram below shows how this two-way traffic can easily make a circle which gets faster and faster when we feel anxious or afraid.

The Mind-Brain-Body Vicious Circle

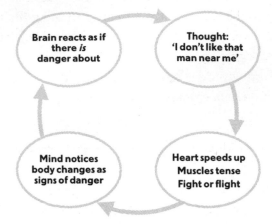

This diagram shows how your mind prepares you to keep safe, maybe by running away. Imagine an aggressive-looking man who you do not know has approached you and is standing very close to you. Your mind (brain) has told your body to get ready to run away as fast as possible. This involves a faster heartbeat to get extra oxygen to your muscles. Those muscles may shake as they prepare to run fast. Your body is now all set to react fast and keep you safe. At the same time your mind is watching and monitoring your body and noticing that it is changing in readiness for action. It is noticing anxiety and some sort of emergency going on in the body world.

Calming your body by talking to your mind

Do you remember Cheyenne in the last chapter? She was frightened by a man in the park. The next day, as Cheyenne left the house she felt panic and fear in case she saw the man again. This made her heart beat fast, and her breathing fast and shallow. She also felt shaky and sweaty. Cheyenne's mind was telling her body that there was danger and preparing it to run away fast. Let us imagine that she did not leave the house but went and sat down in the kitchen. Her heart and breathing would slow. Cheyenne's feeling of panic would disappear. Her body would send confirmation to her mind that there really was no danger. But she would still be at home.

In Cheyenne's example, at the point at which she left the house there was no real danger as she could see that the man was not there. Her mind was looking into the future as she imagined meeting the man. Perhaps Cheyenne will never see the man again, but she may feel fear as she goes through the park gate for many weeks to come. This is known as 'conditioning'. Interestingly, Cheyenne may feel anxiety if she tries to go into *any* park, not just the one where the man was.

Cheyenne values taking care of herself and part of this is taking relaxing walks in the park with her dog. Cheyenne's work on getting her life back includes keeping fit, so she is determined to carry on walking in the park. Sitting in the house all day will not do. For Cheyenne to gain self-control she would need to ask whether her mind was responding to actual danger (the man). If she was just about to leave the house and could see there was no one there, she could have this conversation with her mind. She could tell it that at that moment there was no danger. By talking to her mind she could change the messages her mind sends to her body. This will help her mind to learn there is no danger.

Sometimes people find it difficult to think through how realistic their fears are at the time when they are anxious. It helps to think things through at a calm time then maybe make a note of what you will say to your mind when it gets anxious. You can keep this note and read it when you need it.

Calming your mind by calming your body – breathing

We all breathe all of the time to stay alive. Sometimes we breathe faster than other times. Information about breathing moves up and down along the two-way road between our minds and our bodies. In the previous example Cheyenne started to breathe faster when she was leaving the house. This was because her mind had told her that she may be in danger and may have to escape quickly. Her mind told her this because it could 'time travel' and based its decision on information from the past (rumination) and worries about the future.

One thing Cheyenne could do next time in this situation is to slow down her breathing. This will send a contradictory message to her mind. In other words, the slow breathing will send a different message back to her mind from her body. This new message will say, 'I am OK and the run-away-quickly preparation is not needed'. Cheyenne could do this because there is no man at the door, he was somebody who was in the park yesterday. This slow breathing will have a calming effect on her mind and it will start to re-assess the situation. You can practise breathing exercises very simply and almost anywhere.

- Think about your breathing, feel the air coming in and out
- You may notice things about the air – is it hot or cold, are there smells in it, are you a little blocked up?
- Take deep breaths, feel where the air goes; feel where it fills your body
- Now slow down the speed at which it is coming in, then the speed at which it is going out
- Try to fill the bottom of your tummy and your abdomen with air
- You now need to slow down your breathing to a rhythm. Count to three as you breathe in (count in your mind, not out loud, and about one number per second). Now breathe in, counting one, two, three; hold, counting one, two, three; and out, counting one, two, three
- Keep that rhythm going and breathe at that speed, slowly and deeply

Some people can imagine the message going on the two-way road from their bodies to their minds, saying, 'It's all OK' as they breathe in, hold and breathe out. You can do breathing exercises almost anywhere – in the office, at the bus stop, in the kitchen, even walking the dog. If you find this exercise useful, there is another one you can try in Chapter 19 (see page xx). Like most of these exercises, the more often you do it, the better you get at it.

STOP! THINK!

This skill involves learning to stop briefly before acting, which gives a tiny bit of time to change the way in which you react. It is very good for anger-type problems. Practise saying 'STOP! THINK!' in a calm voice.

Rick got in trouble at work because he had a lot of judgements about customers, which made him angry. He responded very quickly without thinking and was rude to the customers. A similar thing was happening when driving to work: Rick became angry and shouted at other drivers when they cut him up or he thought they were driving too slowly. He shouted before he had even thought about the situation. The 'STOP! THINK!' skill gave him time to think about his response rather than respond automatically. Rick was able to slow down his mind, which stopped an automatic response. The way he did this was to practise saying 'STOP! THINK!' calmly and slowly every few minutes. He became used to saying 'STOP! THINK!' and started saying it almost automatically.

Rick also practised saying 'STOP! THINK!' when driving and at work. It was then quite easy to stop an automatic response at tense moments by replacing it with 'STOP! THINK!' This gave him time to respond differently in a controlled way.

Advance planning

When I decide to go on a diet, I have to decide what to eat. This generally means that I will have to resist custard, cakes and lots of high-sugar, high-fat foods. I also have to decide which size portions I am going to eat. The worst time that I can make these decisions is when I am hungry and looking in the fridge. At this point my decision about the size of portions will be based on satisfying my hunger, which feels like it needs a horse-sized piece of cheesecake at least. The most logical time to decide what I will eat at lunchtime is just after breakfast – my tummy is full, I have high motivation and I am not feeling the need to eat, eat and eat. It is known that if we shop at the supermarket when we are hungry then we will buy more food. Umm, yes, cream cakes, biscuits, cheesecake . . . Oh yes, just a little squirty cream and jam. Many problem behaviours happen as a response to some need or other, such as hunger. The time to decide what to do about the situation is not at the time of need. This is when we use problem behaviours that give us instant relief with long-term pain. For example, when Cheyenne thought about washing her hair, her mind sent her NATs, messages telling her that she was not good enough to use shampoo. The thought of using shampoo filled her with anxiety. To get rid of the anxiety Cheyenne agreed with her mind and washed her hair in washing-up liquid. The anxiety went away but soon afterwards she felt a failure and worthless.

Cheyenne used advance planning to deal with this. Earlier in the day she put the shampoo in the shower and squirted the washing-up liquid down the sink. When it came to shower time it was easier to use the shampoo as there was no washing-up liquid. So we need to plan in advance what to do when difficult behaviours or thoughts come along.

George knew that he was most likely to drink whisky when he got in the car. It is too late to decide what to do about his drinking when the whisky bottle is in his hand. George could take the whisky out of the car earlier in the day or put an alternative non-alcoholic drink inside so there is a choice. If this is too difficult perhaps he could put a small measure of whisky in the car well before 'drink time'. The next week he could make the measure smaller. This is an example of using baby steps to reach a goal of no drink in the car.

Asking for help

At times we all need to ask for help but this is not a sign of being a failure. In earlier chapters we saw that other people often see us differently to how we see ourselves. A kind best friend often sees positive things about us that we cannot see for ourselves. This happens when our minds send us messages that are inaccurate or simply not true. This may be due to past or more recent experiences. It can be important to get a different view on things from somebody else. In Chapter 11 we introduced the idea of the perfect nurturer. Your perfect nurturer may or may not be a real person, but often you can still ask their advice. When you feel overwhelmed with things you may need to ask for practical help or advice. This could be from your perfect nurturer or someone else in real life. You need to plan in advance whom you would ask and possibly what you would ask for. The time of crisis or despair is not the best time to make a plan. Also, it is easier for someone to agree to help when you can talk to them calmly. Make a list here of people who could be helpful when you need help.

People I could ask for help:

_____

_____

_____

What I need help with or advice about:

_____

_____

_____

Recognising NATs

You may remember NATs are negative automatic thoughts. These are unwanted messages from your mind, which we described earlier as junk emails. If you recognise junk emails when they come in you can delete them. If I can recognise that a Russian billionaire who needs my bank account for only a few days and will then give me a reward of £10,000 is nonsense, then I can treat it as such. I do not need to worry whether to take up the offer, whether I might be missing a great opportunity or what I would do with the money, etc. We need to do a similar thing with junk emails from our minds.

Most of us more or less know what our mind junk emails (NATs) are going to say. They tend to be things like 'Nobody will want you', 'You can't do it', 'You're too stupid', 'It was your fault', 'You've tried before', etc. The problem is that these messages tend to arrive at times when you are least able to deal with them – perhaps in a job interview or when you feel alone and low. However, the way to deal with NATs is to write them down when they are not attacking you. Sit down when you are calm and bring to mind the NATs. Write them down and underneath write 'These are NATs and I don't have to believe them or act on them'. Keep this piece of paper with you. When your NATs attack, read it and tell yourself that these are NATs from your mind and you do not have to believe or act on them. It is very difficult to make the decision not to believe and act on NATs when they are at full attack. As with previous examples, advance planning is necessary to deal with NATs.

Have realistic expectations

'I have been abused as a child and felt a constant failure throughout my adult life. I want to read this book by tea-time and be a different person by this evening . . .' This is an example of unrealistic expectations. It is not possible to make such a big change so quickly. Expectations can be seen as goals: if they are too high then we are most likely not to reach them. We need to make baby steps towards our goals in a way that maximises success. Baby steps can be so small that they guarantee success. This may be important if we have tried and tried but only failed each time.

Do you remember that Mandy had problems with walking? Her goal was to sort out her walking problems. This would make a good end goal but probably is too big for a first goal. Mandy needs to think of some baby steps that will take her towards her end goal of sorting out her walking problems. Baby step one might be to walk out of her flat down the road for one minute. This guarantees Mandy success as she knows she can do this. Once she is comfortable doing this, baby step two could be to walk down the road for two minutes. Again, she can achieve success with a tiny bit of challenge. After a few days doing this, baby step three might be to walk down the road for three minutes, again feeling success and a little more challenge. At the end of a week or so Mandy's baby steps have allowed her to experience success and to improve her walking. Each baby step is a realistic goal. This is a great way to start changing: Mandy is starting to walk further and her mind is getting the message that walking does not always mean failure. As time goes on she will be able to increase her walking distances until she can walk as far as the bingo hall.

Decide what you want your end goal to be and then think of baby steps that will get you there. Write these baby steps down so that you can see progress as you move through the steps. This is different from thinking about them. If you just think about them at difficult times then everything can feel like failure. You need to be able to see what progress you have made. Always congratulate yourself on steps made even when it feels as though you are grinding to a halt.

Rewards

Sometimes rewards work well, other times they create problems. Here is an example of how rewards can go wrong. To teach my dog to stop getting on the sofa, I might give him a biscuit reward for getting off. My thought is that the dog will learn that it is nice not to be on the sofa and that it pleases me. As you have probably guessed this plan of rewards is not going to work. The first problem is that my dog only gets a reward if he is on the sofa to start with. This means that I am rewarding getting *on* the sofa, because if he is not on it then he cannot get off it. The second problem is that if this behaviour happens a lot I might have to give him seventeen biscuits in a morning. My dog is now full of biscuits and not interested in my rewards!

Rewarding ourselves can help us to reach our goals by making our new behaviours stronger. Here are some hints and tips on how to make rewards work more successfully. Technically, we could more accurately call these rewards 'reinforcements', but for our purposes calling them rewards is fine.

Rewards always work better if they happen close in time to the event. Let us imagine I am a smoker who is stopping smoking. I might decide to give myself a reward like a sweet, a walk outside or a five-minute break when I manage an hour without smoking. If I do not smoke all day and give myself a reward tomorrow, this is a weak reward. However, if I do not smoke for an hour and I give myself a reward there and then, this is a strong reward.

You can also use baby steps in rewards – this is common with children and star charts. Star charts work by giving a small immediate reward that often builds up to a big reward. I might give my child a star on a chart (small reward) for eating peas at dinner time. When there are ten stars on the chart we can have a trip to the beach. This sort of recording also works well with adults. Often small rewards like stars help because they show you how much progress you are making even when your mind is sending you messages of failure. You can look at the chart and actually see how much progress you have made. The rewards have to be clearly linked to goals, close in time to the event and can add up to a bigger reward.

In summary, the tips are:

- Rewards can strengthen behaviour
- Make sure you reward the behaviour you want to reward (unlike in the dog example earlier)
- Do not reward behaviour you do not want (like sitting on the sofa and eating lots of biscuits, as in the dog example)
- Do not have rewards that create new problems (like eating bags and bags of sweets instead of smoking)
- Link rewards to goals (as in star charts or baby steps)
- Give small rewards close in time to the behaviour, achievement or baby step

Let us go back to my misbehaving dog for a moment. To succeed in getting him off the sofa, I want to reward staying on the floor. I would have been more successful to rub his head (small reward for staying on the floor) every fifteen minutes. This would then only reward him being off the sofa. If he was on the sofa, I could take him off, put him on the floor and ignore him for fifteen minutes. If he was on the sofa he would not get any rewards.

Write here something (small achievement or baby step) that you could reward yourself for and what the reward will be:

_____

_____

_____

Revisit goals

'Why on earth am I doing this?' This is a question we may ask ourselves over and over again. The problem is that we do not always take the time to answer it. It may be easier to think of this as our naughty puppy thoughts, which keep asking us, 'Why on earth are you doing this?' It is not really a question but more of an unhelpful thought. The real message here is: 'It's hard, it's difficult, isn't it time for you to give up again?'

Acting on this message will give short-term relief that feels like 'Phew!' To keep on getting your life back, the way to answer this question is to revisit your goals. Take a little time and look back at what you filled in as your goals and values in Chapter 4. As with most of the ideas we are talking about it is best if you can plan this in advance. Decide that when your naughty puppy thoughts are barking 'It's time to give up' you will look at your goals and values. Write down your goals and values key words here:

_____

_____

Write them on a separate piece of paper and carry that with you or put them on your phone or computer. Visiting your values and goals in your mind can be difficult when your unruly puppies are barking so read your key words and remind yourself why you are doing this when needed.

Grounding

We have noticed the ability of our minds to time travel. Thinking about the past (rumination) and worrying about the future can be overwhelming. We can spend so much time thinking about these things that we do not have room to see or feel what is around us now. Grounding is a technique that is often used together with mindfulness, which makes our minds concentrate and really experience where we are now. It is about focusing on sensations right now even when we are bombarded with rumination and worry. For example, walking in the countryside and passing through a beautiful wood I do not feel or see the beauty as I am overwhelmed with ruminations about the past or about a problem behaviour. These thoughts are coming from my mind; I have not managed to control them. They then get worse as my mind tells me that I always fail at everything. Finally, I walk all the way though the wood and miss all the nature and the beauty.

We can let our minds do things like this in our everyday lives – at home, in the car, at work or anywhere. Thoughts or memories can crash in from the past in an uncontrolled way. Some of these experiences are particularly vivid. They are known as 'flashbacks' and are generally connected to past trauma. Grounding makes you connect with where you are now, not the past, not the future. To practise grounding skills, follow these steps:

- Take note of where you are at this moment – are you standing, sitting, walking, lying down?
- What parts of your body are in connection with the world?
- Describe to yourself what each of these body parts feels like. You may even like to ask it – is this body part hurting, squashed, tingling, hot, cold, numb?
- Name what the world is made of where you are connected with it – is it your bed, the floor, a chair? Describe to yourself the material – is it carpet, wood, fabric?
- Describe the feel of the fabric or material – is it soft, hard, hairy, smooth, itchy, silky?
- Try to notice as many sensations as you can: smells, temperature, sounds, what you can see, etc.

You can take a couple of minutes to try this now.

This is just one example of how to do grounding. Other ideas for grounding are to think mindfully about your body and breath, or to carry something physical with you like a stone that you can touch and describe in detail. Ask yourself is it smooth, cold, etc. Doing something physical that you need to concentrate on is also useful – perhaps gardening, playing the piano, cleaning the house, etc.

Once you practise grounding skills a lot, you might be able to use a reminder to quickly bring yourself back to the here and now without having to do a longer exercise. For example, some people find it helpful to put a loose-fitting elastic band on their wrist and flick it when they need to come back to the present moment, or to just take three breaths mindfully.

Calming yourself, self-soothing

There are times when we all need to feel calm, comforted, nurtured and soothed. Doing things to make ourselves feel this way is called 'self-soothing'. Self-soothing is a skill that we nearly always know about but may not actively use. Actively doing something different is often the last thing on our minds when we are in distress but it is exactly what we need. When our minds are sending us unwanted negative messages it is difficult to decide to do something that soothes us. At this point it seems like we do not deserve it, it is a waste of time, or just a way of avoiding the issues. It is known that when we feel low or depressed everything around us can look bad. At such times it is important to give yourself permission to self-soothe when needed. Self-soothing helps you tolerate distress and also sends a message to your mind that you do deserve this break. Here are some ideas:

- Think about a place where you feel at your calmest and most nurtured. It may be inside or outside – for example, in the bath, on the beach or in the garden. This is the best place to self-soothe.
- Some people feel calm, comforted and soothed whilst doing something like drawing, painting or listening to music. Many people's hobbies are soothing for them.
- Going to be with your perfect nurturer can be a form of self-soothing
- Part of self-soothing is managing your body. Earlier in this chapter we looked at slow, deep breathing and how that can slow down negative thoughts, anxiety and panic. These breathing exercises can also be used for self-soothing.
- Positive self-talk can help with self-soothing. Say out loud in a kind voice three or four positive things about yourself and listen to them. Simply listen to yourself saying positive things. This is different to thinking positive things: talking out loud and listening is much more effective.

Do not try to make a self-soothing plan when you are bombarded with negative thoughts and feeling like you are about to enter the pits of despair. Wait until you are in a calm state, then plan in advance what you are going to do to self-soothe and also when and where. Write your plan here:

What I am going to do:

When I need to do it:

Where I plan to do it:

Tolerating distress and being yourself

The obvious way to deal with negative feelings and pain is to try to make them go away. Feelings can be negative and painful. Sometimes this involves physical pain that seems to get worse when you are distressed or upset. It is not always possible to rid yourself of negative, painful feelings and physical pain. Using your new skills you can accept the pain and also minimise it at the same time. By using these skills you can accept that your pain is here in a controlled way. Does your pain control you or do you control your pain? Step one is to accept your pain is here and then use the self-control ideas that are best for you. The energy you save by not fighting your pain can be put into self-control.

Mindfulness

By now you have practised lots of mindfulness. All of the skills described in this chapter work well with or actually are mindfulness skills so we do not need a separate section here. This is just a reminder to use mindfulness whenever it feels right.

After reading this chapter you may want to think about which skills would work best for you. You may want to blend two or three of the skills to find your best self-control combination. Most self-control skills work better if you pre-plan and practise them when you are feeling good. That way you will be better prepared when you come to a crisis. Write your three favourite skills down here:

_____

_____

_____

Enjoy practising your self-control skills and have a bit of self-soothing time before the next chapter. See you later.

Chapter 14

How to Break the Links in a Behaviour Chain

In this chapter we are going to look at how to break the links in a behaviour chain. At the start of this book most readers had a clear idea of what they wanted to change. The problem was that when we looked at things in more depth they became less clear. Exactly what needed to change looked a little more complex. You may remember that Tom gambled when he was upset. As far as he was concerned, he had to stop gambling as it was wrecking his life. When he tried to stop gambling, he seemed to fail time and time again. This made him more upset and in turn gamble more. Tom often got upset when contact with his children did not work out.

Looking at his behaviour chains in detail, we might suggest that mediation for child contact could be part of his plan for change. Deciding what to change becomes more straightforward when we use our new skills. We cannot think straight when negative thoughts are hitting us in the face and causing distress. This is the wrong time to think about our problems. So, as in previous exercises, we need to do this when we are calm.

Links in a behaviour chain

Chapter 8 was about what needs to change, Chapter 9 concerned the Wheel of Experience and Chapter 10 covered how to understand behaviour. In

Chapter 8 we listed exactly which behaviours we need to change. These were arranged in three main groups:

- Things I do which harm myself or others
- Things I do which stop me from changing
- Things I do which mess up my life or stop me reaching my goals and values

We also thought some more about 'dialectics'. This was about balancing acceptance and change. We saw that we can give up judgements and at the same time still see the need for change. You may want to revisit your My Things to Change list in Chapter 8 before continuing (page 125).

In Chapter 9 we introduced Wheels of Experience to describe the different aspects of experience. These are thoughts, feelings, behaviours (including urges) and body sensations. We also discussed events inside and outside our bodies and how they affect our Wheels of Experience.

In Chapter 10 we looked at behaviour chains. We started to work on the idea that a problem behaviour can be seen as a chain made up of many links. The links involve thoughts, feelings, behaviours (or urges), body sensations and events. Sometimes there are positive links in the chain. These might be pleasant body sensations, positive thoughts or good feelings. There can also be escape or relief links. In other words, at some point, in a small part of a chain, we can move from a painful place to a better place. This can be quite a surprise for many readers. When there are positive parts in our chains they are nearly always short-term. The chain soon becomes negative again and we experience more distress. You may remember the example of drinking until I am 'blotto' to stop myself worrying about being in debt (page 150). This can work really well for a short time: I may feel positive feelings of happiness and being carefree. In a small part of my chain, I have moved from a painful place (worrying about money) to a better place (being happy and carefree). But soon afterwards I feel much worse: I feel sick and I have spent more money on drink. My drinking session has just confirmed what a failure I am and my belief that things can never change. This is an example of a short-term gain from a problem behaviour.

Tom's behaviour chain started with a trigger, which was Sarah saying that she was concerned about money. In the middle of the chain Tom was feeling excited and positive whilst he was gambling (his problem behaviour). At the end of the chain he felt despair and shame when he lost £500 and later lied to Sarah. His contact with his children going wrong was another, different trigger for gambling. Tom could have done a behaviour chain for the incident from his diary on the Monday (Chapter 10, page 153), when his children did not turn up after school. The chain would have looked very similar to the one below, just with a different trigger (children not turning up) and involving gambling online instead of at the casino.

Mandy had walking problems. She discovered that they were at their worst when she went to interviews at the Jobcentre. When she was due to set off, she often heard her mum's voice saying, 'You'll never make it, you can't even walk far enough to get there.' Mandy agreed with her mum's voice and thought that her walking was too bad to get to the Jobcentre. Often she decided not to go. Her feelings of anxiety and panic went down; her mum's voice seemed to go quiet. Mandy said to herself, 'Phew, what a relief now that I've decided not to go!' This was a short-term gain, which she learned about from doing her behaviour chain.

When Barbara from the Jobcentre phoned up three hours later, Mandy felt massive feelings of anxiety and panic as Barbara threatened to stop her payments. Mandy's mind sent her the message that immediate relief was available and she should take it, as it was all too much. Her mind did not send her the message that in three hours' time there would be a crisis. When Mandy did her behaviour chain she could see the short-term gain and the long-term pain she suffered when she avoided things.

Planning to break the links

A chain is only as strong as its weakest link. Some of the links in our behaviour chains are strong (harder to change) and others are weaker (easier to change). As we take actions towards change we may want to look at the weaker links first. Starting with breaking a weaker link can produce an early success and give us hope. It can also disrupt the whole behaviour chain.

There are early links in the chain that build up to the problem behaviour itself. When Tom did his behaviour chain he found there were a number of links in the chain before he actually placed a bet. In the background was his vulnerability cloud – he had had a bad day at the office and was feeling criticised by his colleagues. There was the trigger of Sarah complaining about money; he felt hopeless, sad and guilty. Then he had bodily tension, an urge to get out of the house and so he went for a walk. This took him towards the casino, where he had the thought, 'I'll just nip in for a drink.'

Tom sat down and thought of ways in future to take an action to break a link in his problem behaviour chain. He did this for each link in the chain:

- *The vulnerability cloud.* Tom could look at the things making him vulnerable, the 'bad day' at the office. He could consider stress management such as taking more breaks or mixing with the more supportive colleagues instead of the critical ones. He could even challenge his thoughts that they *were* criticising him by asking himself 'How do I know?' or 'Is there any other way of seeing this? Could there be any other reason why my colleagues were being negative that day, maybe to do with their own problems?'

- *The trigger.* Tom knows that when Sarah talks about money it will probably set off this whole chain. In future, he could sit down with Sarah and share his plans for stopping gambling. Then they could make a plan for how they are going to deal with the money problems together.

- *The naughty puppy thoughts.* 'It's all my fault', 'It's hopeless'. Tom could write down some alternative thoughts such as 'I'm working on this now and we have a plan to deal with the gambling and the money'. He could keep those new thoughts handy on his phone or in his pocket.

- *The feelings of sadness and guilt.* Tom could do a mindfulness physicalising exercise (Chapter 5, page 93). He could take the feelings of sadness and guilt out of his body and have a good look at them (observe and describe, no judgements) and then put them back into his body.

Tom's Vulnerability Cloud

Bad day at the office, colleagues making fun of me, criticising me.

Trigger Event

Getting home to find Sarah complaining about not enough money for bills

Feelings

Sad, angry, guilty

Thoughts

It's hopeless
It's all my fault

Body Sensations

Tense jaw and shoulders
Head throbbing

Behaviour

Urge to get out of the house
Urge to gamble

Problem behaviour

Gambling

Thought

I'll just nip in for a drink

Behaviour

Went for a walk, to the casino!

Body Sensations

Energetic, alert

Thought

Mind focused on game

Short-term gain

Event

Losing games

Thought

Oh no!
This is a disaster

Behaviour

Keep gambling

Feelings

Despair, self-loathing, shame

Body Sensations

Tense jaw and shoulders, felt sick

Behaviour

Left, went home

Feelings

Felt terrible
Hated self
Despair, worry

Behaviour

Lied to Sarah

Long-term pain

- *The horrible body sensations.* Tom could decide to go out for a run when the tension builds up in his body. By doing something active he can change his body sensations.

- *The urge to leave the house.* Tom could mindfully observe this urge and just notice it is there without acting on it. He knows now that urges only last for a short time and then die down, coming and going like waves on the shore. Or he could leave the house but go away from the casino towards his friend's house. Or he could do something instead of leaving the house, like vacuuming, to distract himself.

- *The urge to gamble.* Tom could talk to Sarah and ask her to stay with him when he had an urge to gamble, and do something distracting, like going for a walk together. He would have to be willing to share this with Sarah and trust her to help him. Or he could phone a gambling helpline or a friend until the urge got less.

Behaviour
Went for a walk, to the casino!

Tom was on automatic pilot at this stage, heading for the casino. Somehow he needed to stop and think. But how could he manage this *behaviour*? He could take a picture of the casino on his phone and print it out on his computer, then write 'STOP! THINK!' in red ink across it. He could keep looking at this picture whilst he is calm. Practising this will lead to the words 'STOP! THINK!' springing to mind whenever he sees the casino. Then he will be able to stop for a moment and decide whether to go in or not. He could think about his values key words and ask himself whether this move is going to take him towards being a supportive and reliable husband and father. He could go to his friend's house after doing 'STOP! THINK!'

Thought
I'll just nip in for a drink

This kind of *thought* is known to happen to many of us when we are desperate to carry out our urges. It is a thought that gives us permission to continue. Tom could label this as a 'dangerous thought' and practise spotting the thought whenever it comes along. When he spots it next time he could change direction and walk quickly towards his friend's house.

Next, Tom took a good look at all these options and decided which ones he was actually going to plan to do. It is best to choose options which are easy and early in the chain to prevent things getting hectic. Also, it is good to choose an option which we can do in an emergency when we are well into the chain. He decided to choose the options below to make up his plan:

Tom's plan to break the links

We might make a number of plans to break the links in our behaviour chains and we might need a number of tries at it. Most of us find this. Tom chose to take the following breaking- the-link actions in his first plan:

- Stress management at work – take regular breaks and make sure I eat lunch (to reduce my vulnerability).
- Share my plan with Sarah and ask for her help (to reduce the trigger events).
- Write down some alternative thoughts – 'I'm working on this now and we have a plan to deal with the gambling'. Keep these new thoughts handy on my phone. When I think the thoughts, 'It's all my fault', 'It's hopeless', look at the new thoughts and read them out to myself, if possible.
- Vacuum when I get the urge to leave the house (to manage the urge to leave).
- Use 'STOP! THINK!' when I find myself walking towards the casino and redirect myself towards my friend's house (to control walking towards the casino on automatic pilot).

Tom kept this plan on his phone and looked at it every morning. Whenever the need to use the plan came up, he would do the most useful thing at the time. He did not need to do them in any particular order.

A breaking link action is stronger if it makes it difficult to carry out another link in your chain. When Tom is vacuuming he cannot leave the house as the vacuum cleaner is plugged in!

More plans to break the links

Here is what was in *Janet's* first behaviour chain, with her actions for the first week:

	Links in my chain	**Breaking-the-links actions**
Vulnerabilities	Feeling undervalued at work, eating too much, being overweight	
Trigger event	People laughing at work	
Thought	'They are laughing at me; they think I have no skills'	Challenge the thought – are they really laughing at me?
Feeling	Anger	Make friends with the people I'm angry with
Body sensation	Tension	
Thought	'I should be in a better position'	
Behaviour urge	Urge to shoplift	
Behaviour	Head for the shops after work	
Behaviour	Steal biscuits	Steal fewer biscuits
Thought	'I'm good at this, I'm in control'	
Body sensations	Buzz from not getting caught	

Feeling (short-term)	Excitement	
Body sensations	Tension down	
Feeling (short-term)	Pleasure	
Behaviour	Go home, eat all the biscuits	
Feeling	Feel good	
Thought (long-term)	Wish I had not stolen and binged; I can never succeed and I will always be eating too much	
Feeling (long-term)	I hate myself	

Janet started her breaking-the-links actions with a rather strange step towards her final goal of stopping shoplifting. She was shoplifting two packets of biscuits a day. For the first week she agreed with herself to only take one packet of biscuits a day from the supermarket. For the second week she did not steal any cakes or biscuits. Janet felt joy at achieving this.

When she made friends with the supermarket staff and the office staff, she could no longer see them as the 'enemy'. They seemed quite pleasant and her anger disappeared. Her confidence started growing and she looked forward to shopping after work. Soon, she was strong enough to challenge her thoughts that people at work were laughing at her. Her perfect nurturer helped with this. She began to see that they were not laughing at her and she began to laugh with them. She was feeling appreciated at work, which in turn allowed her to value herself. Her new friends told her that she had a lovely curvaceous figure. She began looking in clothes catalogues with them.

Janet started to get her life back when she tried her first breaking-the-links action of stealing only one packet of biscuits a day. This may be one of the strangest actions that we will look at! She started breaking the chain half-way through, by changing her behaviour. Later, she tackled earlier links, by making friends with the people she was angry with, in the supermarket and at work. Although she started directly with her problem behaviour in the chain (shoplifting), she did it step by step, and she broke the chain in other places at the same time.

Cheyenne's final goal is to be a loving mum to her children. She realised that she could not be the mum that she wanted to be if she could not even care for herself. Cheyenne's children saw a mum who looked scruffy and felt worthless: they were learning that this is what a grown-up should look and feel like. She could not make her children feel special and be an inspiration to them. Cheyenne's beliefs about herself started during her own child-hood when she was neglected and not cared for. She learned that she was 'not worth it' and never would be; these were some of her vulnerabilities.

Cheyenne did her behaviour chain about washing her hair in washing-up liquid. She saw that when she had a shower she tried to fight these worth-lessness thoughts and act as if she *was* worth it by using the shampoo. But picking up the shampoo (trigger) led to lots of feelings of anxiety and panic. When she deliberately neglected herself by using washing-up liquid (problem behaviour) the anxiety and panic immediately went away. By using the washing-up liquid Cheyenne was agreeing with the naughty mind puppies' messages that she was worthless. This seemed to quieten them down. That is why she washed her hair in washing-up liquid – it took away anxiety and panic (short-term gain). About thirty minutes after washing her hair in washing-up liquid she felt worse, as though there was no way forward and her mum had been right to neglect her (long-term pain). These negative thoughts had been going on for about thirty years and would take some shifting.

Thinking about her breaking-the-links actions, Cheyenne knew that she somehow had to stop washing her hair in washing-up liquid (problem behaviour). But she could not do this without feeling panic. The first thing she did was to talk to her best friend, who was surprised about Cheyenne's hair-washing routine. Her best friend suggested that she should just try using the children's shampoo. Cheyenne agreed this was a great idea. She planned to leave the washing-up liquid in the kitchen and not take it into the shower, but when she tried to do this, things went wrong. She felt extremely anxious so she ended up doing the same old thing, using the washing-up liquid. Although her friend had suggested a great first break-the-links action, it was not possible to do it.

In despair, Cheyenne looked again at her behaviour chain. She realised that whenever she used shampoo she was bound to feel anxious so she decided to work on dealing with the anxiety. She realised she had to accept that it would increase when she used shampoo: she would feel worse, not better. But if she could stick with the anxiety and let herself feel it, it would come down again, like a wave breaking on the shore. She practised breathing in for four and out for six, to calm her body a little. Then she made an image in her mind of her anxiety, like a wave which swells up and then comes down. (This exercise is described in Chapter 19.) After a week or so, she could wash her hair with shampoo and feel very little anxiety.

By breaking the links in her chain in several places, Cheyenne achieved success. This started to work against thirty years of neglect and NATs. Cheyenne could tell her best friend how well she had done. This was a new experience for her. Now that she had made her first breaking-the-links action she could start again looking at her behaviour chain and choose something more ambitious. Her first break-the-links action acted as a springboard to greater things.

George was smoking and drinking at work and on the way home. This meant that he had to lie when he got home, which in turn made him feel depressed. He was acting very differently from his values: George wanted to be a loving and supportive dad. Jean did not see this in George and the children seemed to ignore him.

George's behaviour chain made him understand that he smoked and drank whisky when he felt depressed and not appreciated at home (*vulnerability*). He noticed that he never had the urge to smoke or drink at the kids' football club. This let him know that sometimes he did not have the urge to smoke and drink. At home he felt not wanted, not able to control anything in the house, and also depressed. At work and on the way home he had strong urges to smoke and drink. His naughty puppy thoughts were saying, 'Have a smoke if you want to, nobody can stop you.' When he actually did smoke and drink, he immediately felt good (short-term gain). George's behaviour chain also showed him that a little while after he smoked, drank and lied to Jean, he felt depressed and not appreciated (long-term pain). It was at this time of feeling depressed and not appreciated that he had a strong urge to escape these feelings by more smoking and drinking. When George looked at his behaviour chain he could see that this was a vicious circle that was going round and round.

George now understood that if he could break some links in this chain then he could move on towards his values and goals. Some options he thought about were: to do some work on making more of a contribution at home (to reduce his vulnerability); to practise mindfulness to his thoughts of not being appreciated; to stop lying to Jean and just be honest. He decided to choose the break-the-links action below, to work on the actual smoking and drinking behaviours. To break the link in the behaviour chain right at the point of the behaviour itself.

The break-the-links action plan looked like this:

- Keep whisky and cigarettes in the boot of the car all day long
- Keep my values in my pocket
- Practise saying 'STOP! THINK!' when I experience an urge to go and open the boot during the working day, or an urge to stop the car on the way home and open the boot
- Read my values (out loud, if possible) as soon as I do 'STOP! THINK!'
- Notice my urges to smoke or drink and practise mindfulness to the urges and urge surfing
- Reward myself with a mint if I manage to get through a break without smoking, or get home without stopping the car

By keeping the whisky and cigarettes in the car boot, George created a situation where he had time to stop and think and could decide to do things differently before he could get hold of the cigarettes and whisky. He told his mind that he was capable of change as he knew he did not want to smoke or drink at the kids' football club.

When George went into the house after not smoking or drinking, something changed, as he seemed to get a different response from the family. When he thought about this some more, he realised that when he came home he normally avoided contact with the family, as he smelt of smoke and drink. He had been feeling ashamed, which had made him avoid close contact. Now that he did not smell, he did not feel the need to avoid the family. George realised that his first break-the-links actions were also starting to move him towards his values and goals.

Aleena finished relationships because she felt high levels of anxiety and mistrust of men. She made a break-the-links action without realising it. You may remember that she attended mindfulness sessions at the university where she worked. During these sessions Aleena learned to observe her thoughts, feelings, urges and body sensations. She learned to observe her naughty puppy thoughts, feelings, urges and body sensations without trying to change them, push them away, avoid or act on them. By doing this she was able to connect with her feelings of anxiety and her thoughts about men and about her 'unlovable' self.

Before filling in her behaviour chain, she thought that all men were 'after something' and would not find her lovable if they knew the real Aleena, which made her feel anxious. These naughty puppy thoughts and feelings caused her a great deal of pain. Ending the relationship would take the thoughts and feelings away. When she filled in her behaviour chain she understood that ending relationships produced a short-term gain (escape from painful thoughts and anxiety). She understood that she had been actively ending the relationships because this allowed her to escape from her painful thoughts. She also saw that following the short-term gain there was the long-term pain of loneliness. Aleena looked at her goals and values, which included being an available and trusting friend and potential partner. She realised that she needed to change the behaviour of ending relationships.

Aleena made a behaviour chain with ending relationships as her problem behaviour. Looking at this chain, she thought she could work on breaking several links in it. For example, she could have challenged her belief that all men are 'after something'. She could have worked on her belief that she was unlovable and no one could love the real Aleena. She could have worked on tolerating the anxiety without ending the relationship. And she could have worked on reducing her anxiety levels.

Aleena decided to work on managing her thoughts, as her chain showed they were causing the anxiety. Her mind kept telling her that men whom she is attracted to will always be 'after something'. This was a very unhelpful thought. It came along with other thoughts of mistrust and resentment and feelings of anger. And it did not help her to keep what she really wanted – a relationship. She used a technique called 'Naming My Mind'. This involved calling her mind whenever it had these thoughts 'My Suspicious Mind' and imagining it like a parrot sitting on her shoulder, squawking unhelpful things. Aleena learned to say 'Hello, Suspicious Mind' when she noticed the parrot chattering unhelpfully. She used thought challenging on her thoughts that men are always 'after something' and that her real self was unlovable.

Aleena then found Salim, a man whom she thinks she can grow to love. She is concentrating on moving towards that love and asked her best friend what she thought about Salim and the relationship. Aleena found this gave another perspective on the situation. Her friend said, 'Salim and you seem good together. He genuinely likes you and you have lots in common. Stick with it, girl!' Aleena continues to feel some anxiety in the relationship, but is managing the thoughts and feelings successfully.

Pauline felt guilty and ashamed. She had images of past abuse and strong urges to harm herself whenever she was reminded in any way of her past. She felt better when she had harmed herself herself and pulled out clumps of hair (short-term gain). Soon after she cut herself and pulled out clumps of hair, she felt more guilty and ashamed (long-term pain). This was another vicious circle similar to other people's stories. Pauline's self-harm behaviour produced short-term gain but it led on to long-term pain. As a child she was sexually abused and the images in her mind of this abuse were so vivid that it felt like it was happening now (flashbacks). Pauline's uncle had always told her that the abuse was their special time, their special secret. He had told her that she was choosing this special time and if it were to go wrong then it would be her fault. She learned as a child that she was guilty and responsible, even though this is obviously not correct.

You may remember that Pauline went to her doctor, who arranged for some CBT therapy. When Pauline recorded the behaviour of hair-pulling and scratching she found her mind had been full of thoughts about the sexual abuse she suffered. The vivid images and thoughts, feelings and body sensations got worse as she recorded them. Pauline wanted to fill in a behaviour chain but found it too difficult. Her mind told her that she was to blame for what had happened, that she was guilty and a liar. Then flashbacks of the abuse happened. This was too much for Pauline to manage; she felt that her uncle still had control of her and her mind.

During the therapy Pauline's therapist refused to agree that she was responsible for the abuse or that she was somehow guilty. This helped Pauline to see that there were other ways of looking at her past. She told her therapist: 'My uncle is still more powerful than me. I feel like a child whenever I think about him.' The therapist pointed to an empty chair and suggested that Pauline imagine her uncle was sitting in it. She explained that this was an exercise to help deal with Pauline's thoughts that her uncle was still in control and her feelings of guilt and shame.

Pauline agreed to do this and was asked to imagine her uncle in the chair being a bully. She was asked to step in as adult Pauline and defend the small Pauline being bullied. Pauline said she would like to shout at her uncle but felt she could not do this. The therapist encouraged her to remember she was now an adult and she could do this if she chose to. Pauline started shouting and felt she could not stop. She told her uncle it was *his* fault, not hers, and she told him to get lost. For the first time ever she was in control of her past.

Pauline learned to remember that she was an adult when she had flashbacks. The therapist showed her how to enter the flashback situation as a grown-up and protect little Pauline. So now when Pauline has flashbacks she remembers she takes size-six shoes and is a grown-up who can deal with bullies. Pauline's therapist told her the flashbacks may still happen but now she has a way of dealing with them. This was a big break-the-links action and she needed someone to help her make it.

Pauline could now start looking at her behaviour chain as she could manage her feelings, thoughts and flashbacks. She did this with her best friend Katrina.

Rick had anger problems. He felt that most people in the world were useless, whether drivers, rail customers or family. When he filled in his values bull's eye (see page 72) he was shocked to see how far away from his values he was living. The crisis point came when he was given a final warning and found himself in danger of losing his job. Now the panic and worry were too much. Rick decided to do a behaviour chain for the event that led to the final warning.

Rick's behaviour chain

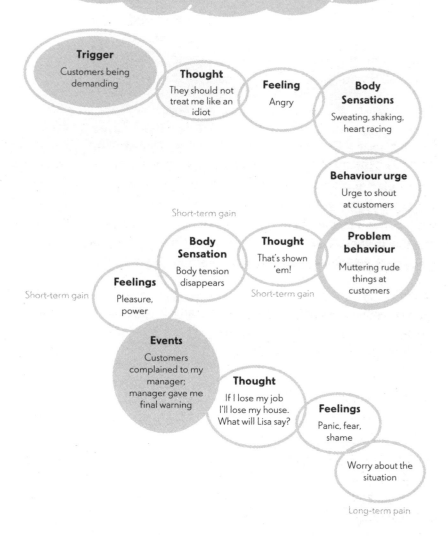

Interestingly, we noticed in Chapter 12, page 185 that one of the thinking errors people make is called 'shoulds'. Having 'shoulds' is having a list of ironclad rules about how you and other people 'should' act: becoming angry at those who break the rules and feeling guilty if you yourself break the rules.

This was definitely the case for Rick and it made him vulnerable to all the anger problems he had. One of his 'shoulds' was 'I should be in the army, like my dad'. This made him vulnerable to becoming angry whenever he thought about his job. He believed that his job issuing tickets at the railway station was somewhat embarrassing and beneath him. Rick managed to put all this in his vulnerability cloud.

Rick checked out his values and goals key words. He found that they were about being a loving and supportive husband and father, having more control of his anger and understanding it. He discovered that they did not mention being in the army, like his dad! This was a breakthrough for Rick when he began to notice all the rules he had for himself and for other people. He called these 'My Shoulds'.

Breaking-the-links actions had to be big – this was a life emergency. Rick decided to go to an anger-management group. He bought a self-help book too.

Rick noticed that most of his behaviour chains contained 'should' thoughts at the start. For example, in the chain on the previous page he had the thought, 'They should not treat me like an idiot.'

- Rick decided that when he noticed a 'should' thought he would use 'STOP! THINK!' and count to five before doing anything. This became easier to do as time went on and even became an automatic response to 'should' thoughts.
- Rick practised mindfulness each evening at home. He imagined giving each angry thought to a soldier marching out of his head and pictured them lining up to get in a boat. This made him laugh as he had had issues about being in the army and there he was, imagining soldiers! The anger problem felt just a little silly and more manageable.
- When Rick went to his perfect nurturer, the sea, he imagined a boat

setting off with the angry soldiers in it. You may remember he also used to let his anxiety float away on the sea.

- Timetables rule Rick's life all day at work – he is very skilled at using them – so he made his own timetable for work. At five minutes before each hour he took time to stop and think about his values and his family. Rick learned that the more times you do something, the more naturally it comes.

Rick came to realise that his ironclad rules came from his childhood. He had been acting as if he still needed the approval of his dad. This was keeping him in a prison made of 'shoulds' so that he was endlessly angry. As an adult man what he really needs to get his life back is to be a loving and supportive husband and father.

Mandy had walking problems. As we saw earlier in this chapter, she discovered that her walking problems were at their worst when she went to interviews at the Jobcentre. As she was setting off, she often heard her mum's voice saying, 'You'll never make it, you can't even walk far enough to get there.' When she decided not to go to the Jobcentre, she felt relief from anxiety and her mum's voice went quiet. This was the short-term gain, which she learned about from doing her behaviour chain. The long-term pain started when Barbara from the Jobcentre rang up and threatened to stop her payments. Mandy learned that her walking problems and her mum's voice both played a big part in her pattern of avoiding things. They were important links in her behaviour chain.

People often hear voices when there is no one there – research shows that many people have experienced this. It is important to know that voices can say positive or negative things. Those who go to therapy generally hear voices saying negative things, which causes them distress. It is very rare to find somebody in therapy because they hear voices saying positive things like 'You are really great and I think you are going to do well in your career'. This voice is likely to be thought of as a friend. The people who are the most distressed by hearing voices tend to believe their voices are very powerful and that they can do nothing to challenge or change them. They tend to believe that the voices must be obeyed.

Mandy looked at her values and goals key words: they were about having somewhere nice to live and having a job. She realised if she carried on avoiding she would never get these things. All of this was too much for her to manage alone and her family doctor arranged for Mandy to go to a support group for people who hear voices. Going to the group helped her to realise that she was not alone. She saw that other people understood what she was going through; they also experienced very similar things. The group helped her to learn some skills for working with voices.

At the group she did the exercise of talking to an empty chair whilst imagining her mother in it. She said goodbye to her mother, explaining that she (Mandy) was no longer a child: she was an adult now and getting her life back. She said her mum was wrong when she told Mandy she would fail at everything. She also learned how to practise mindfulness to voices. The group showed her how to create and hold onto more realistic thoughts that were different to her mum's opinions. They suggested that she should give herself relaxing treats like a long, hot bubble bath.

Mandy looked at her behaviour chain. In her vulnerability cloud she wrote that she feels anxious and ill the closer she is to her interview date. She saw that when she was setting off to the Jobcentre, she heard her mum's voice saying, 'You'll never make it, you can't even walk that far.' She had body sensations of walking being painful and feeling tired and sickly. Mandy had a strong urge to stop walking. She thought (NATs), 'I'll never get there. I can't walk, how can I do a job? I'm ill.' She felt hopeless, afraid and anxious.

Mandy decided not to go to the Jobcentre (thought). At this point she stopped walking and turned around (problem behaviour). As soon as she turned around she felt instant relief (short-term gain). Things changed again when Barbara rang from the Jobcentre. Mandy's short-term gains came to a sudden halt and long-term despair set in. Barbara threatened to stop Mandy's payments. Mandy noticed that her mum's voice was saying the same things as her NATs. She also noticed that her walking problems and how she reacted to her mum's voice both played a big part in her pattern of avoiding things – they were important links in her behaviour chain. Mandy decided to work on these two things. Breaking these links would help her avoid things less often, she thought. With all of this in mind, Mandy made this plan:

Vulnerability cloud

Just before the interview time I will:

- Talk to my cats, who are also my perfect nurturers
- Have relaxing treats like the bubble bath, as suggested
- Use mindfulness to voices skills

Breaking links

On the way to the Jobcentre I will:

- Tell Mum's voice that it's wrong about me
- Take a friend to the interview
- Surf the urge to turn around and not go
- Imagine myself in the gym with the staff, where I can walk quite well

Mandy did work with an empty chair at the hearing voices group to challenge the hold she believed her mum had over her, but she needed help from others to work on her walking and voice hearing. She got help from her family doctor, the gym and the hearing voices group. Her breaking-the-links actions continued to get bigger until she was able to walk to the florist shop that we read about in Chapter 3 (page 52). Mandy started getting her life back by wanting to be able to walk more easily. She achieved this partly by saying goodbye to her mum. Mandy had to admit that the young family doctor from the 'University of Wherever-it-was' knew what she was talking about!

Sally had learned during her childhood that only perfection was good enough. Now an adult, she continued to act as if this were true. Most evenings Sally vomited at home to rid herself of calories and toxins, and this was really messing up her life. Her goals and values were: wanting to be a loving partner; be honestly herself; stop vomiting and using laxatives; manage her anxiety. Unless Sally could stop vomiting (her problem behaviour) she would never be able to get her life back. After meeting Rosemary, she decided things had to change. She started work on her behaviour chain. It looked like this:

Sally's behaviour chain

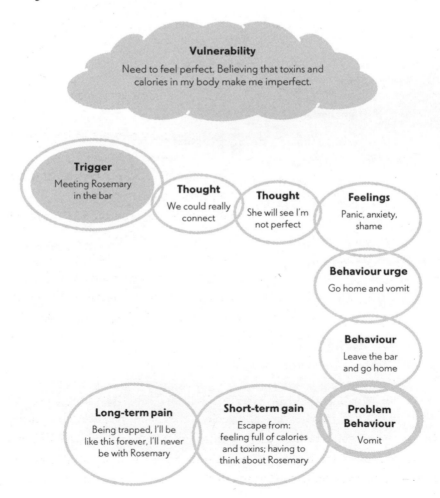

After looking at her behaviour chain Sally thought about which links could be worked on first. She knew that any work she did would have to be realistic and achievable. This reminded her of SMART goals, which she was quite skilled at as she used them at work. She thought that her break-the-link actions had to be SMART (Specific, Measurable, Achievable, Realistic, Time-limited). With all this in mind Sally decided these were the links that she could work on:

Vulnerability cloud

- Check how many calories an average woman needs for a healthy diet
- Check whether my diet does in fact have a lot of toxins in it
- Write down what is 'good enough' rather than perfect

Link breaking

- Mindfulness to feelings – notice feelings of being ashamed and imperfect, just let them be
- Mind reading – how do I know that Rosemary sees me as imperfect? Am I a mind reader?
- Urge surfing – I will use this in two different places in my chain, when I want to leave the bar and just before I am about to vomit
- Use 'STOP! THINK!' when I need to and practise this during the day at work
- Use self-soothing when I'm in the bar – calming breaths
- Imagine myself happy with Rosemary, even if I am imperfect
- When I get home, promise myself that I can vomit later on, then wait thirty minutes. During this time use my mindfulness and notice that I feel full of toxins and calories. Do not vomit during these thirty minutes!

Although Sally thought of quite a few things to try, most were small so she could fit them all into her day. She decided that in her last idea the waiting time to vomit could be increased by thirty minutes each day – she did this until eventually she had to set her alarm to get up to vomit. Doing this seemed crazy and Sally started to question whether she really wanted to vomit or just go back to bed. When she changed the arrangements for vomiting she started taking control: Sally was now giving orders to her vomit urges. This was the first action towards stopping vomiting altogether.

Now we have looked at a few behaviour chains, it is time for you to decide which links in your chain you will work on. This will be in the next chapter, so before you move on, take a break and we will meet up again soon.

—

Chapter 15

Breaking the Links in My Chain

This chapter shows you how to use your own personal vulnerability cloud and behaviour chain to plan to reduce your vulnerability and break the links.

My behaviour chain

In Chapter 10 you had a go at filling in your own behaviour chain. Now we would like you to copy your own vulnerability cloud and your own behaviour chain into the spaces overleaf. You may want to add some more things to your cloud and chain. Remember, for the vulnerability cloud you can think of the background to the problem. Things in your life that make you vulnerable to carrying out your problem behaviour. These might include all sorts of things like lack of sleep, not getting the right food, using drink or drugs, not having enough money, problems at work, etc. The cloud might also contain beliefs like needing to be perfect or having to please people. Regrets and ruminations about the past, background anxiety and feelings or worries about the future could be in the cloud. It could contain memories and images from the past of trauma or abuse. It might contain specific stressful things such as waiting for a court judgement, an important appointment, a stressful event or maybe having an argument with a friend. Copy your own cloud here. Do not forget that you may want to add to or change what you wrote before.

My behaviour chain

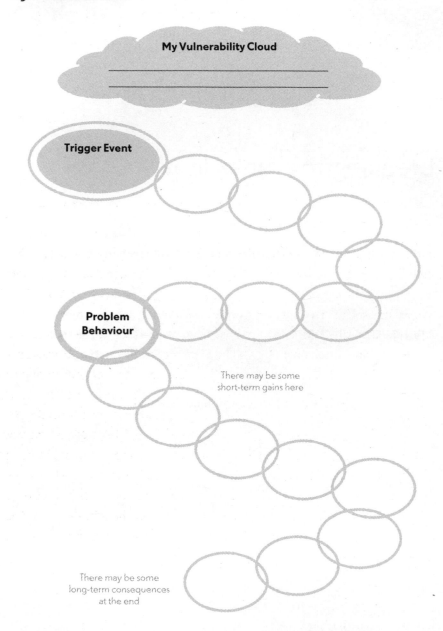

My Vulnerability Cloud

_____

_____

Trigger Event

Problem Behaviour

There may be some
short-term gains here

There may be some
long-term consequences
at the end

Well done! You might think of or notice more vulnerabilities as you go along over the next few days. If you do, you can add them in.

Next, copy your own behaviour chain below your vulnerability cloud. Again, just as with your vulnerability cloud, you may want to add some more things. You do not have to use every link we have provided, or you may want to add a few more.

My breaking-the-links plan

Now you can clearly see your vulnerability cloud and your problem behaviour chain, we would like you to copy each of them into your 'My Breaking-the-Links Plan Table'.

First, copy what you have written in your vulnerability cloud into the 'What was in it?' column in the table. Next, fill in the behaviour chain part of the table. Starting with the 'Trigger event' link from your behaviour chain, put this in the first box in the 'Links in my chain' column of the table, next to the 'Trigger event' box. Then have a look at the second link in your behaviour chain. Copy this into the second box in the 'Links in my chain' column. This second link will be a thought, feeling, behaviour or body sensation. Circle which one you think it is in the box to the left. If you do not know whether it is a thought, feeling, behaviour or body sensation, just have a guess. If you have an urge to do something but you do not actually do it, circle the behaviour anyway. For example, you might have an urge to move but not actually move, or you might feel an urge to smoke but not actually smoke. In this case the link in your chain will say 'urge to smoke' and you will circle behaviour in the box on the left. Put all of the links from your behaviour chain into the table. Do not fill in the other two columns just yet.

My Breaking-the-Links Plan Table

Vulnerability cloud			
What was in it?		What could I do to reduce my vulnerability? (actions)	My reducing vulnerability plan

Behaviour chain			
Type of link	Links in my chain	What could I do to break this link? (actions)	My breaking-the-links plan
Trigger event			
Thought Feeling Behaviour Body sensation			

Behaviour chain			
Type of link	Links in my chain	What could I do to break this link? (actions)	My breaking-the-links plan
Thought Feeling Behaviour Body sensation			
Thought Feeling Behaviour Body sensation			
Thought Feeling Behaviour Body sensation			
Thought Feeling Behaviour Body sensation			

Behaviour chain			
Type of link	Links in my chain	What could I do to break this link? (actions)	My breaking-the-links plan
Thought Feeling Behaviour Body sensation			
Thought Feeling Behaviour Body sensation			
Thought Feeling Behaviour Body sensation			

What could I do to break each link?

The next step is to come up with lots of possible breaking-the-links actions, sensible and otherwise. These could involve challenging our thoughts, changing our feelings, asking for help or using another new skill we have learned. You might decide to accept rather than change some thoughts, feelings and body sensations using mindfulness or self-soothing. Perhaps you remember some of the things people did in Chapter 14 that appeal to you too.

Start with your vulnerability cloud. Fill in column two under the heading 'What could I do to reduce my vulnerability? (actions)'. Think of anything you could possibly do to make yourself less vulnerable to carrying out your problem behaviour. It might be something as simple as going to bed an hour earlier, putting a limit on your alcohol consumption or getting more exercise. It could be getting some help from your perfect nurturer to develop some kinder ideas about yourself.

Now move on to your behaviour chain. Fill in column three under the 'What could I do to break this link? (actions)' heading. Try to come up with an idea for each link in the chain. Later we are going to select the ones that appeal to you most to make up your breaking-the-links plan. For now, let yourself go and be as creative as you can. For example, you may have a link in your chain that says 'Urge to smoke'. In column three you could write 'Sit on my hands', 'Suck a sweet', 'Go for a walk' or 'Stand on my head'. If you find it hard to come up with ideas, look back at Chapter 14, or ask a friend. You could look at Tom's list on page 219 of Chapter 14. Each of the ideas you have written in column three is a possible action in your final breaking-the-links plan.

How am I going to reduce my vulnerability?

Have a look at the ideas you had about how to reduce your vulnerability in 'What could I do to reduce my vulnerability? (actions)', column two in the Vulnerability cloud part of the table. Ask yourself which one most appeals to you. Which one would be relatively easy to carry out? Or there might be a more adventurous idea which will take a lot of work but which seems very important to you. Choose just one action and copy it into the

'My reducing vulnerability plan' in column four in the table. Copy what you have written in the 'My reducing vulnerability plan' column one more time below.

My Reducing Vulnerability Plan

What I'm going to do to reduce my vulnerability (action)

When I'm going to do it

Excellent. Taking this one action should reduce the background stress which makes you vulnerable to carrying out your problem behaviour.

What am I going to do to break the chain?

Go back and look at the 'Behaviour chain' part of the My Breaking-the-Links Plan Table. You have already listed actions you could take to break each link in column three 'What could I do to break this link? (actions)'. Have a look at all the actions in column three. In a moment you are going to choose up to four to go into column four 'My breaking-the-links plan'.

Column four will be the list of actions you are deciding to actually take. Here are some tips to help you choose as you look at column three:

- Is this action realistic?
- How practical is this action?
- Does the action appeal to me?
- Do I feel I could do this action?
- Try to choose actions which will break links early and later in the chain.
- You might include an action to deal with your long-term pain (after the problem behaviour has happened, if it does). It can help to deal with this, especially if it involves beating-yourself-up thoughts and feelings. They can make you feel depressed and hopeless, and so make you vulnerable to more problem behaviour.

Go back to the table and fill in column four 'My breaking-the-links plan', just copying over from column three the actions you have chosen to take. There should not be more than four breaking-the-links actions in column four.

My breaking-the-links plan

Copy out your chosen actions from column four 'My breaking-the-links plan' into your My Breaking-the-Links Plan below. Make a note of when you are going to take these steps. For example, you might write 'STOP! THINK!' as a break-the-links action and 'When I get the urge to shout' under 'When I'm going to do it'.

My Breaking-the-Links Plan

1. What I'm going to do (action)

_____

When I'm going to do it

_____

2. What I'm going to do (action)

_____

When I'm going to do it

_____

3. What I'm going to do (action)

_____

When I'm going to do it

_____

4. What I'm going to do (action)

_____

When I'm going to do it

_____

Great, nice work! If your naughty puppy thoughts are barking that this will never work, or other unhelpful things, pop them on the lead and read on.

Troubleshooting

The last step in making our plan is to ask ourselves, 'What could go wrong with my plan?' For example, *Tom* had an action of vacuuming when he had urges to leave the house. This was a good action because it made it difficult to leave. But when he asked himself the question 'What could go wrong with my plan?' he discovered the answer was 'I could just turn off the vacuum cleaner and leave the house anyway'. This is true, of course. Most people can wriggle out of a plan if they want to. We need to think about some troubleshooting ideas. Troubleshooting ideas are for dealing with what could go wrong with our plans.

In Tom's case, he decided to practice *willingness*. Willingness is where we make ourselves willing rather than wilful. When we are willing, we are open to new ideas and accepting of discomfort and urges in a mindful, accepting way. When we are wilful, we work hard at keeping our problems going and refusing to change. Tom decided to be willing to hang onto the vacuum cleaner so that his plan would work for him.

Another example is *Mandy*'s plan of asking a friend to come with her to the Jobcentre. When she asked herself what could go wrong with her plan, she came up with 'I could tell my friend I'm poorly that day and then she won't make me go'. Mandy realised that if she asked for help, she had to be willing to take it.

George planned to put his cigarettes and whisky in the car boot. When he asked himself what could go wrong with the plan, he noticed he might 'forget' to do this in the first place. So his troubleshooting idea involved setting an alarm on his phone at 8.30 a.m. to remind him to put the cigarettes and whisky in the boot.

Have a look at your reducing vulnerability and breaking-the-links plans and ask yourself, 'What could go wrong with my plan?' Write your answer here:

_____

_____

What is your troubleshooting idea to deal with what could go wrong?

_____

_____

Now you have action plans to reduce your vulnerability and also to break some of the links in your chain. You have a troubleshooting idea to deal with what might go wrong and you are ready to take action. As you do this, be kind to yourself and remember it is all very new. It will take time and practice to put your actions to work. The good news is, your problem behaviour will always happen again until you have cracked it, so there will always be another chance.

To share your vulnerability, breaking-the-links and troubleshooting plans, or to get support as you put them to work, visit www.getyourlifeback. global/getyourlifeback. Here, you can also download the tables and work-sheets above. Other ways of getting help and support might be to share your plans with a friend and involve them in helping you with it. These are just your first plans. Once they are working, you may want to go back to column three 'What could I do to reduce my vulnerability (actions)?' and 'What could I do to break this link? (actions)' in your My Breaking-the-Links Plan Table and decide to do some more.

My Breaking-the-Links Plan Diary

Here is a diary to record whether or not you manage your actions each time there is a chance to try them out. You will need this diary each time you are tempted to carry out your problem behaviour. Be kind to yourself and remember it will take time and practice:

Date and time	My action	Did I manage this step?		Did I carry out my problem behaviour?		What do I need to do differently next time (if anything)?
		YES	NO	YES	NO	
		YES	NO	YES	NO	
		YES	NO	YES	NO	
		YES	NO	YES	NO	

Thank you for reading this chapter and doing a lot of work for yourself. Congratulations on getting this far. It will take a few goes until you manage to take all of your actions. Do not be discouraged. We hope you will stay kind and patient with yourself as you go along – we are sure your perfect nurturer will help with this. You probably need a break by now, and we will see you soon.

Chapter 16

Taking Action to
Get Your Life Back

In this chapter we will revisit the values and goals that we identified earlier, shape them up a bit and break them down into more manageable steps. Then we will decide to follow these steps towards our goals in our everyday lives. This is the way to get your life back. When we do this, there is no longer a need to live in a world full of avoidance. We can use our new skills to deal with painful thoughts and feelings.

Taking action towards getting your life back is not always easy. Things happen that get in our way. In this chapter we will look at how things get in the way and can stop us from taking the steps we really want to take. We will look at how to get past these problems by laying out some specific short-term goals. These build on the baby steps we decided to take in Chapter 4. They are bigger steps that we can take towards getting our lives back. We will make sure these goals are SMART (Specific, Measurable, Achievable, Realistic and Time-limited). Then we will look at how to make sure we actually take these steps, not just talk about them.

Take a look back at Chapter 4, where you first made a note of your values and goals. These are the reasons why you have been willing to work towards change. You boiled down your values into some key words for each area of your life (page 69). Write these key words here:

Relationships

_____

_____

Health

_____

_____

How I occupy my day

_____

_____

Leisure/Growth

_____

_____

We are going to link these big aims with the baby steps that we have already taken. Your baby steps are in your My Baby Steps Diary (page 79). We are going to plan bigger strides towards your values and goals but first, let us look at what can hold us back.

Things that get in the way of taking action

You started taking baby steps towards your values and goals in Chapter 4, using your My Baby Steps Diary. Did you manage to do this exercise? If the answer is 'Yes', skip the next bit and go to the part on page 256 marked with asterisks ***. If the answer is 'No', you need to read this next bit.

Think about when you did not fill in your diary. Did you forget about it or did you remember but something got in the way of doing it? If you forgot, how can you remember to do it this week? Some ideas may be putting a reminder on your phone, a sticker on your mirror or perhaps asking a friend to remind you. Make a decision about how you are going to remember and have a go at it this week.

If you remembered, but things got in the way, ask yourself, 'What got in the way of me doing my diary?' If it was a thought or feeling, for example, 'This is a waste of time' or 'This makes me feel anxious', just notice this. Then choose one of the skills we have been learning to help you go ahead and fill in the diary. You could decide to thank your mind for the thoughts and feelings that get in the way and do the diary anyway, or you could choose to give yourself a reward whenever you fill in the diary – for example, a five-minute break from work, fifteen minutes reading a novel, or a walk outside. Then decide when and where each day you plan to fill in your diary and where you are going to keep it. Fill it in for a few days, at least once a day.

When am I going to fill in My Baby Steps Diary?

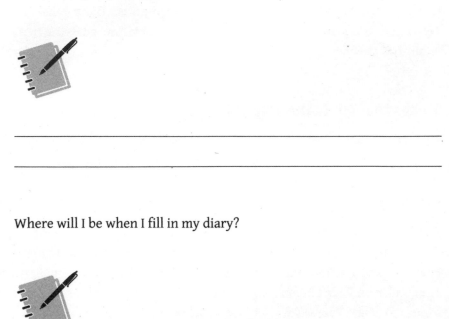

_____

_____

Where will I be when I fill in my diary?

_____

_____

Will I fill in the diary in this book or keep it somewhere else (perhaps on my phone or computer, etc.)?

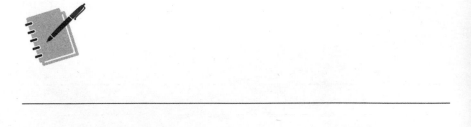

_____

_____

What is my reminder?

_____

_____

What stopped me from filling in my diary?

_____

_____

My plan to get over things that are stopping me from filling in my diary

_____

_____

When you have filled in your diary, move on to the next section. If you are at the stage where you have not yet filled in your diary from Chapter 4, you can imagine what you would have put in it, if you want to continue below.

***For those who did fill in the diary already, here it is again from Chapter 4. Copy your diary from Chapter 4 into the table opposite or imagine what you would have put in the spaces.

Great, so now we are going to take a look at the column in your My Baby Steps Diary called 'Things that got in the way'. You can see in the example that I had the thought 'Mum will think I've gone soft'. We could call this an 'internal obstacle' thought – it is something happening inside my head that could stop me. It could have stopped me taking my baby step of thanking Mum for the cake but this time it did not. I might have had other thoughts and feelings, like 'I don't want to do this' or 'Mum will just laugh at me'. If I let myself really listen to these puppies barking, I would not make the baby step.

In Chapter 12, we learned that we can handle thoughts in many ways. I could be mindful, letting the puppies bark away and just go ahead and do it anyway. I could start training my puppies by asking myself, 'How do I know Mum will laugh at me?' or 'What would my perfect nurturer say to me?' I could sing the negative thoughts in the shower to my favourite pop song. I could helicopter up and look down and see the bigger picture. From up there I could see the thought puppies barking away. I could see past them to my goal of showing respect for my mum. This would help me to go ahead and say 'Thank you' to Mum.

Internal thought obstacles can stop us from stepping towards our values and goals. Sometimes there are outside obstacles too, like not having enough time to do something. But often the problem is that it is our naughty thought puppies are telling us that we do not have time.

Do you remember George? He was depressed and had NATs; he was also smoking and drinking a lot. When George decided he wanted to spend

My Baby Steps Diary

Day	Baby step	Did I do it? Yes/No	Things that got in the way	Things that helped
Example	Thank Mum for cake	Yes	Thought she'd think I've gone soft	Practised saying thank you first before I did it with Mum
Monday				
Tuesday				
Wednesday				
Thursday				
Friday				
Saturday				
Sunday				

(please see page 256)

quality time with his family, he decided to take a baby step of doing the washing-up most nights. In his baby steps diary George filled in his 'Things that got in the way' column. He noticed NATs like 'It's pointless, washing-up is just a naff thing to do. Anyone can wash up, that's not going to make me into a good dad.' When he listened to these untrained puppies barking, he found he really did not want to do his baby step of the washing-up and actually even forgot to do it.

George learned how to 'helicopter up' above the situation and look down on it. From up there he could notice the barking puppies and he could also see his family and his own values and goals. When he could see things from above he could keep his reasons for doing the washing-up in sight.

At first when George washed up, Jean would thank him for it and the kids would come over and be astonished about it. This made George really think that he was contributing. After a while the family took it for granted. Then George's thought puppies got off their leads again. They started barking, 'No one notices, no one says thank you' and George began to have angry feelings about this. He began to get strong urges not to do the washing-up. His body tensed up when his puppies started barking. But George had become pretty good at noticing things without judging them. He noticed what was going on in his head and his body so he went back to his values and remembered that he wanted to be a supportive husband and dad, contributing to family life. He remembered that this meant doing the washing-up, among other things. So, with a sigh, he did the washing-up. He made a nice image in his head of himself giving this action to his family as a present. This made the washing-up a lot easier. He also noticed that being thanked all the time is not how it works in families.

Using your My Baby Steps Diary, copy down any thoughts or feelings that got in your way or could have got in your way when you started taking your baby steps. You can find them in the fourth column in the diary, 'Things that got in the way'. You may want to add some more things here as well:

_____

_____

_____

_____

Take a minute to think about how you might handle these things that get in the way when they come up again, as they will. Mindfulness? Helicoptering? Reviewing and challenging your thoughts? Perfect nurturer? Singing the thoughts in the shower? Any other ideas? Write down your plan here:

_____

_____

_____

_____

That is great. Do not forget to take a bit of time today to try out your plan. Bring the obstacle thoughts to mind, then try out your chosen idea for handling them. You may have to do this a few times as you get better at using your plan.

Moving from baby steps to short-term goals

Next, we are going to look at how to design more and bigger steps that will build on our baby steps and take us faster towards getting our lives back. These steps are shown in the illustration below:

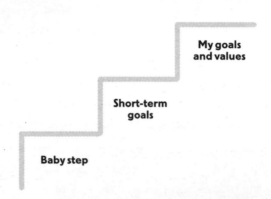

George felt that his most important values and goals were to be a loving and supportive dad and husband. His first baby step was doing the washing-up. By taking this step he learned a lot about how it feels to move towards his goals and values. He noticed that his untrained puppies could bark discouraging obstacle thoughts at him. He learned more about how to handle them too. Washing-up can easily seem trivial and irrelevant, but actually taking these baby steps teaches us many skills and how to keep going. We could notice that doing the washing-up in itself does not make George happy. That is why focusing on whether we *want* to do something or *like* doing something, or whether it makes us *happy* is of little use. It is getting our life back that makes us content and at peace with ourselves in the long run. To get there we need to be able to handle all kinds of thoughts and feelings, some wanted, others unwanted.

George could now think about some short-term goals, which are bigger steps towards being a loving and supportive dad and husband. He decided on the following short-term goals:

George's short-term goals

1. Be involved in the children's outside school activities

2. Join in the household chores and duties

3. Look after myself physically

He made a list of specific actions he could take towards each short-term goal:

1. Be involved in the children's outside school activities

    Take the children to football practice Saturday morning (hooray, I already do this, so I can tick it off!)
    Do homework with each child for half an hour twice a week

2. Join in the household chores and duties

    Do the washing-up (hooray, I can tick this off already!)
    Mop the bathroom and shower twice a week
    Make the bed and make sure the children do theirs

3. Look after myself physically

    Take a thirty-minute walk each day
    Swap shop-bought pies at lunchtime for homemade, healthy sandwiches

George also wrote that he would remember to smile whilst doing these actions whenever it occurred to him. He knew that helicoptering is a good skill for him to deal with loudly barking puppies so he carried a packet of mentholyptus sweets in his pocket. When he got one out and sucked it, this reminded him that he needed to helicopter up and take a clear look at the situation he was in. The taste and sensation reminded him of what to do and why.

Another thing George found helpful was singing his negative thoughts, both in the shower and in his head. He chose 'In the Summertime' by Mungo Jerry. He sang his negative thoughts in a jolly way: 'It's a waste of time, it's a waste of time, you're just no good, you're just no good, you will never do it, you will never ever, ever, manage it'.

These are some of the obstacle thoughts the puppies barked at George. The singing gave him some good distance from the thoughts, taking the power out of the puppies' barking. The barking was still there in his head, but it seemed less powerful and a bit silly when he sang the thoughts.

When George thought about these practical actions to take him towards his short-term goals, he checked that his actions were SMART. He could see that each action was clear, he knew when, where and for how long he had to do it. George made a chart with his short-term goals and SMART actions on it, which looked like this:

George's short-term goals and actions plan

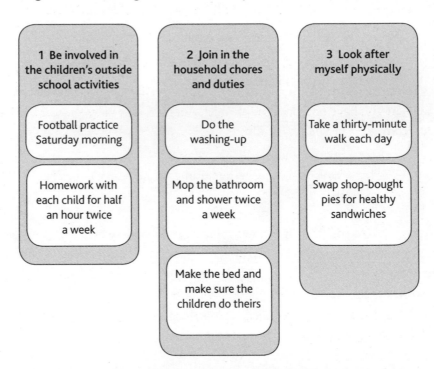

Each day, George takes a look at his chart, which hangs on the back of the kitchen door. Before he goes to bed, he ticks off those actions that he has done. For those actions that he has not managed to do he makes a plan to deal with them the next day. He always has an image of his perfect nurturer about, to encourage and speak kindly to him; he is learning to be kind to himself. George found it helpful to hang his chart on the kitchen door where everybody could see it. He felt that this was showing the family how hard he was working towards being a good dad. It also encouraged him to do his planned actions as he knew the others could see if he had not done them.

Now it is time to decide on your own short-term goals and actions. First, write your goals and values keywords here:

_____

Next, write a baby step that you have already taken towards your goals or values. You can find this in your My Baby Steps Diary, in column two (page 257). If you have not managed this yet, imagine your baby step and write it down:

_____

Next, write down the things that get in the way of making your baby step, from column four:

_____

Now write your most useful idea to deal with the things that got in the way:

Decide on three short-term goals you would like to achieve to move towards your values:

Short-term goal 1

Short-term goal 2

Short-term goal 3

And some SMART (Specific, Measurable, Achievable, Realistic and Time-limited) actions you can take to get to step towards each goal:

Short-term goal 1

Action

_____

Action

_____

Short-term goal 2

Action

_____

Action

_____

Short-term goal 3

Action

Action

Before continuing, check that all of your actions are in fact SMART. If they are not, go back and change any that you need to. You may want to make a chart like George's and hang it somewhere like on the kitchen door. Here is a chart that you can fill in. Blank charts can also be downloaded from www.getyourlifeback.global. Just copy your work above into the spaces in the chart.

My Short-term Goals and Actions Plan

1 _____	2 _____	3 _____
_____	_____	_____
_____	_____	_____

We are guessing that you have been experiencing some pretty loud barking from your own personal thought puppies by now. Perhaps you have some thoughts and feelings of reluctance or hopelessness, or maybe you are just totally optimistic and fired up. Decide on a time of day when you are going to take a look at your My Short-term Goals and Actions Plan. Tick off your achievements each day and remind yourself of actions planned for the next day. If you have not managed to do one of your actions, think about what got in the way and how you will get over this next time. Make a picture in your mind of your perfect nurturer, who will help you stay kind to yourself whilst doing this.

Using short-term goals to get your life back

Short-term goals are the stepping stones towards your values and getting your life back. George's values were to be a loving and supportive father and husband. His short-term goals and actions were moving him quickly towards these. When George had reached his short-term goals, he was able to set some more. Each of George's short-term goals moved him nearer to getting his life back. When George reached his short-term goals, he was ready to make some new ones.

As George continued to set goals and take action, he noticed that his place in the family was changing. His actions had changed the way in which the family reacted to him. Jean started to see George acting in new ways, like the George she was originally attracted to. The children began to expect their dad to be a part of their everyday life. These actions tamed the naughty puppy thoughts that made George want to smoke and drink. The naughty puppies seemed to growl less as he reached his short-term goals. He was losing the need to take time out to feel 'in charge' and to think that no one could stop him. You may notice that this is the opposite of the vicious circles that we looked at earlier in the book: George was now experiencing a *positive* circle.

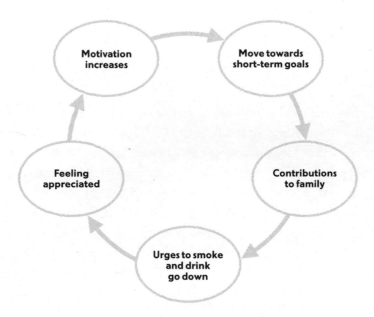

It is interesting to note that George first said that his problems were drinking and smoking. As time went on he learned that drinking and smoking were only two of his problems. He began to understand his behaviours and could see that there were other things that had to change for him to stop drinking and smoking. He learned that drinking and smoking were not his biggest problems at all: his biggest problems were that he felt excluded from his family and not appreciated or loved. When George worked hard on his short-term goals he no longer felt excluded from the family and his urge to drink and smoke went down. This meant that he did not have to lie to Jean. He no longer had negative thoughts about himself being a liar and letting Jean down.

Now you have set short-term goals, you can take SMART actions to step towards them. As you do this you will move towards your values. You will get things into your life that you want to be there. In previous chapters you have worked to understand your problem behaviour and planned actions for breaking the links. Trying to change problem behaviour without doing this usually does not work. Now you have two action plans: one to step *away* from your problem behaviour (Chapter 15); another to step *towards* the life you want (this chapter). These two plans together are the master plan for getting your life back.

Well done for reaching the end of this chapter. It must be time for a break so have a cup of tea or take a walk and get ready for the next chapter.

Chapter 17

Keeping Going

We have done a lot of work together so far, taking a long hard look at your problem behaviour and getting to know it very well. We have made plans to reduce your vulnerability and to break the links in your behaviour chain. We have also planned short-term goals and taken SMART actions to step towards your values. At about this stage along the road to getting our life back most people feel a bit tired. We may feel overwhelmed and confused and need some support to continue. This chapter is here to offer part of that support.

Motivation

In the *Oxford English Dictionary*, the definition of motivation includes 'Willingness to do something'. Willingness is defined as 'The quality or state of being prepared to do something; readiness'. This chapter will tell us how to manage our motivation. Motivation or willingness is known to come and go, depending on many things. Things such as how we feel physically and mentally; what is happening around us; what we are being asked to do, or what we are asking ourselves to do. You will have heard the word 'willing' a few times throughout this book. You may have learned that willingness is something we can practise. That is, we can learn to be willing. It is part of mindfulness practice. And if we are willing, we will be motivated.

It is true that we can feel more or less motivated at different times. It is not a steady state kind of thing. Even if we start out very motivated, our motivation can flag as we go along. Bring to mind a time when you made a resolution. Perhaps to stop smoking, start going to the gym or to go on a diet. Think about your motivation just before you started (probably high). Then, at the beginning of your programme (still high), but then a few weeks later (ouch! lower). Usually, our motivation journey goes like this:

The Motivation Journey

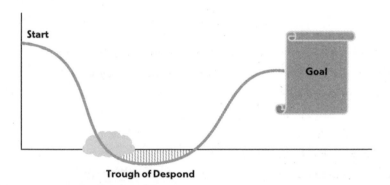

We start off our gym programme, for example, full of enthusiasm, motivation and willingness. As we go along, the novelty wears off. We find it is tiring. We have made progress and then our motivation gradually drops. It feels like we are going nowhere. At a certain point we reach the cloud on the graph: the cloud is the point where our motivation falls to the point where we want to quit.

Our motivation drops down below the line. Now we are in the Trough of Despond!

We are likely to experience very strong urges not to go to the gym. We will find excuses why we cannot go today. We might even 'forget' to go. Our unruly thought puppies might be barking at us that are weak, losers, we can't follow anything through, etc. Our puppies seem to direct this at us personally. But science shows it is not just about us. This is a journey most humans take as they work on change, on learning new things. And there is a key secret to remember about this: to get through the trough we *just have to keep doing what we started doing and then we will come up the other side.* If we can get through this Trough of Despond and up the other side, back up above the line again, we are very likely to reach our goal. The rest of this chapter looks more closely at motivation issues and how to deal with them.

Balancing my thoughts and feelings about striving for goals

Remember the thinking errors in Chapter 12 (page 183)? Some of us are 'black and white thinkers': things are either black or they are white, with no shades of grey in between. Extreme thinking like this makes us feel and behave extremely. For example, if I have only two alternatives, 'I love you' or 'I hate you', I am in danger of being completely clingy or very hostile. It is easy for me to swing from love to hate. Black and white thinkers could imagine that their thought puppies are either black or white. We need to practise changing the colour of these puppies to grey. We can do this by finding a realistic or balanced 'grey' thought. 'I like you most of the time' would be a grey puppy thought.

When it comes to motivation, this can involve black and white thinking too. Either 'I'm doing great at this' or 'I'm a complete failure'. If we have extremely positive thoughts we will not be prepared for the Trough of

Despond and it will take us by surprise. If we have extremely negative thoughts our motivation will start off low and the Trough of Despond will put an end to our efforts. Whichever extreme of black and white thinking we have, when we hit the cloud part of the graph and enter the Trough of Despond, we are going to give up and get desperate and wish we had not even started in the first place. Our thought puppies about success and failure are too black and white. So what does a grey puppy look like? It might look like this: 'Some days are easy and some are difficult' or even 'Everyone has to struggle to get to where they want to be'.

When my expectations are too high

Interestingly, both colours of puppy can be equally problematic. If I have thoughts that are extremely positive, my puppies might bark, 'Yeah! This is going to solve all my problems!' or 'This is going to be dead easy.' These kind of very positive thoughts give us *unrealistic expectations*. Starting off with unrealistic expectations means we are bound to fail. Some of us might have had parents who had unrealistic expectations of us. If we grow up with unrealistic expectations we have two options. We can bust a gut to try to meet the expectations and fail, because they are, after all, unrealistic. Or we can duck, dive and dodge so that we never try, and get labelled lazy or selfish.

Just take a moment to look at your own motivation and expectations. Do you see any thought puppies telling you it is going to be quick and easy moving towards your goals? If so, get that puppy on a lead and paint it grey. It is not going to be quick and easy or you would have already done it. On the other hand, it is not going to be horribly painful all the time, either.

A saying or two might help us here:

- This is a marathon, not a sprint
- We're on a long journey, there'll be ups and downs
- Change is like learning to play a musical instrument, you have to start by making funny little noises which don't sound too good before you can play a solo
- When you learn to swim, you should start at the shallow end

Have a go yourself at making up a saying that captures your ups and downs of change and the fact that it takes time. Write your own saying here:

_____

_____

Do not worry if you cannot think of a saying, just choose one from the list that suits you best.

When my motivation gets low

The first thing to remember is we have predicted we will *definitely* suffer from low motivation at some point on our journey. So when it happens, notice it and remind yourself that you knew you would arrive at this point sooner or later. Take a look at the graph at the beginning of this chapter and mark on it where you think you are. Here are some tips for getting though the Trough of Despond.

Not following the urge to quit

When our motivation gets low, all our urges are about giving up, but we have learned how to observe our urges and how to choose not to follow them. We can do this with the urge to give up. We can 'surf' our urges to give up and stay on top of the urge wave until it subsides. We can 'helicopter up' and look down on the thoughts, feelings and urges, see our values and goals at the same time and choose to carry on.

Checking for black and white thoughts

Often when we reach a low point, our naughty puppy thoughts go bonkers:

they bark loudly all the extreme and negative things they know. Check for this, take a look at what they are saying to you and ask yourself, 'Is this helpful to me right now?' If the answer is no, deal with them. Get those puppies onto a lead behind you as you walk along your chosen road, do not let them lead the way. You are in charge of where you go. There are a few ways to do this, such as singing the thoughts to a pop tune or saying them in a cartoon voice. You could paint the puppies grey by coming up with more realistic thoughts, like 'I've come a long way, this will pass'.

Encouraging ourselves with baby steps

To give ourselves encouragement through the Trough of Despond, we can go back to baby steps. Just think of one or two very small things you can do each day to keep moving towards your goals and not get frozen. Write them down, and tick them off each day.

Helicoptering up

Getting a bigger picture view is always helpful. We can use our helicopter-ing skills to hover up and look down on the situation. We can get a view of the whole process, from starting off to where we are now, and we can see the goal in front of us too. This view will us help us to see that we are in a temporary trough.

Metaphors

Being in a trough is a metaphor for this phase of low motivation, as if we are doing an assault course and have dropped into the mud. Other meta-phors which might help are:

- Being in the bunker on the golf course
- Reaching the pain barrier in a race
- Running out of fuel in the car
- Coming to a block in the road
- Getting stuck at an airport

In all these situations we are frustrated and the solution is to take action to keep going, not to stop.

Asking for help

At this time asking for help is a really cool thing to do. It is difficult though, especially if our thought puppies are barking loudly. We can plan in advance to ask for help. We can share with a partner or friend that we think we will get to the Trough of Despond and we need their help to keep going. There are some things which make asking for help work better. Make a troubleshooting plan to get you through the Trough, using some of the tips listed here. Share the troubleshooting plan with your friend. Agree that the other person will talk you through the troubleshooting plan but you need to be *willing* to listen to and follow their advice.

Perfect nurturer

Even if you do not have a friend you can easily talk to, you can always use your perfect nurturer. You can go to your safe place and have a pow-wow with them. Your perfect nurturer will give you kind words and compassion to help you along the road.

A story of motivation

Here is a Wheel of Experience of Aleena's thoughts and feelings. Aleena was struggling towards her value of being available to be in a relationship with someone. She had set a short-term goal of spending some time every other weekend with Salim but as she did this, she found herself becoming anxious as she grew to like him more. This was because she had a deep fear of being rejected or abandoned. She felt a strong urge to call off the relationship altogether. As the time to do things together approached she was filled with dread and a very strong urge to find an excuse not to see him. If she had followed this urge she would have experienced the short-term gain of relief from her anxiety but she would have stepped away from her values and goals.

Aleena's Wheel of Experience

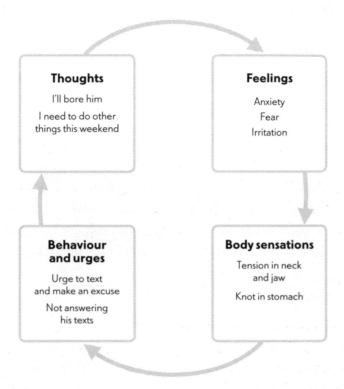

As well as these things going on inside Aleena's mind and body, there were also thoughts and feelings about giving up. Noticing that she was struggling to resist urges to dump Salim and that life was hard, her thought puppies barked:

- 'What's the point? This is never going to change'
- 'I will end up messing up, I might as well just do it now'
- 'Salim will see the real struggling me and won't want me'
- 'All men are after something'

As you can see, listening to these puppies barking and believing they are correct would make it likely that Aleena would give up on her goal. Aleena was aware that this was happening. Her mindfulness skills helped here. She observed her thoughts whilst giving them to soldiers marching through her mind. She noticed the hopeless thoughts popping up time and time again. She knew the thoughts were not helpful; they were pulling her away from her goal of spending time with Salim. She also spotted that she was in the Trough of Despond, just as predicted. She put her troubleshooting plan into action to deal with this:

1. Aleena made a list of the things she had achieved so far. These were:

    •   Spent time doing things with Salim for three weekends so far
    •   Resisted the urge to dump him
    •   Practised mindfulness to just observe my thoughts

2. She continued the mindfulness practice of giving hopeless thoughts to soldiers marching through her head

3. She painted the black and white thought puppies grey, by writing down and reading out the following balanced thoughts:

    •   'Sometimes it's easy and at the moment it's hard'
    •   'I can only do my best'
    •   'Salim knows that I struggle and he still respects me'

4. She set some smaller goals to keep herself going:

    •   Answer Salim's texts at least once a day
    •   Put reminders on my phone to remember to keep weekends clear
    •   Do a yoga class twice a week

Aleena kept going. Her Trough of Despond lasted three weeks – it felt like forever. But then one day it was as though the sun had come out. Something inside of her relaxed. She still had the thoughts and feelings but they seemed more distant somehow, less powerful. Some of the unruly puppies in her mind yard had turned grey and the black and white ones seemed to be less sure of themselves.

We always get another chance

Sometimes, when we get to the Trough of Despond we do actually give up. OK, it is not our shining moment but it may not have been the right time or the right circumstances for us at that particular moment. The thing to remember if we have given up is that we always get another chance – hooray! Because we are still living our lives, these problem behaviours and habits will return. We can decide to give it another go, any time, anywhere. We can build in what we have learned from our previous attempts. We know what obstacles are likely to come along and we can plan in advance how to deal with them next time.

So, if you have got stuck in the Trough of Despond and given up once, twice, three times or more, gather yourself up, plan how you will get through it next time and try again.

Chapter 18

Revisiting Your Story

Stories and meanings

In Chapter 2 we looked at stories. We introduced Janet, Tom, Cheyenne, George, Aleena, Pauline, Mandy, Rick and Sally. Each had a story which lead to them being the way they were. We looked at how we could each tell our own story, and how to make it a more compassionate one. Later, we talked about feelings and learned how to handle them, including anger. Anger could be the right thing to feel about our story but it is also very important to observe and handle anger so that it does not ruin our lives.

We hope that you have managed to move on from what might have been a judgemental story, blaming yourself or others. Telling our stories without judgements can make the basic facts clear. We discussed how to use validation in Chapter 6. Validation gives us a much more compassionate view of our story. It says, in effect, 'It's understandable that I am as I am, and I struggle with the problems that I have'. Our perfect nurturer (see page 168) can help here by showing compassion towards us.

As we re-tell our stories, first without blame and then with compassion, the meanings change. Our feelings and thoughts about our stories change as well. You have done some of this work already, using validation and your perfect nurturer. In this chapter we invite you to complete the work of re-telling your story, allowing yourself to focus on your values and goals. To help you do this, we are going to look at three of the stories from Chapter 2.

Revisiting Pauline's story

Let us look at Pauline's story. It is a sad story of abuse at the hands of her uncle, and of not being believed by her parents. It has lead to many years of self-harm and self-loathing. Pauline came to understand that it was not her fault (for what child can ever be responsible for abuse?). She felt more and more angry towards her abuser, and towards her parents for not believing her. Now, as an adult, she felt the need to confront them. She went to meet them and told them again about the abuse. Again, they did not believe her. So Pauline got stuck with anger, frustration, and thoughts going round and round in her head. Pauline's round and round thoughts sounded like this:

'They've ruined my life'

'If only they hadn't . . .'

'I can't ever have a relationship because of my past'

'I'm depressed because I was abused'

'It's impossible to recover from this'

Let us helicopter up and take a good look at the thoughts and feelings Pauline had about her story. Actually, from up here, we can see that they were just untrained puppies running wildly around the yard of Pauline's mind. The central question was, were they helping? Were they helping Pauline to step towards her values and goals? Another pack of puppies was also hurtling around the yard of Pauline's mind. These puppies were saying things like:

'I shouldn't have to deal with this'

'I should not be struggling with harming myself'

'Why me?'

'They were wrong'

And even 'They should be punished'

The puppies were barking these judgements loudly. Again, the question here was not, 'were these thoughts justified or were they true?' but, 'were they helping Pauline to step towards her values?' Her values and goals included caring for herself without self-harming, being a good friend and being more balanced about her opinions of men. The untrained puppies were in danger of pulling Pauline away from all of these goals. They were also taking up all her time and energy as she allowed them to pull her around the yard.

Pauline had two choices. She could either keep getting pulled away from her values and goals by her thoughts and feelings about her story. Or she could get them on a lead and step boldly towards her values and goals.

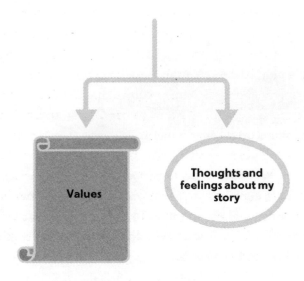

But she felt that if she did not focus on the angry thoughts and feelings she would be letting her parents and uncle 'off the hook'. Letting them get away with it would be an injustice on top of existing injustices. So she carried on focusing on these thoughts and feelings and they carried on running riot around her mind and generally running her life.

Eventually, Pauline 'got it'. She got that, true or not, right or wrong, these strong thoughts and feelings were just that – thoughts and feelings. She noticed that they were taking all her time and energy, so that she did not have time to become a good friend or to care for herself properly. Also, the strong thoughts and feelings produced urges to harm herself, just to make them go away. She realised that she could use her mindfulness skills to let these thoughts and feelings be so she had a chat with the puppies. Pauline said, 'Look, I know what you're saying. You might be right, but you're not helping right now.' She got the puppies on a lead, trotting behind her as she took steps towards her values each day. She did not try to get rid of the puppies (we know that never works) but she did not treat them as if they were in charge of her life either.

You can see that how we relate to our own stories is important. In Pauline's original story she blamed herself. You may also have a story where you blame yourself. Often, we feel angry with those who did badly by us, as we see it. Sometimes we can swing back and forth between blaming ourselves and blaming others. In this book we have learned to feel compassion towards ourselves and to be non-judgemental. We have learned to allow ourselves to feel anger and also how to handle our anger. Now we need to 'let go' of our stories. That is not to say that they are not important but it is to say that we need to focus forward, on our values and goals. We also need to focus on the obstacles to be overcome on the way. There is a saying in Dialectical Behaviour Therapy (DBT): 'You may not have caused all your problems, but you still have to sort them out'. Acceptance and Commitment Therapy (ACT) also talks about the need to let go of our stories, after we have worked on them.

Revisiting Mandy's story

Mandy's story went like this: 'I'm useless and not good enough. I can't do anything. I'm weird because I hear my mum's voice even though she is not there.' Mandy never did get so far as feeling angry with her mum for being so critical, unsupportive and emotionally abusive, but by going to the gym, and in the hearing voices group, she learned that she was the same as many other people in the world. She was not weird after all. Also, she gradually learned that her mother had been wrong about her: she was *not* useless. She noticed that whether she listened to her thoughts or whether she listened to her mum's voice, it was the same – they were all untrained puppies running around in her mind. They did not help. So she got them on a lead and got her life back. She began to grow into a new healthy self who could do things. Every day Mandy makes a choice: she can follow her values or she can do as before and believe her mum's voice.

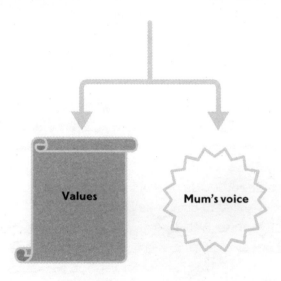

Some days, this choice goes badly and she finds herself really letting the puppies take over. On those days she struggles and feels bad. Other days, she gets in charge of the thought and voice puppies. She can still struggle and feel bad on these days too, but she is comforted because she knows she is getting her life back. Mandy is proud of this.

Revisiting George's story

George's story was not based on an abusive childhood; it was based on the beliefs he held about his place in the family. He felt he was entitled to respect because he was the 'Man of the House'. He felt he had a right to be the centre of attention in the family. And yet, he felt left out because no one spoke to him much at home. Because Jean was a teacher and 'cleverer' than him, he could not deal with feeling inferior to her. He could not understand why his friends were not interested in plumbing because he certainly was. He thought he deserved his smoking and whisky because he felt left out and lonely, and no one respected him.

If we helicopter up at this point and look down at George's story, what can we see? Regardless of whether he is right or wrong, George has an awful lot of 'being entitled to things' thoughts but he is not getting the things to which he believes he is entitled. Because of this, George's mind yard is full of puppies saying he deserves cigarettes and whisky:

George noticed that these were just thought puppies and realised he had to change his behaviour. If he waited for all his 'entitlements' to come true, he would wait forever. Also, a thought like 'You deserve a smoke' is never going to help George stop smoking, regardless of whether it is true or not. George's thought puppies are still there, but for the most part on the lead. He is focused on the direction he wants to take, to be part of the family and contributing to it. One day, George's puppies got out of control again when he had a couple of ciggies at work. He felt terrible and then he noticed his puppies running riot:

George was learning that his out-of-control puppy thoughts were always there in the background. They seemed to catch him when he was not watching them and not ready for them. He now had a choice, whether to follow his naughty puppy thoughts and feelings, or to step back and decide to follow his values. George was learning that some days were more difficult than others and some days he listened too much to his puppies. This is when he needed all his new skills to get them back on their leads and see the bigger picture. As time went on George became more skilled and these difficult times got less. As part of dealing with his judgement thoughts George decided to re-write his story. He wrote it without judgement words and 'entitlements', using his new understanding of his problem behaviours.

George's new story looked like this:

> 'Because I am a dad and a husband I believed that I had an automatic place in my family. These thoughts had developed over many years. My thoughts were unhelpful and made me feel excluded from my family. When I smoke and drink whisky I feel better for a short while and then I feel worse. I know that with my new skills I can change this situation if I work hard.'

Your new story

We now invite you to revisit your own story. Close your eyes and helicopter up. Look down at your own story from this high place where you can see the big picture. From up here, see if you can spot blame thoughts, angry feelings, sad feelings or other thoughts, feelings and judgements about your story and in your story. Now open your eyes. Write the thoughts, feelings and judgements that you spotted in your story and about your story into the puppies' callouts below:

These thoughts and feelings puppies are probably barking pretty loudly and they may feel very important, as they were part of your story. Now write your goals and values keywords here:

_____

_____

_____

_____

_____

Are your thought puppies helping you step towards your goals and values? If not, how do you plan to handle the thought puppies next time they try to take charge? Write your plan here:

_____

_____

_____

_____

_____

This is great progress. You may struggle putting this plan into practice and the puppies may take over now and again. When they do, and you notice they have, stop, pause, then get them on the lead behind you as you step towards your goals.

My new story

You now have new ways of looking at your problem behaviours: you can understand why they are there and how you can deal with them. You have also learned how being judgemental is so damaging to yourself and those around you. Using your new understanding of your behaviour in the same way as George did, write down your new story here, without judgements or blame, just sticking to the facts:

My new story

_____

_____

_____

_____

_____

_____

Take a moment to check that your new story is free from judgements and 'shoulds'. If any of these things are in your new story, take a moment to change them and take them out. Check that you are being kind to yourself. If you are not being kind, ask your perfect nurturer for help.

My new success story

After all your hard work you will have a new set of skills so that you can think about a different success story to the one that you started with in Chapter 3 (page 56). Your new success story will be realistic and with goals that are reachable. These new skills will equip you to live by your values and reach your goals. George wrote a new success story that looked like this:

> 'Over the last few months I've worked hard and now I feel a part of the family, which was my main value and goal. I had to learn to understand that my thoughts were driving my behaviour. When I got my thoughts under control, I could manage my problem behaviours. I now do household chores and help the children with their homework. I still use my new skills to keep on task. I do not have the urge to drink and smoke very much at all now. It is three months since I last had a smoke or a drink and I do not feel depressed.'

Now it is time to write your new success story. It may well be that you have already started your success story in real life, as you have worked through the chapters. If you have, you can include these things in your new success story. Take a moment to think about all of your new skills before you start. OK – go for it. This is where you see that you really can get your life back. Write your new success story here:

My new success story

_____

_____

_____

_____

_____

_____

You now know the way forward and how to get there. There will be hiccups on the way, but you have the skills to deal with them as they come along. In the next few chapters there will be ideas about how to keep practising, what to do when things go wrong, and more resources to use. Be kind to yourself and take a little break before moving on to the next chapter.

Chapter 19

Practise, Practise, Practise

We are going to start this chapter with a bit of science about practising. Then we will discuss how we can use what we know about practising to help us break old habits and build new ones.

Practising gets us onto automatic

When we practise something many times we seem to be able to do it automatically, without thinking about it. This includes many everyday activities like riding a bike, driving, writing or even drinking a cup of tea. Much of everyday life involves automatic actions. When we walk, we do not need to think which leg to move next. Our legs just seem to move automatically – left, then right, feet angled correctly, and wow, we are walking along!

We all started learning to move our legs soon after birth and then went on to crawl. Some time after crawling we all learned to stand, before setting off and taking our first steps. The action of walking took a lot of practice before we were able to do it smoothly. After taking thousands of wobbly then steady steps we now do it automatically. Our brains and bodies have put together complex information about balance, perception, muscle movements, thinking ahead and so on. This automatic action of walking has been 'hardwired' in our brains. Science tells us that when hard wiring happens, long strings of nerve cells join together for fast automatic action. Hard wiring is like ring roads that go around villages and towns. It involves super highways that bypass conscious thoughts. We have many super highways for the different things that we do on automatic. Scientists have found that when we use our specialised hardwired super highways, we use very little of our brain's capacity. This leaves our brains available for other things.

Think about all of the actions you need to carry out in order to drink a cup of tea:

- Look at the object on the table in front of you. Is it round, hollow and can it hold liquid? Does it have a handle?
- Recognise this object as a 'tea cup'
- Estimate how far away it is from you
- (Messages are now passing to and from your brain at amazing speed, although you are not aware of them)
- Extend your arm for the exact distance required towards the cup
- Open your hand
- Close your fingers exactly around the cup handle, using enough pressure to hold it
- Pick up the cup using your hand and arm moving together
- Adjust the angle of your hand so as not to spill the tea as your arm moves
- Locate exactly where your mouth is
- Calculate the distance from the cup to your mouth
- Start moving the cup towards your mouth at a speed which does not spill the liquid
- Decide when to stop your arm from moving
- Stop moving the cup when it reaches your lips, or if the tea is too hot, stop before your lips and blow gently on the surface of the liquid
- Press the nearest edge of the cup gently to your lips
- Open your mouth
- Suck gently, with your lower lip placed against the cup and your upper lip placed slightly away from the cup, allowing liquid to enter your mouth. This is called 'sipping the tea'
- Stop sipping when there is enough liquid in your mouth

- Close your mouth to prevent the tea from escaping
- Swallow the tea
- Reverse all the movements of the cup to replace it on the table
- Re-calculate the weight of the cup to adjust the speed and distance for a safe landing back on the table the right way up

This list is just a small sample of the automatic actions that take place when we drink a cup of tea. Millions of nerve impulses and actions are hidden from us as we do things automatically. When we drink a cup of tea we do not have to think about each of these stages – we just pick up the tea and drink it. Our brain has a super highway for drinking hot liquid. All of these actions are hardwired so as to bypass our conscious thought processes. When we practise, we repeat and repeat new behaviours. We develop hard wiring and build super highways for new automatic actions.

But first you have to get off automatic

Practising new behaviours gets us onto automatic, so that we can do new things. But our problem behaviours have also been practised many times, so they too are automatic. In order to change them we have to become more aware of them, to gradually get them off automatic. This usually happens in three stages:

1. We notice we have 'done it again' *after* the behaviour has come and gone
2. We notice we are doing it *during* the behaviour
3. We notice we are in danger of doing it *before* the behaviour starts

We build up our awareness of our problem behaviours by doing Wheels of Experience, drawing behaviour chains, planning to break the links and taking actions to step away from our problem behaviours. But even this takes practice. At first, because our problem behaviour has been on automatic for years, we cannot notice the behaviour until after it has happened, which can be very frustrating. But as we carry on working on our problem behaviours, we get better at spotting them earlier. The sooner we can spot the behaviours, the more we can do to change them.

Rick's shouting when he was annoyed was an automatic action. He did not have to think about whether to shout or not, he did it on automatic. By the time he actually thought about what he had done, it was old news. He had repeated this shouting behaviour many times in his life. He had a shouting super highway that bypassed thinking.

To start working towards changing, Rick had to slow down this process to give him time to consider his response. He had to bring the process into conscious awareness and get off automatic. After a few goes he managed to notice that he was shouting *during* an outburst, though he still could not stop shouting. He kept trying and finally noticed his strong urges to shout *before* he actually shouted. Saying 'STOP! THINK!' interrupted the traffic along his brain's super highway and gave him time to think about his choices. When Rick kept practising saying 'STOP! THINK!' his brain gradually built a new super highway. When he had angry thoughts, feelings, body sensations and urges to shout, he reacted automatically with 'STOP! THINK!' Our brains' super highways need traffic; they work in a 'use it or lose it' way. As Rick's new 'STOP! THINK!' super highway got more traffic, his shouting super highway got less traffic. Now his brain directs most of the traffic along the 'STOP! THINK!' route.

Practise handling NATs

Many of us have been listening to the unruly puppies in our mind yards for a long time. We have accidentally built super highways for our negative thoughts. They just keep coming along automatically – they are negative automatic thoughts (NATs). When you get NATs you can practise putting them into trash, like junk emails. Or you can respond by sending your own message back. Your replies can be curious, questioning or confrontational. Think about how you will reply to your NATs. Some examples are:

- How do you know?
- What is your evidence?
- What would someone who disagrees say?
- Does everyone think that?
- A-ha, you are a thinking error! (You could name which kind if you liked)
- I don't agree!
- Well, my opinion is . . .
- That is just not true
- I'm too busy to listen now
- Come back in ten minutes, I'll deal with it then
- No, I think you are wrong – this is what really happened . . .
- Thank you for that, it has been noted
- You may think that about me, but I think I'm . . .
- Stop going on and on
- Hello, naughty puppies
- Will you behave yourself!
- I see my Negative Mind has come for a visit

You could practise singing the NATs in the shower or giving them to your favourite cartoon character to say. You also have your balanced replacement thoughts to read aloud or repeat in your mind. Whichever way you prefer, as you practise more your new responses will become easier, stronger and faster. The aim is to make them into automatic responses. Then your brain will stop using the old NATs super highway and send traffic down the new, more effective super highway.

Practise controlling your body

In previous chapters we have seen what an important part our body sensations and reactions play in our problem behaviours. What goes on in our bodies is very important: they react to threat to keep us safe. Our brains help our bodies by warning us that threat may be about.

A man in the park had threatened Cheyenne. After this Cheyenne was afraid and anxious about going into any park, not just the one where she was threatened. Her brain sent signals to release adrenaline, gearing up her body for running away ('fight or flight'). Cheyenne's brain had spread her fear of the man to include the place where it happened (the park). Then it spread her fear further from the park to include *any* park. She did not need to *see* the man to feel afraid and anxious; her brain was labelling any similar places and people as dangerous. Now her body had the fight or flight reaction in all of these situations. It was a vicious circle:

Many problem behaviours are due to our minds time travelling. Ruminating about the past or worrying about the future can produce fight or flight changes in our bodies. Our brains monitor these changes and take them as a sign that we really are in danger. Actually, there may be no danger; it may all be due to our time travelling minds and to vicious circles.

As with most skills the more you practise, the better you will get at controlling or changing your body. Buddhist monks have been using mindfulness skills for centuries to control their bodies. They have shown us that it is possible to control responses such as breathing, heartbeat, blood pressure and the experience of pain. Here are some skills you can use to control your own body responses.

Paced breathing

The body has two nervous systems, the sympathetic and the parasympathetic. The sympathetic nervous system activates fight or flight responses and increases arousal. When we are upset and worked-up, the sympathetic nervous system is very active. The parasympathetic nervous system works to regulate feelings and calm things down. Paced breathing works by increasing the activity of the parasympathetic nervous system and decreasing activity of the sympathetic nervous system. One system is in charge of breathing *in* and the other is in charge of breathing *out*. When we breathe in, the heart beats slightly faster, and when we breathe out, it beats slightly slower, so we want to increase the amount of time breathing out using paced breathing.

In paced breathing we slow down the breath to about five or six breaths per minute, so that each breath lasts about ten seconds. We work on breathing in for four seconds and out for six seconds. We can choose to pause for a couple of seconds at the top of the breath, between in and out, if we want.

Paced breathing exercise

- Take a clock, watch or phone which shows seconds
- Place it in front of you and practise breathing in for four seconds and out for six
- Decide whether to include a pause at the top of the breath. You might want to change the numbers you count, say to five instead of four or seven instead of six
- Just keep counting seconds in and out until you get comfortable with the feel of this
- Notice the differences in your body before and after doing this exercise

Practise this as much as you can when you are fairly calm. If you do not have a clock to hand, you can estimate seconds by saying in your mind, 'One elephant, two elephant, three elephant' and so on. Eventually, your brain will make a super highway so that you can do this whenever you need to calm down. This breathing pattern activates the parasympathetic nervous system to calm your body down. The more you do this, the better at it you will be as a new automatic super highway develops.

Dive reflex

We are mammals, and all mammals have a dive reflex. This reflex slows our heart rate right down and calms the body. It can help us calm down from extreme feelings. We can use a bag of frozen peas covered in a cloth, or a gel pack cooled in the fridge to trigger this reflex. Whatever we use, it needs to cover our face as completely as possible.

Dive reflex exercise

- Stand or sit down
- Take a breath in and hold it
- Put the peas or cool gel pack over your face
- Hold your breath and count to thirty seconds
- Remove the bag of peas or gel pack from your face
- Release the breath

You should find that your heart and breathing rate have slowed, especially if you are worked-up beforehand. If you do not have frozen peas or a cool gel pack, try splashing your face with cold water. As with most of the exercises in this book, the more you practise it, the better you get at it. As new super highways develop, this new skill can become automatic.

Practise using your skills where and when you need them

This section is about making sure that the skills that you have practised work in the places and at the times when you need them. We know that skills need to be practised in every setting and situation, not just in the therapist's office or in your own home. It is best to start practising skills when you feel safe and calm as it will be easier to concentrate and learn. Repeating the practice creates new super highways for coping.

Next, put yourself into more challenging situations and practise your new skills there too. Skills need practising in all the different settings and situations you move in and with all the different people you know. They need practising when you are calm and when you are upset, when you are stressed and when you are tired.

For example, Cheyenne practised paced breathing in her lounge at home. She found this quite easy. The problem was that as soon as she thought about going to the park, the old fears and anxiety flooded back: her mind had decided that parks are dangerous places. She realised that just thinking about going to the park was a trigger for her fight or flight reaction so she started by using her imagination. She formed images in her mind of herself leaving her house through the front door, walking towards the park and going around the park. She used her paced breathing to control her body when she needed to as she did this, noticing that as she practised, she was able to stay in the park in her mind and her anxiety levels gradually came down.

Cheyenne had sent her mind another message about parks. When she was ready, she actually did this journey, using her paced breathing when needed. Her anxiety went up again, of course, but then came down pretty fast as she had already practised, practised, practised. This is called 'exposure' and it works by allowing our brains to learn that the feared situation can be safe.

You may have feared situations in your life that are stopping you from stepping towards your values and goals. If you have a feared situation that you have been avoiding, and you really need to go there, this is how you can practise like Cheyenne:

Feared situation exercise

- Practise paced breathing somewhere safe and calm.
- Once you are good at it, move on to the next step.

- In a safe and calm place, form images in your mind of going into the feared situation; try to make them as clear and vivid as possible.
- Rate your fear from 1–10 as you do this.
- Hold the image of the situation in your mind.
- If your anxiety reaches 10, practise paced breathing to control your body reactions until the rating is 8 or less.
- Stay with this image until your fear calms down. Often, your fear may be at a rating of 8 or 9 out of 10 at the beginning. You are looking for a reduction to 3 or 4 out of 10.
- Repeat this exercise in your imagination a few times, not trying to escape from the situation and not being overwhelmed either.
- Next, actually go out and put yourself into the feared situation, using your paced breathing when needed (anxiety = 10), and staying in the situation until your fear calms down to 3 or 4.
- If you feel you have to leave the situation, see if you can hang on for just a couple more minutes. If you still cannot manage, then leave.
- If you have had to leave the situation before calming down, go back to doing this in your imagination until you are good at it, then try again in real life.

Hints and tips for practising

This section is about basic skills and ideas to help you keep going as you practise. Some of them are reminders about things you will recognise from earlier in the book. The aim is for your new skills to become as automatic as writing, riding a bike or drinking a cup of tea. Practising controlling your body sends messages to your mind that all is well and it does not have to prepare for danger just at the moment. Practising controlling your thoughts gives you mental space to concentrate on taking actions towards getting your life back.

Remind yourself about values and goals

'Why on earth am I doing this to myself?' This is one of the most common things we say whilst working towards getting our lives back. When you hear yourself saying this, stop for a few seconds and revisit your goals and values key words (page 208). These key words are the answers to your question. Some people find it useful to note down their values key words on a piece of paper, computer or phone. You can remind yourself of why you are on this journey whenever you need to by looking at your key words.

Plan your practice

Always plan what skills you are going to practise. Also, be clear about how often, at what time, and where you are going to practise. What are you actually going to do? Take a minute to imagine doing the practice in advance. For example, you may plan 'I am going to walk mindfully to the bus stop each morning'. Then you can imagine what this will look and feel like in reality. Write your practice plan down here:

My Practice Plan

What I'm going to practise (skill)	When	Where	How often

Be realistic

'I will change my life next Tuesday and be a new person on Wednesday'. This is a great goal that has everything in it that you want. However, as you can see, it is not realistic and is doomed to failure. So look back at your plans to step away from your problem behaviour and towards your values. Are they realistic?

Baby steps

Getting our lives back nearly always involves taking some small steps towards a goal. Mandy had a goal to walk to the centre of town. If she had tried to make it all the way first time, she would have failed and told herself it was an impossible task. By walking for just one minute then gradually increasing time and distance she finally made it. You can set small goals in your practice plan and tick them off as you go along. This helps us notice the progress we are making and gives us encouragement to carry on.

Record your progress

If you record your progress, using one or more of the diaries in this book, you can see how well you are doing. This record will be available at difficult times when encouragement is needed. You can even use your diaries to make a simple graph on a piece of paper or on your computer. Here is Mandy's graph:

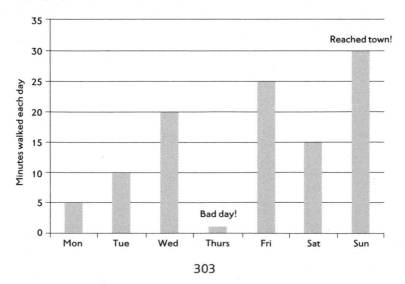

Sally was working on stopping vomiting when she got home each night. During the day her mind was sending her NATs about her body being full of toxins. She was practising treating these messages as junk emails and deleting them but because she still had NATs quite often she felt as though no progress was being made. Sally decided to spend a morning putting a tick on a piece of paper every time she had a NAT about toxins. A few days later, she spent another morning doing this. She did this at intervals for a couple of weeks. Eventually, she made a graph and could see that the number of NATs had actually halved. She needed the graph to see her progress. Sally suddenly thought that if she could keep this progress going, the NATs would have more or less faded away by the end of the next week. It was the graph that helped her to keep going.

Check your Breaking-the-Links Plan

Your Breaking-the-Links Plan from Chapter 15 (see page 240) contains some skills you can practise to step away from your problem behaviour. Take another look at it now and think whether there are more places you could break the chain and more skills you could use to do this.

Mindfulness

When you are practising skills you may find yourself thinking about your problem behaviours. This may involve a whole chain of thoughts, feelings, body sensations and urges. Mindfulness can allow us to observe all this without getting hooked into it. When you practise skills, it is great to start practice times with a mini-mindfulness exercise. This could be a three-minute mindfulness of breath, or a mindful stretch, or just observing the soles of your feet. It helps us really be in the here and now, the present moment. Our practice will be more focused and effective.

Use images

When we imagine doing something we activate the same parts of our brains which would get active if we were *actually* doing the thing. Making images of ourselves doing things is a great way to practise. Our brains will learn a lot about how to do the things in real life that we imagine when we are practising.

Images can put you in positive places. Your perfect nurturer is an image that can be compassionate and validating during your practice. You can also create positive images of yourself. A calm or positive image can send a message to your mind telling it there is no need to panic. Try this exercise:

Positive image exercise for dealing with a stressful situation

- Make an image of yourself in a stressful situation; imagine this picture on the wall in front of you
- Shrink the image into a dot, which disappears
- Make a new image of yourself in the same situation, but this time calm, confident and coping well
- Make this image as big and colourful as you can
- Whilst gazing at the positive image, squeeze your left hand by pressing your right thumb into the palm and right fingers down onto the back of your hand
- Practise this many times whilst calm
- When you actually go into the stressful situation, just squeeze your hand; you will not need to actively make the image, it will just be in your mind, helping you along

Ask for help

Getting or asking for help is not a sign of weakness but a sign of strength. Being able and willing to ask for help means you are accepting and acting on changing your problem behaviours. We saw in the early chapters of this book that a kind friend often sees things a lot more positively. Other people may think of good ideas which have not occurred to you. They may understand what you are thinking, so that you do not feel alone. Having somebody else walk next to you along the road is great for staying on track and not giving up. You can also ask for help from your perfect nurturer. One thing to remember if you ask for help is that you need to be *willing* to take it. If you 'yes, but . . .' or reject ideas and help, the helper may give up and go away.

Is practising helping?

The plans you have made and the skills you are practising may not always lead to the changes you want. For example, Janet knew that she was not popular in the office so she decided to practise agreeing with all her colleagues. She thought that this would make her more popular, but it did not work – it just irritated the life out of everyone in the office. Janet decided to practise at home. She practised making an image in her mind's eye of herself chatting to the people she worked with. In this image, she was asking them questions about themselves and making the effort to be interested in what they had to say. The activity of taking interest in what is going on around us is a form of mindfulness called 'participating'. Eventually, Janet tried out her new skill in the real office. She found she was able to chat and people responded well to her interest in them.

The brick wall

Sometimes a situation just cannot be improved and this needs to be recognised and accepted as the 'brick wall' that it is. For example, someone you love may reject you, or you may find yourself suffering an illness or chronic physical pain. You might have an accident, which leaves you disabled in some way. In these situations we need all of our acceptance skills, including mindfulness and compassionate self-validation. We can self-soothe and be as gentle and kind towards ourselves as we can. We can do things to look after ourselves and improve our lives moment to moment, but we cannot actually change the situation. Strangely, accepting that we cannot change it, really accepting it from deep within our hearts, can bring us peace. It can also open up new ways forward that we might not have been able to see before. Banging our heads against brick walls gives us headaches, takes up a lot of our precious time and makes it hard to see anything except the wall.

Start again the next day

There will be times when you end up carrying out your problem behaviour despite all your best efforts not to. You should know that this happens. Watch out for catastrophising thoughts about this, like 'I've totally messed up, I'll never be able to manage this in my whole life'. You may have a strong urge to give up; you may even *decide* to give up and feel some short-term relief. When the depths of despair hit you, stop fighting for the day and take a holiday. Tomorrow is a new day and you can start again: there is always another chance tomorrow. We must be careful to recognise when we are in a hole and stop digging.

Rewards/treats

We all like rewards and treats. A small reward or treat gives a feel-good factor. If we reward our own work and effort, we help to strengthen our chances of working hard in future. Do not be tempted to reward yourself with a lavish world cruise for a small step! Rewards work better when they are small and close in time to the work and effort done. A square of chocolate with your coffee at 5 o'clock after some hard work is generally a more powerful reward than going to the cinema at the end of the month.

Summary

To sum up, the message in this chapter is that practice is the key to success. When we practise, we go through a process of getting our problem behaviours off automatic. Through practice, our new skills and behaviours become automatic. Our brains make new connections, building new super highways and redirecting our minds' traffic down these new roads.

Handling NATs and controlling our bodies are important things to practise. We start practising in safe, calm places then build up to practising in more difficult and even scary situations. Hints and tips for practising include making a plan, using mindfulness at the start, making sure our plans are working for us, being kind to ourselves and knowing when to accept what we cannot change. We can only get our lives back through patient and repeated practice, making it easier for ourselves by taking a compassionate, self-validating approach as we go along.

Be kind to yourself now: take a break and do something you enjoy.

Chapter 20

Handling Flashbacks

This chapter is for readers who experience flashbacks. If you do not, move on to Chapter 21.

What is a flashback?

Flashbacks are vivid images that our brains send us of past trauma. These images can include anything that a person found traumatic, for example childhood abuse, accidents, seeing other people harmed, receiving shocking news, etc. It is not possible to list all the situations that may be connected to flashbacks as there are so many. Flashbacks usually come when we do not want or need them. They can be very vivid and feel as if the awful thing is happening all over again, right here and now. Sometimes we can even lose touch with where we are and the world around us. Most people experience flashbacks as images. For example, if you have been in an accident with a red car, your flashback may be a visual image of a red car hurtling towards you. But flashbacks can also come as sounds, for example the sound of squealing brakes. Flashbacks can come as smells, such as the smell of burning rubber. They can also come along as body sensations, such as a pain in the ribs where the seatbelt tightened. Lastly, flashbacks can come as feelings, for example intense anger or panic. Sometimes flashbacks involve all of our senses at once, which can make us feel as though we are reliving the trauma.

Flashbacks happen because our brains tend to store information about traumatic events in a different place to normal information. It is as if they have filed away trauma in a cabinet marked 'here be monsters'. Our brains can refuse to take us to the trauma cabinet when we want to go there, when we are trying to deal with them. Then our brains will open the cabinet and let out information as flashbacks, when we do not want them. Normally, information about what has happened to us in the past is stored so that when we remember it, we are aware that it happened in the past, not now. Because trauma information is stored differently, we do not have that sense of the past when we recall it.

Some people suffer flashbacks from a single trauma, say a car accident. Other people have flashbacks from many traumas, perhaps from when they were small. A single trauma is easier to deal with, though still not very easy. You may need to find help for flashbacks from a professional. Trauma-focused CBT and EMDR (Eye Movement Desensitisation and Reprocessing) are tried and tested methods that help.

Handling flashbacks

Flashbacks are generally very upsetting as they 'take us back' to trauma. Here are some ways you can help yourself to deal with them:

Imagery re-scripting

This works well if your flashbacks are due to earlier abuse. Imagery re-scripting is when we revisit the trauma and change the details of it in our imagination. We do this to teach our brains that we are safe now and do not need to be scared any more. If you are still living in a traumatic situation, for example in a domestic abuse situation, do not use this technique. You first need to get out of the situation.

In imagery re-scripting we make a new image of ourselves as bigger and more powerful than we were during the trauma itself. We use our new strength to act differently in our imagination. For example, Cheyenne could have used an image of herself as a giant, bopping the head of the man who threatened her. If you were abused as a child you might make yourself into a giant child in your mind's eye. Then when you are threatened in your flashback, you can do as you wish to the abuser. This might involve throwing him or her out of a window. Sometimes if you loved the abuser you will not want to hurt them, so you might just want to lock them up in a room somewhere and walk away.

Other people decide to handle flashbacks by taking a mental image of themselves as adults into the flashback of the abuse. The adult self can then rescue the child self from the abuser. Here is how to use this technique. Start as we suggested in Chapter 19 (see page 305), with making the negative abuse image and shrinking it to a dot. Then make a positive image of yourself being powerful, say as a seven-foot-tall child, or as an adult rescuing the child. Use the technique of squeezing your hand whilst you make this new image. Follow the steps below:

- Make an image of yourself in the flashback situation; imagine this picture on the wall in front of you
- Shrink the image into a dot which disappears

- Make a new image of yourself in the same situation, but this time big and powerful and able to do anything you want
- Make this image as big and colourful as you can
- Whilst gazing at the positive image, squeeze your left hand by pressing your right thumb into the palm and your right fingers down onto the back of your hand
- Practise this many times in a calming, safe place
- When you next get a flashback, just squeeze your hand; you will not need to actively make the image, it will come along to replace the flashback image

Making the flashback into a film

It often helps to get a bit of distance on a flashback, so that you can see it for what it really is, a fragment of information about the past. Try making an image of the flashback as a film, preferably an old black and white film. When you watch it, in your mind's eye remember it is just an old movie, nothing more.

Recognising the feelings

When flashbacks happen they are horrible experiences. They are horrible because it feels as though we are reliving the trauma that caused them. This in turn produces a whole lot of feelings that we do not want. Recognising the feelings that happen is the start of dealing with them. Recall and name as many feelings as possible and write them down. Stand back or helicopter up and take a good look at them. There is more about dealing with these feelings later in the chapter.

Grounding

You will probably remember grounding exercises from Chapter 5 (see page 95). When using grounding a message is sent back to your brain that you are here, now, not back at the time and place of the trauma.

Knowing when you need help with flashbacks

Many of us do not willingly take a look at the content of our flashbacks – it seems too terrifying – so we spend a lot of time avoiding flashbacks if we can. We might deny ourselves sleep in case we have nightmares, which are similar to flashbacks. We may avoid certain places, people or activities. This is understandable given that we are scared stiff. The problem with this way of coping is that our lives become focused on avoiding rather than getting our lives back, so actively making the flashback images when we are not having them may be necessary to overcome them. Because this is a scary and difficult process it is important to know when you need help with it. If you struggle with the exercise above, or you just do not feel able to do it, you may need help. Here are some more exercises that help with flashbacks. You can also do these whilst you wait for help, to make life easier for yourself.

Notice what you are avoiding

Just helicopter up and take a look at what you are avoiding in order to try not to have flashbacks. Perhaps you have given up work or travelling. Maybe you avoid relationships. Ask yourself, 'Is this actually preventing me from having flashbacks?' Our guess is not. Give yourself permission to go to the avoided places and do the avoided things. Use your new skills and think about SMART actions. An example of this could be if you want to go back to the place of an accident, you may have to use baby steps to get there. So on day one, travel a quarter of the way there (baby step 1). Day two, halfway there (baby step 2) and so on. At each stage think about the feelings that happen and use your new skills to manage them.

Check out your thoughts about having flashbacks

As well as having flashbacks, we can have a lot of naughty puppy thoughts about having flashbacks. The puppies may be barking:

- 'I'm going mad, I'm such a weirdo'
- 'This is not normal'
- 'I'll never get over this'

- 'No one can help me with this'
- 'I can't stand it'
- 'If I stay in bed all day I won't get a flashback'
- 'I can't deal with this without drugs'
- 'It was all my fault'
- 'It was all his/her fault'
- 'They were wrong to have sent us there'
- 'I should have done more'

Notice that these thoughts are just thoughts. Because you think them does not make them true. Ask yourself if these are accurate or helpful thoughts. If not, how could you handle them?

Write your thoughts about your flashbacks here:

_____

_____

Now write how you plan to handle the thoughts about your flashbacks here:

_____

_____

Check out the feelings that come along when you have flashbacks

When we have flashbacks we experience all the feelings that we had at the time. Sometimes we were just numb whilst it was happening, other times we may have had feelings of terror, anger, rage, shame, disgust, hatred or self-loathing. None of these feelings are things people want to feel. How could you handle these feelings using your new skills? For example, self-soothing, distraction, physicalising exercise, opposite to feeling action.

Write your feelings here:

_____

_____

Write how you plan to handle these feelings:

_____

_____

How are you coping with flashbacks at the moment?

You may be coping well with your flashbacks and not need any assistance. However, many people use ways of coping that give the short-term gain of escaping from flashbacks, but long-term pain. Some examples of this are using drugs or alcohol to excess, binge eating, self-starving, self-harm, gambling, spending, thinking about killing yourself, spacing out, or avoiding situations. All of these, as we have seen, become problems in themselves and stop us getting our lives back.

Write down how you are coping with flashbacks now:

_____

_____

Write down how you plan to cope in future. This should include your plans from above about dealing with thoughts about flashbacks and the feelings that come along with them. Will you, for example, try re-scripting, making the flashback into a film, grounding or recognising the feelings or recognising when you need help?

My flashback plan

_____

_____

Well done! It is important to know that flashbacks can be normal after trauma, that many people suffer from them and that they can be cured. You can help yourself using the techniques we have outlined and by managing the thoughts and feelings which come along with flashbacks. You need to be aware of when you need help with flashbacks and be ready to find help, even if you have to wait to get it.

Perhaps it is time for a little break or treat, maybe a cup of tea or a walk in the garden, before moving on to the next chapter.

Chapter 21

When Things Go Wrong

This chapter is about how to survive when our plans do not work out as we had hoped. It is impossible to think in advance about all that could go wrong. Even the best plans come up against glitches. Here, we tell you how to get over these. We illustrate using familiar characters from this book. At the end of the chapter are FAQs about when things go wrong.

Here is a story about a marathon runner. Well, she was not actually a marathon runner; she wanted to be one. She wanted to be one because achieving difficult things was important to her. She realised that her best chance of success lay in good preparation and training so she set herself a period of sixteen months to get in shape and ready to run a marathon. Her name was Aleena and we know her well.

Aleena did some research on the net and downloaded a beginner's marathon plan. It told her she would need to run three to five times a week regularly for at least a year before starting a sixteen-week training plan to build up to a marathon. The plan had lots of useful hints and tips about diet and clothing and energy drinks. Aleena was very excited and imagined herself running gracefully along the road. She also noticed her thought puppies waking up and saying, 'What if you don't manage it?'

Aleena thought about her diet. She realised she would need to eat plenty of nutritious food to support the extra physical effort she planned to put in so she changed her shopping list and cooking habits. She also knew she would have to start running, and that she would have to plan goals and baby steps on the way to her marathon run. She decided she would ideally want to be able to run a half-marathon distance after nine months of training. This was one of her SMART goals. After twelve months she would want to be able to run a half-marathon relatively easily. Then she would choose her race and be ready to start her sixteen-week beginner's marathon training plan.

This was her big picture plan:

Aleena broke down each step into smaller steps, as she had learned to do. These were her goals for the first nine months:

Aleena looked at this and found her puppies were barking very loudly now. When would she fit it in? How would she keep going? She felt some problems with motivation so she read Chapter 17 of this book, Keeping Going, and used a couple of tips from there. Aleena then *made a public commitment* on social media and to her work colleagues and friends. She also broke down the first three months' goals into *baby steps*. These were:

- Get some good running shoes
- Get some running clothes
- Decide on a route to run first
- Decide which times and days to run
- Go for first run

So on 15 September Aleena set out for her first run. And she found she could go half a mile, then she had to walk: she was out of breath and she got a stitch. A lady walked past and looked at her with pity. This is what her thought puppies were barking at her:

At this point, the story could go one of two ways:

> Aleena agreed with the puppies. She could not see the point in carrying on – the road ahead was too long and too difficult. She went home and had a nice bath. Running was not really for her, she thought. She sold her running gear. She felt bad about being a failure and did not try again.

> Aleena did not give up. She got round the three miles by walking and running then she went home. Afterwards, she made a star chart for herself and proudly ticked off the first box. She let the thought puppies bark away behind her, on their leads.

Aleena decided not to give up and she found herself thinking about her run repeatedly. She noticed a very strong urge not to do it again the next time. 'Hmm,' she said to herself, 'I have a few options here. I could let this urge dictate to me. I won't go for a run and I'll feel bad about it. Or I could just surf this urge not to go out running tomorrow, or I could make the task easier.' As soon as Aleena thought about making the task easier, she relaxed. This would be a good solution. She crossed out 'Run three miles' and put in 'Run one mile'. She could do this. Then she remembered that she had had to walk some of it so she put in 'or walk' next to 'run'. Aleena felt her motivation rise again; she had made her plan more realistic.

Aleena managed to keep up her running almost every time. Then her mum got ill. She rushed off to her mum's house and forgot her running gear. She stayed for a few days until her mum was better. Back home she felt depressed about running: she had not been out for a week, she did not feel like going out at all. But Aleena had learned that doing what we feel like all the time is not the way to reach a goal. She remembered her value of achievement and her goal of the marathon. She decided to go running the next day however she felt, but the day after she forgot to go.

Aleena came to a number of these low points as she went along. At these low points she took steps to deal with problems of motivation and with the noisy puppies.

- She found a colleague at work who went out running with her

- She gave herself a reward of a fruit smoothie when she finished her run
- She published her progress on social media and got messages of encouragement
- She started buying a running magazine
- She put this quote on her bedroom mirror: 'Do not despise the bottom rungs of the ladder, they are just as important as the rest'

She had lots of highs too – when things went well, she experienced joy and contentment. Over time, her body began to change and running became easier and smoother.

Then Aleena fell over: she was out running and tripped over. She lost her balance and came down hard on her backside, hurting her coccyx bone. The next day, she could not sit down or walk without pain. It took Aleena over two weeks to recover from this injury. She went to see a physio for treatment. The physio also taught her some exercises for strengthening her core muscles so that she would not strain her back when running. She also joined a yoga for runners class where she learned how to loosen up stiff muscles and met some other runners. When she recovered, she had the same choice: listen to the puppies telling her it was too difficult and hopeless or go out running again. She reduced the mileage and off she went.

We could tell you more of this story, about how she had to get over her race nerves and how she felt when she came last in her first ever race, but it would take too long. We can tell you that on 26 April, eighteen months after starting her programme, she completed the London Marathon. She could not believe she had made it. It was fabulous. Yet even then, one of her puppies said, 'Yes, but you were at the back.' She resisted the urge to strangle that puppy and told him to sit down and behave himself. Aleena enjoys running now, and has a whole new set of friends to go with it.

Every journey involves handling thought puppies. If we struggle with them and yell at them, spending all our energy on them, we will not have enough resources to get our lives back. If we believe what they tell us as if it is true, we will never get our lives back. So, we have to tame them and constantly step forwards.

Many of the 'bad' things that happened to Aleena on her marathon journey actually turned out to be 'good' things. For example, her fall led to her meeting a good physio and getting extra advice and help. It also led to her joining a yoga for runners class, where she found more friends to motivate her and to run with. Aleena learned and gained a lot from what might be seen as a setback.

More examples

Janet

Janet got off to a flying start. She stopped shoplifting quite quickly and this change was rewarded when she made friends with the cashier. Previously, Janet had tried to avoid contact with the supermarket staff. The most difficult times were when she was home alone: her naughty thought puppies got very busy. Janet felt hungry and annoyed that she was cutting down on eating – it seemed like an injustice. It was not really an injustice but her thought puppies were telling her this. These messages sent her to the fridge and she ate anything she could find. This immediately shut up the thought puppies. You have probably guessed that this short-term gain gave Janet long-term pain and a sense of failure. She was doing well, except for when she was alone.

Quick ideas from Janet

Try not to be alone at home at 'high risk' times. If I have to be at home, phone a friend, do something interactive on the internet, or go for a walk. Or give myself a task with a time limit on it, for example, 'I will clean my skirting boards before bedtime'. Complete a task that makes it difficult to eat at the same time. Put fresh healthy foods in the fridge.

Tom

Although gambling caused Tom all sorts of problems it gave him a short-term high. At the time of his success story he had not gambled for six months. It was a rocky road to this point. Although he did not admit it at the time, progress was stop and go. When Tom made a secret bet he felt as though he could never kick his habit. Very soon after this bet, he felt ashamed and had thoughts that it was all hopeless.

Quick ideas from Tom

Accept that this was a gambling setback and life starts again tomorrow – a new day, a new start. Keep a gambling diary to record when I place bets. Look at my diary when I am feeling hopeless, so that I can see my progress. Make it difficult for myself to place a bet. For example, plan walks that do not go near the betting shop, do an activity at betting time.

Cheyenne

Cheyenne never felt that she was worth it. Because of this she could not feel attractive or skilled as a mother. Things moved on and she started using nice shampoos and skin products. She began to be more confident with parenting. The problem was that some days Cheyenne got exhausted at work and the children just did not cooperate, wanting crisps and sweets all the time. At these times Cheyenne just gave them some sweets. Her thought puppies were very busy at these times, saying, 'Give them the sweets and they will shut up.'

Quick ideas from Cheyenne

Remember, many other people have hit these moments with their children. Tell myself this is normal life. Accept my exhausted feelings and giving the kids sweets. Start again tomorrow. Have some healthy snacks prepared so that there is no negotiation with the children.

George

Drinking is George's most difficult problem. Although he has other problems, when George drinks, he loses the will to deal with his other problems and stops trying. Sometimes George made great progress but when he had had a drink he could not be bothered to try.

Quick ideas from George

Find out when I am most likely to drink. Look at trigger events for my drinking, check out my behaviour chain. Go back to my My Breaking-the-Links Plan and choose to take some steps away from drinking. Make it difficult for myself to get the whisky by keeping it in the car boot. Put some lemonade on the path on the way to the car, write my key values words on the lemonade bottle. Make myself drink the lemonade first and decide whether to carry on to the whisky in the car boot or do something different.

Pauline

Pauline had self-harmed for a few years. It was a strong behaviour that Pauline's brain had a super highway for. She pulled her hair out and scratched her skin until it bled. Her behaviour chain showed that this happened when Pauline had flashbacks and thoughts of self-loathing and self-blame. When she was working towards stopping self-harming, she sometimes felt overwhelmed by her feelings and slipped back. At these times Pauline felt like giving up altogether.

Quick ideas from Pauline

Do my homework from therapy with my friend Katrina. We can buddy up to support each other. Agree to call each other when the urge to self-harm feels overwhelming and talk each other through our My Breaking-the-Links Plans. Tell Katrina about my self-loathing and self-blaming thoughts. Get her to repeat out loud what she has heard, so that I can get some distance on it or argue back. Helicopter up and take a look down at these thoughts. Use my perfect nurturer tree if Katrina is not available.

Mandy

Mandy heard her mum's voice criticising her and causing her distress. After a year of hard work, Mandy had a new life. During that year there were moments when she felt that it was impossible to reach her goals. If you hear voices it is often difficult for other people to understand what is happening. Friends may think they are helping by telling you that the voices are not real or they are just from your mind. This rarely helps. Mandy needed some quick ideas to use when she felt that her mum's voice was in charge of things.

Quick ideas from Mandy

Practise mindfulness to Mum's voice. Observe the sounds it makes and do not get hooked into believing it. Just let the voice go on and on and focus my mind on what I am doing right now. Write down what the voice says and put the paper in the Demon Chest. Write some replies and put them on the table: 'I'll deal with this in a moment, Mum'; 'Hello, critical Mum, you are grumpy today'. Read out these replies when the voice bothers me. Make a recording of my replies and play them aloud. Turn on the radio at a high volume and dance around the room.

Rick

Rick had anger problems: he shouted at people. When he understood more about his problem behaviour, he was able to control his anger. Rick was angry with everybody around him and angry with himself. He also had moments of thinking about giving up. At these moments, he felt as though he was a balloon that was about to burst with anger. There are points when it is time to stop fighting such strong feelings. Rick's ideas for himself included shouting. This is like pricking the balloon with a pin so it does burst, but in a safe place. You cannot harm yourself by shouting or screaming in a place where you will not panic other people.

Quick ideas from Rick

Go to the beach – my perfect nurturer, one of my favourite places. Shout loudly for as long as I can until I am exhausted. Congratulate myself on not shouting at a real person. Look at My Breaking-the-Links Plan and my action plan. Start again.

Sally

Sally went for a total life change. She described the fear and anxiety that she felt as like being on a roller coaster ride. As she rode the roller coaster, her progress was affected too. When she was up, she was confident, and when she was down, she came very close to giving up. Roller coaster experiences are quite common during change: you will feel on top of things many times, yet it can feel like a disaster at the low times.

Quick ideas from Sally

Keep a diary of progress to show myself that the low times are short-lived and come and go. Keep it in my pocket so I can look at it in a crisis. Write all my achievements so far on a sticky note and stick it to my mirror.

All these stories describe how we feel like giving up when things go wrong. There are many ideas and they are different for each person. When each character noticed how things tended to go wrong, they took a step back or helicoptered up and took a good look at how this happened. Then they made a plan to deal with it next time. In real life things *do* go wrong and we all feel like giving up sometimes. Think about what is most likely to go wrong in your journey of change. Make a plan of what you are going to do when this happens. Write your own plan for coping with setbacks here:

My plan for when things go wrong

What is likely to go wrong?

_____

_____

_____

What I plan to do when things go wrong:

_____

_____

_____

_____

Good. Now you have a troubleshooting plan you can come back to when you have a setback.

Here are some FAQs about dealing with setbacks:

FAQs

Q – What if I start (smoking/drinking/gambling/self-harming, etc.) again once I've stopped?

A – Well, most people need a few goes before they completely make it. Replacing a problem habit with a new habit takes time and practice. You could do a behaviour chain (see Chapter 10, page 155) to check out what was the trigger for this setback. Put the setback behaviour (smoking, drinking, etc.) as the problem behaviour in the chain. Or you could do a Wheel of Experience from the time you had the setback. Next time the trigger happens, how will you handle your thoughts and feelings and behave differently so that the setback does not happen? Notice any unhelpful thought puppies telling you that you will never make it? Get them on the lead. Go back to your values and goals and remind yourself why it is important to you to carry on.

Q – Does everybody think they are going to give up at some point?

A – Yes! Feeling like giving up often indicates that real hard work is going on. It is not necessarily a sign that things are going wrong. When you start changing, your thought puppies may tell you it is not worth it, it is too difficult, etc. This can make the initial change quite tough.

Q – Have I failed if I feel like giving up?

A – Feeling like giving up is a part of the changing process – it is a feeling most people have at some point. Build into your plan what you will do when these thoughts and feelings come along then it is not a shock when they arrive.

Q – If I have a setback and have to start again will I lose the progress I have already made?

A – You keep the skills that you learn from this book – it is like learning to ride a bike. If you know how to ride a bike, you could still ride even after a long break from it. Your riding skills may need to be brushed up but this will happen quite quickly. This is similar to learning the skills in this book. If you have a setback and give up for a while, your skills will still be there and you can quickly strengthen them again. So if you do have a break, do not panic, pick yourself up and start again.

Q – Could I just cut down on my problem behaviour rather than give it up altogether?

A – No, not really. If it is a problem, it needs to stop. We just need to be clear exactly what the problem is. For example, eating is not a problem behaviour in itself but binge eating is. So you need to stop binge eating altogether. Self-harming is never acceptable as a way of coping, it is too damaging. The basic issue is why we do these behaviours in the first place. We usually do them to avoid painful feelings and thoughts so once we have the skills to manage these, we should not need our problem behaviours any more. If you hang onto a bit of a problem behaviour it is very likely to get out of hand at times of stress.

Put your plan for when things go wrong somewhere you can easily find it, or put a marker in this book so that you can flick to it when you need to. This is excellent progress.

There are two more chapters in this book: one has more FAQs and the other more resources. You can read these when and how you want. The resources chapter contains further reading, organisations where you can find support, our website where you can download materials and our blog, as well as information about the Get Your Life Back Community.

We would like to leave you with our warmest wishes and to share that you are not alone in your work. All of us deal with challenges on a daily basis. If we could give you a gift, it would be that your life brings you joy, meaning and a sense of purpose. The skills that you have learned from this book will stay with you for ever. There will be some difficult times ahead when you will need all of your new skills. Our last message is to encourage you to never give up getting your life back.

All the best,

Fiona and David

Chapter 22

FAQs

Many of the answers in this chapter also appear in other places in the book. They are based on common questions people ask when we work with them. We hope they help you.

I did not feel better after doing mindfulness exercises

Yes, this is something that people say. Mindfulness is a great tool to have in your Get Your Life Back tool belt. It is about training your mind to focus your attention where you want it to be. This skill is very useful for handling thoughts, feelings and body sensations without having to act on them. Mindfulness is not about relaxation or feeling better. If you go to the gym you will have some enjoyable sessions and others when you hate being there, but you will still be training your body. Mindfulness practice is the same so go back and look again at the mindfulness sections and practise some more. If you have thoughts telling you 'I can't do this' or 'I hate this', notice that they are distracting thoughts and bring your mind back to whatever you are focusing on in your practice. Even if you are not sure about mindfulness, keep practising.

I can't seem to motivate myself to get started

Making the first step is often the most difficult. We tend to cover up our problem behaviours in various ways. We can try to ignore them. We can have thoughts that help us pretend there is no problem really. We can hide our behaviour from others. To get started we have to challenge these well-established cover-up habits. Having difficulty in getting started calls for baby steps. You do not have to try to achieve everything in your first step. The smallest baby step could be thinking about getting started and writing down the pros and cons.

Can I damage myself by looking at old memories?

You cannot damage yourself by looking at old memories. Old memories are being stored somewhere in your mind and could be locked away as they are upsetting. When you look at old memories they may be painful. Getting upset in a controlled way can be part of the healing process. It is important to have skills for calming yourself down and controlling your problem behaviour before looking closely at old memories.

I can't remember my history

Your history could be locked away in your mind. If you have trouble accessing memories, they are probably tucked away in a safe place because they are painful. We know the brain stores difficult memories differently from other memories. Make sure you do the exercises in this book to make it safe before trying to access painful memories. Your mind is protecting you, so you need to build up skills to manage your thoughts, feelings and behaviour before moving that protection to one side.

I didn't find my problem in the book or the stories

There are so many different problems that we could list. When you look at the stories in this book, try to think about what is similar to your own problem behaviour. For example, does your problem involve doing too much of something or hurting somebody? The Get Your Life Back stories and chapters are designed to help with general types of problems rather than trying to list individual ones.

My feelings seem to be mixed up and happen in the wrong place at the wrong time

Mixed-up feelings can be due to developmental problems or neglectful and abusive experiences. They can also be part of a reaction after traumas such as a car crash or assault. Here is one example of mixed-up feelings coming from childhood learning. Pauline was sexually abused as a child. She was told (and so learned) that this was a 'special time', it was 'love', a 'special secret'. Actually, being abused was really painful and disgusting. So she learned that love and special times involved feeling pain and disgust. Now Pauline feels pain and disgust whenever she feels sexual love; her feelings are confused.

Here is an example of mixed-up feelings after a car crash. George had been involved in a car crash when a lorry came across the carriageway and hit his car. Afterwards, he felt massive rage towards the driver, even though he knew the tyre had blown and it was not the driver's fault. He felt rage towards all the lorry drivers in the world. At home, he felt withdrawn and distant from his family and unable to enjoy anything. The good news is that mixed-up feelings can be sorted out with brave work.

When I start working on my problems I seem to become a young child again

This is called 'developmental collapse'. Developmental collapse can happen when there have been abusive experiences or neglect during our childhood. These experiences can make our development wobbly and uneven. Each developmental stage is then built on weak foundations. Rather like a house with weak foundations, our adult self can fall down or collapse back to childhood. Things like smells, sounds, sights and other sensations can trigger developmental collapse. It is usually short-term and might happen when you try to think about the past or when there is a trigger that reminds you of the past.

I feel better when I don't think about my problem behaviour

This is a great example of short-term gain. It is true that if you do not think about your problem behaviour you can feel better. On the other hand, this does not make your problem go away. We have learned in this book that problem behaviours are usually short-term solutions; they help us avoid emotional pain. Because they work so well, we do them again and again and they cause long-term pain by making us feel even worse, wrecking our lives.

I feel better when I've had a couple of drinks – is this bad for me?

The answer to this is nearly always yes. Drinking gives short-term gain for maybe two or three hours. Drinking also stops your ability to control thoughts, so your naughty puppy thoughts can run riot. Drinking to forget our problems just makes things worse in the longer term. It can also give you a new problem of a reliance on alcohol. All in all, it is not a good solution.

If I don't check things (lights, door locks, plugs and things like that) I will worry too much to be able to do the things in this book

You may not feel like it, but you are at a great starting place. You have already realised that checking is stopping you from getting your life back. Write down your values key words and ask yourself whether checking things is stopping you from stepping towards your goals. If the answer is 'yes', draw a behaviour chain and put checking things in the middle *as the problem behaviour*. Try to notice the relief you get after checking (short-term gain). This relief might be very brief, but it can keep your checking behaviour going. Then try to notice the longer-term consequences of all the checking (long-term pain). There will be links in your chain, which you can break, and things in your vulnerability cloud you can work on, using the skills you have learned.

Give yourself permission to check things at a level a little lower than the number of times you are doing it at the moment. So if you have to check the door locks three times before you can do something, give yourself permission to check them only two times. Use your new skills to manage the anxiety that will come up. This is a baby step that will move you towards getting your life back.

If I'm addicted to something, I can't change, can I?

This is a common myth. Addiction describes a very strong urge that feels impossible to resist. Addictions can be described as psychological – for example, 'If I don't do something, I will panic' – and physical – for example, 'I shake and sweat if I don't take substances like cannabis'. As with many other behaviours that we have looked at, baby steps are the starting place. All addictions can be changed.

My mind is a mass of endless chatter – I can't write all that down!

This is an interesting statement and one we often hear. Do not make a thought diary that is the size of a novel, this is of no use. You need to record just a sample of your thoughts. Some people can record a whole day of thoughts, others just describe a minute or so and still fill the page. We are looking for typical patterns of thoughts and feelings. Patterns tend to repeat themselves, which is great for us. It means we can study the patterns and work out how to change them. Thought catching is a skill. Have a look back at Chapter 12 for more hints and tips.

How long will it be before I'm better?

This is a question almost everybody asks. You will probably not be surprised that there is no clear answer. Generally, long-term problems take longer to fix compared with short-term problems. If a problem started in childhood and you have lived with it since then, it will take a while to change.

Why do things that happened in my childhood make me have problems now?

'Why have I not got over it?' In 2010 researchers used global World Health Organisation figures and showed that people who had bad things happening in their childhoods have more problem behaviours as adults. You can see this in action in Chapters 2 and 3. The good news is that research has also shown that these problem behaviours can be changed.

How come I have to see a therapist when my problem is physical pain?

Physical problems like pain may have many reasons for being there. Some reasons could be to avoid bad feelings or to form relationships with those who help us. We may not be aware of these reasons. We can make a behaviour chain with pain as the problem behaviour. Scientists have found that all physical problems also seem worse when we are distressed or feeling low. We could put being distressed or being low in our vulnerability cloud.

I couldn't fill in all my links in my behaviour chain

This is not a problem so do not worry. Sometimes there are many links before and after a behaviour and sometimes there are not. If you can only think of one or two links write them down and see whether more links get filled in as you get going.

I keep crying when I try to think about my problem thoughts

This has probably been one of the reasons why you have not dealt with your problem thoughts. Try using baby steps – how many thoughts can you think about before you cry? Is your mind sending you the message that these thoughts are too painful so do not approach them? Do you need to send messages back to your mind saying that you can manage the pain? What happens to you if you cry, is it a disaster or can you manage it?

I can't resist biscuits, so should I just carry on eating them?

No!

Are you sure that validation is not just agreeing with bad things?

This is a common mistake. Validation is showing that you are listening and understanding. Understanding is not judging or agreeing.

I keep spacing out

Spacing out is often known as 'zoning out'. Spacing out can be on a scale starting from daydreaming to a total cut-off from your world. A total cutting-off can happen when thoughts and feelings become overwhelming. If they are overwhelming, you may close down and not feel or recognise them. A good starting place would be to keep a diary of when this happens. Record things like triggers for spacing out, how often you space out and for how long. This will help you to decide whether spacing out is a problem or not. If you decide it is, then think of spacing out as a problem behaviour.

Is it OK to use this book if I am in therapy?

There is nothing in this book that will clash with things you are doing in therapy. There may be some different ideas and ways of looking at things. These will help to strengthen your therapy.

I am on a waiting list for CBT. If I use this book, will it mess up my therapy?

The more skills you get from this book, the more skills you can take to therapy. The things in this book may not be exactly the same as your therapy but the skills will be complementary. Your new skills will strengthen your therapy.

I've had CBT and it didn't work

CBT, like other main therapies, is based on research. This means that we know they can work. Because we know this you will have learnt useful skills from your CBT sessions. Hold on to these skills and work your way through this book. As you gather more new skills, think about how to apply them to yourself, together with the CBT skills that you have. Do not give up hope – see your CBT sessions as your new starting place and start working through this book, getting your life back.

Won't using baby steps just slow things up?

What really slows things up is taking a massive step and failing. Small steps build in strong success. If you are struggling, make your steps even smaller – this is not a failure. As we have seen before, changing is a marathon, not a sprint.

My mum was very emotional – does this mean that I will be too?

Some of these things are linked with inheritance, but the links are not strong. It is more likely that you have learned problem behaviours during your childhood. Either way, we can learn to manage our thoughts and feelings.

I don't have time to commit to doing all the stuff in this book

Ask yourself whether you really want to change or not. You may have to treat not having enough time as a problem behaviour. You can solve the problem by changing things in your life or by training naughty puppy messages in your head.

Should I tell my family that I'm using this book?

This is a matter of personal preference. If you can share that you are working through this book, this will help with commitment. If you feel that you would rather not, this is not a problem.

What I did was really bad, so I should feel like this

This is an untrained mind puppy message. Think of this thought as a problem thought as you work through the book.

My thoughts and behaviours are too out of control to change

Many problem behaviours feel like this and that is why you have kept them. This is a clear case of needing baby steps. If you try to change your out-of-control behaviours in one go they *will* be out of control! Start thinking about what can be changed using SMART goals, no matter how small. Many small steps are better than one big failed step. No behaviour is unchangeable.

But I have been like this for as long as I can remember, even in early childhood

Long-term problems usually take longer to change so set realistic goals and do not give up hope. As a rule of thumb, the longer you have had a problem behaviour, the longer it takes to deal with. All problem behaviours can be dealt with. Start with baby steps and keep moving forward.

When I thought about my problem behaviour there seemed to be more pros than cons so shouldn't I just stick with it?

There are generally short-term gains that come with problem behaviours but there are also long-term pains. The pros and cons may not carry the same weight. That means that some things are more important than others. So I may have six small pros and one huge overwhelming con that is messing up my life.

My problem behaviour is too painful to look at

You may be experiencing feelings like shame or grief when you think about your problem behaviour. These feelings are very unpleasant and we usually want to avoid them. We try not thinking about the things that give us these feelings. Try to identify the feelings you have when you look at your problem behaviour. Give them names (shame, anger, sadness, fear, etc.). Use the physicalising exercise from Chapter 5 (page 93). You can get better at accepting the feelings without letting them overwhelm you. Then you will be able to look at your problem behaviour more clearly.

I think I may harm myself if I try to change things

Ask yourself where this thought has come from; is there any evidence for it? What would someone who disagrees say about this? Is this just your naughty puppy thoughts barking away? If you notice an increase in urges to self-harm as you work on your problem behaviour, add this to your list of Things I Need to Change. Go back and do a behaviour chain for having urges to self-harm. Then use this to plan how you will deal with the self-harm urges.

I can't trust anyone to talk to about my problem behaviour

If this is a problem for you, use your perfect nurturer. Go to your safe place and share your problem behaviour and your thoughts and feelings about it. You can ask your perfect nurturer to stay with you whilst you work on your problem behaviour.

How do I know whether to change or accept my feelings or behaviours?

This is different for different people. As a rule of thumb, it is better to change problem behaviours rather than accept them. You may find that some thoughts, feelings and body sensations are not going to go away if you fight them. If you use acceptance in the ways we have learned, then they often get easier to bear.

I'm OK until I see my whisky bottle, then all my good intentions disappear

Seeing the temptation is usually a trigger event. This may be whisky, cigarettes, doughnuts, a betting shop or a razor blade. Make it as difficult as possible to access your demon tempter. Put it outside or in the bin, if possible. For example, if your problem is drinking, ask people in pubs not to serve you. If your problem is gambling, do not drive past the betting shop.

I was abused as a child and I might have sort of enjoyed it for a short time – so was it my fault?

Because our bodies are hardwired for pleasure, including sexual pleasure, we can sometimes feel this for a short time, even during abuse. This does not mean it was your fault – it is never a child's fault. Abuse involves a power imbalance with the adult using their power to exploit the child.

I think that I want to live by myself – is that wrong or avoiding things?

Some of us are very happy living by ourselves. Do not feel forced into any position.

I was diagnosed with a mental health problem – does this mean that I can't change?

Mental health diagnoses are ways of labelling behaviour, thoughts, feelings and body sensations which cause distress to ourselves or others. Because you have a label does not mean that your problems have become more serious or that they will last forever. Mental health diagnoses are made by an expert having an opinion rather than through things like blood tests. These labels can be useful if they help us get the treatment we need and understand more about how to help ourselves. They are not useful if we feel helpless to change as a result.

Why do I feel better for a short while when I self-harm?

Self-harming is difficult to understand when you see it or experience it. Your behaviour chain may have shown you the answer to this question. Self-harming leads to short-term gain. The gain is often relief or escape from painful thoughts and feelings. Self-harming can also release natural painkillers (endorphins) into the bloodstream, which can give a good feeling. It may also work in other ways, such as people looking after me after I harm myself. People who self-harm are generally not aware of how it works.

If I think I need therapy, what should I do?

This is a good time to ask somebody else what they think. Your family doctor is used to being asked such questions and can refer you for therapy. If you go for private therapy, make sure the therapist is registered with a professional organisation and that they offer a proven therapy.

If I want to see a therapist, do I need to see them face-to-face or does the internet or phone therapy work?

This is a personal choice. The internet offers a range of options, including therapy by using email, therapy using secure chat rooms and Skype or another voice-over internet protocol. You may be offered interactive therapy at your family doctor's surgery, using programmes like 'Beating the Blues'. There is evidence that all of these methods are effective, as well as phone therapy.

I have been told that if I hear voices I have to take medication for the rest of my life

This is an old-fashioned way of looking at things. Research evidence has shown that both CBT and ACT can work well for managing hearing voices. Sometimes medication and therapy together can be appropriate. Never stop taking medication without expert advice and careful planning.

Is this book based on CBT, DBT, ACT or CFT?

This book draws on all of these therapies for you to Get Your Life Back. They all have much to offer.

Chapter 23

Resources

This chapter aims to equip you for the journey ahead as you get your life back into your own hands and stride on down the road towards your values and goals. Here, we list some related self-help books, organisations which offer support and advice and a description of the website linked to this book.

CBT self-help books for anxiety, anger and everything else

Anxiety

Overcoming Anxiety: A Self-Help Guide Using Cognitive Behavioral Techniques. By Helen Kennerley. Published by Robinson (2014).

This is the classic self-help book for anxiety and has sold more than 130,000 copies. It is on the 'Books on Prescription' list in the UK.

http://the-reading-agency.myshopify.com/products/reading-well-books-on-prescription-2014

Anger

How To Deal With Anger: A 5-step CBT-based Plan for Managing Anger and Frustration. By Isabel Clarke. Published by Hodder & Stoughton (2016).

This is a book outlining a step-by-step approach to managing anger.

Everything else

All the books in the 'Overcoming' series published by Robinson. By a variety of authors, all of these books take a CBT self-help approach to many different problems.

ACT

ACTivate Your Life: Using Acceptance and Mindfulness to Build a Life that Is Rich, Fulfilling and Fun. By Joe Oliver, Jon Hill and Eric Morris. Published by Robinson (2015).

This book gives loads of help in managing intense feelings and being clear about your values.

DBT

The Dialectical Behavior Therapy Skills Workbook: Practical DBT Exercises for Learning Mindfulness, Interpersonal Effectiveness, Emotion Regulation, and Distress Tolerance. By Matthew McKay and Jeffery Wood. Published by New Harbinger (2007).

This book has hundreds of great exercises for developing more skills like the ones we have learned in this book.

CFT

The Compassionate Mind: How to Use Compassion to Develop Happiness, Self-Acceptance and Well-Being. By Paul Gilbert. Published by Constable (2010).

If you have problems with beating yourself up and hating yourself, this book will be terrific for helping you.

Mindfulness

Mindfulness: A Practical Guide to Finding Peace in a Frantic World. By Mark Williams and Danny Penman. Published by Piatkus (2011).

This book has become a classic guide for all those who want to deepen their understanding and practice of mindfulness and apply it to everyday life.

Organisations that offer support and advice

It is not possible to list all of the organisations that may be able to offer you information, advice or support so here is a short list of UK websites that you may find useful. If you feel that you need help, probably the best place to get started is with your family doctor or GP. Family doctors have a wide range of experience in mental health issues and distressing situations. They can often refer you for therapy with a professional if that is needed.

NHS Choices (UK) – offers a huge range of information and organisations for both mental and physical health.
www.nhs.uk

When you get onto this site, go to the 'Choices' home page or go to www.nhs.uk/conditions/stress-anxiety-depression/pages/ways-relieve-stress.aspx

Mind – promotes the views and needs of people with mental health problems, offers advice and information.
www.mind.org.uk

Citizens Advice – offers a wide range of free practical advice, including financial, legal, income advice, etc.
www.citizensadvice.org.uk

Young Minds – provides information on child and adolescent mental health for individuals, parents and professionals.
www.youngminds.org.uk

Nightline Association – a confidential listening service for support and information, run by students for students.
www.nightline.ac.uk

Samaritans – Twenty-four-hour support and advice for those who are experiencing despair.
www.samaritans.org

Cruse Bereavement Care – support and advice for those who have experienced bereavement.
www.cruse.org.uk

www.getyourlifeback.global

This is the website linked to this book. Here, there are copies of the tables, which you can download for your own use. There is no copyright on these tables, so feel free to share them with friends or colleagues.

On the website you can also join the Get Your Life back Community, where you can share your experiences of working on problem behaviours, blog, receive support from each other and some feedback from us.

You can also download MP3 files of mindfulness exercises and other exercises, and videos of us talking about topics from the book.

Chapter 24

Glossary – Terms Used in this Book

Abdomen – The part of the body just below your tummy.

Acceptance – Accepting something rather than trying to change it, often applied to feelings.

ACT – Acceptance and Commitment Therapy.

Addicted/Addiction – A term applied to an urge which appears to be almost impossible to resist. It can be psychological and/or physical.

Adversity – Poor environment and damaging experiences.

Anxiety – A set of feelings and body sensations that happen to protect you. An easy example of anxiety is the set of experiences that you may feel if you have just been almost run over when crossing the road.

Assertiveness – The ability to make choices or statements and see them through.

Awareness – To be able to perceive or see what is around you and your inside experience.

Baby steps – Small steps that work towards a bigger step or goal.

Behaviour – Almost anything that you can observe, see or measure a person doing. This may include moving, breathing, laughing, etc.

Behaviour chain – The chain of links (thoughts, feelings, body sensations) that happen before and after a behaviour.

Behavioural urges – The urge to do a behaviour which is often driven by feelings.

Binge eating – Eating a huge amount of food in one go, much more than is usual. Often the food eaten is of a random selection, e.g. whatever is in the fridge.

Body sensations – Things that can be felt in your body, such as pain, warmth, heartbeat, etc.

Bull's eye exercise – An exercise that helps you recognise your life values and measures how near your life is to them.

Calorie-rich food – Foods that are packed with calories, which usually taste delicious but are very bad for us and pile on fat and weight.

CBT – Cognitive Behavioural Therapy.

Cerebellum – A part of the brain that is connected with muscle movements.

CFT – Compassion Focused Therapy.

Chain – A series of events that are connected to a behaviour, what happens before and what happens after.

Chain analysis – This is similar to a chain but adds meaning to the events just before and after a behaviour. It can help us understand a behaviour.

Childhood abuse – Abuse that happens during childhood, which can be sexual, emotional or physical. Usually abuse happens at the hands of an adult.

Childhood neglect – Neglect describes a situation where care is, or has been poor. Severe neglect can cause developmental damage, which can be long-term.

Coccyx bone – a small bone at the bottom of your spine.

Coming out – Being public about being gay, or being sexually attracted to a person with the same gender as yourself.

Compassion – Attaching love or kindness to a person or situation.

Compassionate self-validation – Validating yourself by listening and using reflection. Compassion is added to this validation.

Conditioning – Anxiety or other responses moving from one place or situation to another.

Condoning – Agreeing or supporting something.

Conscious choice – A decision that is made after considering many things that are important to the decision.

DBT – Dialectical Behaviour Therapy.

Demon chest – A place where things (demons) can be safely and securely kept, such as NATs.

Depression – A mental health problem that includes low mood, negative thoughts and poor motivation.

Developmental damage – Damage that happens during childhood that stops development from moving forward in an expected way. This can also affect later development from happening.

Dialectical – Holding two positions at the same time, even if they appear to be opposites.

Diary – A record of things. This can include thoughts, feelings or behaviours.

Effect – The end result of something, often thoughts or feelings.

Emotions – Automatic feelings that often drive behaviours. Emotions can be very strong and get connected to the wrong things; they include changes in our bodies.

Empathy – The ability to see things from another person's point of view and wanting to support them.

Empty chair – A technique where you can imagine a person sitting in an empty chair. Important messages can be given to the imagined person. This is often used for giving messages to a seemingly powerful person, e.g. an abusing adult from the past.

Exposure – Experiencing a feared situation until the fear reduces to see that it can be safe.

Fatigue – A feeling of mental or physical exhaustion.

Feelings – Feelings are messages that come from your mind; things like happiness, sadness, anger, etc. Although it is not strictly true, feelings can be seen as the same as emotions.

Fight or flight – A fast decision that your mind makes to protect you. In the face of danger a fast decision has to be made to fight or run away as fast as possible. This is an automatic response.

Flashback – A vivid image that has the feeling of being real. Flashbacks are connected to past trauma or bad things; it can feel like reliving the trauma.

Frozen – Not being able to move or even think due to severe fear.

Function – The reason why a behaviour happens.

Functional analysis – A system to work out why a behaviour is happening and what may be keeping it going.

Gay – Being sexually attracted to a person of the same gender as yourself.

Goals – The final thing that you may be working towards.

Grounding – Recognising what is here and now, it includes your surroundings such as where you are.

Hardwired – A direct connection in your nervous system which allows very fast actions.

Hearing voices – Hearing a voice or voices when there is no voice spoken.

Helicopter view – Getting an overview of a situation just as though you are looking down from a helicopter.

Here and now – Being aware of the here and now; focusing the mind in the present moment.

Image –A picture in your mind of a person, place or situation.

Impulses – Describes messages coming from your mind through your nervous system.

Intention – Making up your mind to do something.

Judgements – Being judgemental is making a decision on whether something is good or bad.

Junk email – Email that arrives without invitation and can be harmful.

Laxatives – Drugs or mixtures to make your bowels open (having a poo).

Learned helplessness – Reaching a position when you stop trying to do something because there seems no hope of managing to do it.

Long-term – Something that lasts for a long time.

Manipulate – Do something to change things for personal gain.

Medication – Chemicals that we take to change things in our bodies. Medication can be used for changing things like mood and lowering anxiety, etc.

Mental health – Also known as psychological health or psychological well-being, it involves mood, thoughts, feelings, emotions and the interaction with our physical bodies.

Mental well-being – Often known as psychological well-being, it describes good health regarding thoughts, mood, feeling and emotions.

Metaphor – A small story which helps us understand something.

Mind – Our minds are how we refer to the parts of ourselves that do thinking and feelings.

Mindful listening – Listening very carefully, focusing on what the person is saying without judging.

Mindful stretch – Stretching the body whilst mindfully paying attention to body sensations.

Mindfulness – Focusing on the present moment with awareness, without judging.

Mindfulness muscles – These are your mindfulness skills and the more you use them, the stronger they get, just like going to the gym to tone up your muscles.

Mobility – The ability to move about as you want to.

Mood – A term for your current state of psychological well-being.

NATs – Negative Automatic Thoughts.

Negative reinforcement – see reinforcement.

Neurons – The 'wiring' in your nervous system.

Normalise – Help ourselves or other people realise that something is more normal than we previously thought.

Observing mind – Looking or thinking about things without necessarily acting on them.

Panic – This is a set of feelings or emotions that are preparing you to take fight or flight.

Panic attack – When you have a panic attack, you experience feelings or emotions that prepare you for fight or flight. Panic attacks happen when your mind mistakes a safe situation for a dangerous one.

Parroting – Repeating something precisely just as a parrot would.

Perfect nurturer – An image which you can go to for non-judgemental support.

Physical health – The health of your physical body.

Physical sensations – See body sensations.

Physiological regulation – Systems in your body which keep things at a constant level, e.g. body temperature.

Physiology – How things work in your body, e.g. how your blood gets from your heart to your toes.

Positive reinforcement – see reinforcement.

Positive self-talk – Talking to yourself in a positive way; this can involve talking back to your mind when you get negative thoughts or messages.

Psychiatrist – A doctor who specialises in mental health. Psychiatrists generally have skills in medication.

Psychologist – A person who specialises in understanding and changing behaviour without medication.

Psychology – The study of human behaviour.

Psychosomatic – Something physical that happens due to a psychological reason.

Quicksand – Soft sand that you will sink in if you stand on it. Used as a metaphor for sinking further the more you struggle.

Reflecting – Repeating back what you have heard in your own words to show that you are listening and understanding.

Reinforcement – Something that increases the likelihood of a behaviour happening again. It is not necessarily pleasant. Positive reinforcement does this through reward, negative reinforcement does this through escape.

Reward –A pleasant thing, which you get when you have done something.

Rumination – Worrying about the past or the present.

Schemas – Views that we form about ourselves, the world and others, usually over a long period of time.

Self-criticism – Negative judgements about yourself and what you are doing.

Self-harming – Causing yourself harm; for example, scratching yourself, pulling out hair, cutting yourself, etc.

Self-neglect – Not looking after yourself well enough.

Self-soothing – Having the ability to calm and support yourself when needed.

Short-term – Something that lasts for a short time.

SMART Goals – Goals that are Specific, Manageable, Achievable, Realistic and Time limited.

Spacing out – Mentally switching off or your mind going blank. You may feel detached from the world.

Star chart – A chart which can have stars drawn or stuck on it as a reward; it can also be used to record progress.

STOP! THINK! – Stopping an automatic response by saying 'STOP! THINK!' and giving yourself time to choose how to respond.

Surf the wave – Feel what is going on but do not respond. Can be used for dealing with feelings and urges.

Survival of the fittest – The strongest of a group survive but the weakest do not. This is how evolution works over very long periods of time.

Target behaviours – These are the behaviours that we need to change. The target behaviour is part of a behaviour chain.

Therapist – A person who provides therapy.

Therapy – Working through a process of change, usually with a therapist.

Thought catcher – A way of recognising and then writing down thoughts so that they can be worked with.

Thought diary – Same as thought catcher.

Thought record – Same as thought catcher.

Toxins – Damaging chemicals often found in small quantities in or out of your body.

Treatment – Taking action to improve physical or psychological health. Usually treatment is directed at an illness or problem.

Trigger – Something that starts a behaviour, thought or feeling. You may not be aware of the trigger or understand it.

Trough of Despair – A metaphor for reaching a point during change when you feel desperate and have strong urges to quit. It feels as though there is no way forward.

Urges – A desire or need to do something.

Validation – Shows that you are listening, concentrating and understanding what is being said. Listening with mindful focus and without judging. You can validate yourself (self-validation).

Values – These are the things that you think are very important in your life. They describe the way you want to be. Getting your life back involves making sure your values influence the way you live.

Vicious circle – A circle of events, thoughts and behaviours that seems to drive itself. Vicious circles generally create and then maintain problems.

Vulnerabilities – These are things in our lives that make us more vulnerable to carrying out our problem behaviours. Examples may be lack of sleep, poor diet, using substances, recent negative events.

Vulnerability cloud – A way of listing the vulnerabilities which contribute to us carrying out our problem behaviours.

Wheel of Experience – A diagram describing thoughts, feelings, body sensations and events that go along with our problem behaviour.

YouTube – A video sharing website.

Zoning out – See spacing out.

Acknowledgements

We would like to acknowledge the pioneers of the four therapies on which this book is based:

Aaron T. Beck, founder of CBT

Stephen Hayes, founder of ACT

Marsha M. Linehan, founder of DBT

Paul Gilbert, founder of CFT

Each of these therapies has been developed and shaped by many great clinicians, too many to name here. We are deeply grateful for all of their work. We hope we have done it justice.

Secondly, we would like to thank the people who read this book during its development. We learned from their comments and were cheered up and kept going by their encouragement. They are:

Val Fish

Ronnie Hermiston

Adele Hyde

Dan Roberts

Jackie Watts

Thirdly, we thank Andrew McAleer, our editor at Robinson, for his assistance and support and for risking his career by publishing this book!

Thank you to Helen Kennerley, Joe Oliver and Frank Bond for their encouragement, support and inspiration.

Fiona Kennedy and David Pearson

Index